DECEIVING

THE

DEVIL

DARBY KATHLEEN RAY

DECEIVING THE DEVIL

Atonement, Abuse, and Ransom

THE PILGRIM PRESS   CLEVELAND, OHIO

The Pilgrim Press, Cleveland, Ohio

Grateful acknowledgment is made for permission to reprint the following:

From *The United Methodist Book of Worship*. Copyright © 1972 by The Methodist Publishing House; Copyright © 1980, 1985, 1989, 1992 by The United Methodist Publishing House. Used by permission.

From Bernice Johnson Reagon, "My Black Mothers and Sisters, or On Beginning a Cultural Autobiography," *Feminist Studies* 8, no. 1 (spring 1982): 81–96. Reprinted by permission of the author.

From the *United Church of Christ Book of Worship*, p. 46. Reprinted by permission of the United Church of Christ Office for Church Life and Leadership.

Biblical quotations are from the New Revised Standard Version of the Bible, © 1989 by the Division of Christian Education of the National Council of the Churches of Christ in the U.S.A., and are used by permission

Library of Congress Cataloging-in-Publication Data
Ray, Darby Kathleen, 1964–
    Deceiving the Devil : atonement, abuse, and ransom / Darby Kathleen Ray.
      p. cm.
    Includes bibliographical references and index.
    ISBN 0-8298-1253-9 (pbk. : alk. paper)
    1. Atonement.   2. Feminist theology.   3. Liberation theology.   I. Title.
BT265.2.R38   1998
232'.3—dc21   97-44077
                                                                       CIP

Contents

Preface

How is it that God in the life and death of Jesus acted to confront evil in a decisive and redemptive manner? Christian tradition offers two main explanations. In one line of thinking, Christ's death on the cross atones for human sin because he substitutes for or represents the sinner (substitutionary atonement). In another, Jesus' life and ministry offer a radically new alternative or example for living without sin (moral influence). Both of these classical models have their contemporary detractors. Feminists are concerned that they permit—and even encourage—violence and abuse, and liberationists are concerned that they undermine human efforts to combat injustice and oppression by encouraging ethical passivity. Even Christians who are unsympathetic to feminism or liberation find that the two classical models leave them without adequate theological resources for understanding and confronting the myriad evils that crowd their daily lives.

In this book, I retrieve and refine a third, classical model that meets the objections of feminist and liberation theologians and better meshes with the piety of most Christians. This model underscores how God in Christ rejects the tools of evil, but without glorifying passivity or suffering. It is based on the intuition of many of the early church fathers that the powers of evil cannot be easily or forcefully defeated but must be creatively and cunningly subverted—an insight whose contemporary relevance and potential are astounding. Their idea was that in the life and death of Jesus, God acted to "deceive" or outwit the devil. This notion may strike some as unnervingly heterodox or disturbingly immoral, and yet it is an idea that, when demythologized, preserves a firm, if unexpected, anchoring in Christian tradition; at the same time, it provides a narrative about the saving work of Christ that can speak to the concerns of contemporary feminist and liberation theologians about the reality and scope of human evil.

Such a narrative about the work of Christ requires a thoroughgoing reevaluation of traditional concepts of sin and evil, God, and Jesus the Christ. It demands that we move away from the atonement orthodoxy most Christians have imbued since birth—an orthodoxy characterized by paternalism, patriarchalism, and militarism—and toward models for understanding our world, our God, and ourselves that encourage responsibility, compassion, courage, and creativity. The model presented in this book seeks neither to degrade human agency nor to ignore its theological and ethical limits. It safeguards the infinite Otherness of God while boldly witnessing to the grace of divine incarnation and intimacy. Most important, it is a model that can help Christian women, men, and children recognize and confront evil in our everyday lives, for that is where we encounter it.

The idea of God's deception of the devil is both dangerous and promising. It is dangerous because like all models, it is amenable to perversion and typification; and like all models, its relevance and appropriateness depend upon the context within which it is placed. Despite these caveats, I find it to be a promising idea because it offers an ancient, yet refreshingly novel, way to understand divine power and activity—an approach that can avoid the major pitfalls of traditional models while offering a sanguine word of hope and a savvy strategy for resistance to those who seek to oppose evil in their everyday lives.

Feminist and liberationist concerns about atonement force me to grapple with difficult questions: How can I, on the one hand, agree with the conviction that traditional construals of the work of Christ constitute theological violence and, on the other hand, maintain that the life *and death* of Jesus have redemptive efficacy? Why do feminist theologians tend to dismiss all notions of atonement as irretrievably problematic, while most liberationists insist that some such notion is essential to Christian identity and community? Is there a way of thinking about the salvific work of Christ that can satisfy the need of ordinary Christian people for a theology that is both rooted in tradition and open to the transforming winds of the Spirit? These questions prompted the writing of this book; they motivated me to treat with absolute seriousness the critiques of my fellow feminists and liberationists as well as the foundational Christian claim that somehow, Jesus' suffering and death are part of God's salvific response to evil.

Numerous people and institutions have shaped my thinking about these issues. While a graduate student at Vanderbilt University in Nashville, I was privileged to learn from such fine scholars as Peter Hodgson, Sallie McFague,

Fernando Segovia, Eugene TeSelle, Ed Farley, Charles Scott, Nina Gove, and Mary Ann Tolbert. Equally important were the insight and support provided by a host of friends and student colleagues, especially Nancy Victorin-Vangerud, Mark Justad, Laurel Schneider, Denise Gyauch, Anne McWilliams, Jeanine Dorfman, Melissa Donahue, Dan Deffenbaugh, Noelle Wainwright Warner, and Victoria Krebs. As I left the familiarity of Nashville for upstate New York, I was blessed to find incredible intellectual and spiritual cama-raderie among my students at Hobart and William Smith Colleges in Geneva. Though our time together was brief, I treasure the lessons I learned with them about teaching, learning, and creating community. At various times I found solace and hope in church communities, notably Christ Episcopal Church and Brookmeade United Church of Christ in Nashville, and St. James Episcopal Church in Jackson, Mississippi. The women I have worked with through Rape Crisis in New York and Mississippi have given me insight into both the tragedy and the possibility of living with and against evil in this world. I am grateful to Timothy Staveteig of Pilgrim Press for taking interest in my book and helping me bring it to fruition, and to Millsaps College in Jackson for pro-viding me with a summer research grant.

I would not have been able to envision and complete this project with-out the unflagging love and support of my beautiful best friend, Angie, or without the encouragement of my sister Amy or the insight of my mother, Pamela, to whom this book is dedicated. Finally, to my partner, Ray Clothier, whose passion, patience, and good humor have accompanied me from Nashville to New York to Mississippi, at considerable personal and profes-sional cost, I owe a debt of gratitude.

Introduction:
Atonement, Abuse,
and Ransom

Understandings of atonement are as varied as the people who articulate them. At the heart of most construals of atonement, however, are two convictions: first, that things are not as they should be between God and world; and second, that this situation *can* be resolved, that right relationship *is* possible. Within the parameters of these broad convictions an enormous degree of variation is possible. And indeed, the history of the doctrine of atonement reveals an endless stream of difference, nuance, continuity, and antithesis as various accounts of both problem and solution are proposed and debated.

In ancient Israel the ritual of sacrifice was believed to effect atonement. Depending on the context, the emphasis may have been on sacrifice as a human gift offered to God, as a sin offering, or as a memorial and celebration of divine–human communion; but in every case it was understood to be the point at which the Divine and the human came into contact and the covenant relationship was renewed. For biblical Judaism the process of atonement, centered on sacrifice, functioned positively, to make human beings acceptable for participation in Israel's religious life, and negatively, to avert the evil created by sin.[1]

The early Christians inherited this dual focus that provides the basic framework within which Christian thinkers have understood atonement through the ages. Within the context of Judaism and Christianity, then, atonement involves the establishing of right relationship between God and world *through* the confrontation of evil.

1

In Christian tradition, atonement (at-one-ment) is most broadly defined as "reconciliation," whose root, *katallage,* means "making otherwise."[2] Implied is a situation of separation, distortion, brokenness between God and world. This relationship is variously understood to include one or more of the following relationships: divine–human, divine–nonhuman, human–nonhuman, and human–human. Atonement refers to the process by which those who are separated are brought near, what is distorted is untwisted, and what is broken is mended and made whole. Metaphors and images used to express this process range from the battlefield to the courtroom to courtly love, while key concepts include justice, mercy, sin, love, obedience, compensation, substitution, and representation.

Within Christian tradition, there is further consensus that talk about atonement involves the broad claim not only that right relationship is brought about through the confrontation of evil, but also that the event or process of atonement is necessarily connected to the figure of Jesus of Nazareth. The incarnate God, Christianity claims, acts in such a way as to bring about reconciliation where there was estrangement, liberation where there was enslavement. The consensus comes to an abrupt halt at this point, however, as an irreducible variety of interpretations is offered about what separates God and world, why and how reconciliation occurs, and when this reconciliation takes place.

Despite the multiplicity of interpretations, Christian tradition has yielded what might be called an atonement orthodoxy—a set of images and claims regarding the saving work of God in Christ that stands at the center of popular Christian theory and practice, exerting influence through sermons, hymns, liturgies, and church school curricula. This atonement orthodoxy is the offspring of two major models—the Anselmian and the Abelardian— both given classical expression in medieval Europe. Although usually the *differences* between these models take center stage in studies of atonement, I am concerned with their commonalities because together they have bequeathed contemporary Christians with a highly problematic doctrine of atonement. At the center of this doctrine stands the claim that through the voluntary obedience and self-sacrifice of Jesus the Christ, perfectly exhibited in his life and especially his death, the disobedience and willfulness of human existence are overcome once and for all; as a result, God's honor and authority are renewed, humanity's sin absolved, and right relationship between the Divine and humanity restored. We will see that this doctrine is based on assumptions about the nature of sin, God, and salvation that, together, actually create and sustain what many today recognize as evil. Ironically, the very doctrine whose job it is to attempt to understand and articulate God's response to evil perpetuates evil in the lives of many women, men, and children.

Voices of Dissent

The critique of this atonement orthodoxy is not new. In every age, and particularly since the Enlightenment, notable dissenters have taken issue with various of its claims and implications. In our day, two sets of voices and experiences have emerged with special clarity to sound the alarm. For feminist theologians, the centrality of atonement language and imagery in patriarchal theologies, which militate against the full personhood of women, children, and disenfranchised men, and which, more specifically, appear to contribute to sexual and domestic violence, requires a reevaluation not only of atonement but also of Christianity itself. For liberation theologians, the collusion of Christianity and imperialism—of cross with sword or, in neocolonialism, of cross with capitalism—demands scrutiny. Both perspectives raise serious questions about the legitimacy of Christianity's foundational claim that in the life and death of Jesus of Nazareth, God has acted in a decisive way to confront evil and to reconcile the world to God's self.

Sexual and domestic violence occur with astounding frequency in all social classes and ethnic groups.[3] Although these kinds of violence are believed to go unreported more than any other crime, conservative estimates suggest that in the United States, more than 50 percent of all women have been raped or have experienced an attempted rape during their lives. A woman is beaten every twenty seconds and is raped every two minutes. Estimates are that 20 to 40 percent of all children are subjected to some kind of sexual violence by the time they are eighteen, the most common form being father-daughter molestation.

From a theological perspective the reality of sexual and domestic violence represents a horrible abuse of power, a corruption of the Christian ideals of love and justice, a perversion of right relationship between victim, offender, and community and, perhaps most important, a destruction of the victim's belief in the fundamental blessedness and trustworthiness of the world, of other people, and even of herself. The Christian church has been painstakingly slow to recognize and denounce these types of violence as evil.

While reasons for the church's acquiescence abound, one of the most pointed charges focuses on the doctrine of atonement. It is argued that many of the concepts and images that have traditionally been used to talk about the redemptive significance of the life and death of Christ do more harm than good because they contribute to an "erotics of domination" that can work to justify violence against women and children.[4] As we will see, many key elements of traditional construals of atonement—including certain interpretations of love, fidelity, honor, power, justice, obedience, punishment, suffering, and sacrifice—can and do lead to the theological sanctioning of sexual and domestic abuse. For this reason, increasing numbers of women and men who agree that the church and Christian tradition have been partners, however unwitting, in creating a theological milieu conducive to violence are faced with a difficult choice: to view Christianity as irredeemably complicit in structures of violence and evil and thus to leave it altogether; to see atonement as ancillary to Christianity and thus opt to embrace Christianity sans atonement; or to recognize the centrality of some understanding of atonement to Christianity and thus choose to reconfigure the doctrine in ways that contribute to an "erotics of liberation" rather than of domination.

At different times in my theological thinking and feeling I have embraced each of these choices as legitimate. And I must admit that even as I opt for the third response, I find myself pulled toward the first by my awareness of, and contempt for, the numerous ways in which Christianity—the religion of my upbringing and of my choice—has been and continues to be complicit in structures and discourses of injustice, ignorance, and indifference. To believe in the essential and/or potential goodness of Christianity is for me a leap of faith that my experience has thus far tentatively confirmed.

Even as I waver for a moment between what I set forth as choices one and three, however, let me be firm in asserting my growing conviction that the second option is not as viable as I once thought. When we talk about "atonement," we are talking about the process of reconciliation that is possible between God and world—a process in which evil is confronted in a decisive way, opening up the possibility of right relationship. Furthermore, within *Christian* tradition, this liberative dynamic is understood to be uniquely manifest in the life and death of Jesus of Nazareth. To claim that atonement is ancillary to Christianity is to deny either the centrality of the process of reconciliation to Christianity or the important role that Jesus plays in this process, or both.

My understanding and experience of Christianity lead me to argue for the necessity of both elements. On the one hand, a Christianity without the recognition and confrontation of evil for the sake of right relationship becomes a spineless, "feel good" religiosity that perpetuates all manner of injustice and oppression because of its inability to model and empower resistance to such evils. On the other hand, a Christianity that fails to recognize the theological significance and centrality of Jesus of Nazareth—the particularities of his life's teaching and praxis; the community of men and women who supported him and continued his mission; and his death understood in negative terms, as the tragic outcome of a life of compassion and justice making, and in positive terms, as the signifier par excellence not only of the shape and consequence of human evil but of a resistance to evil in which the Divine and human find common ground—is an ahistorical religiosity offering little relevance or hope in a world in desperate need of concrete words and acts of transformation, of liberation from evil.

Atonement, understood as the reconciling, redeeming, liberating activity of God in Christ, is essential to Christianity. The task at hand, I argue, is not to dismiss the problems and perversions of atonement language and ideas, as if by deeming them dispensable the damage they do will simply disappear. Rather, the problems and perversions need to be addressed directly and unapologetically so that alternative images and ideas can emerge to support Christian individuals and communities in their struggle to confront evil and to renew and sustain right relationship. This book is a modest effort to do just this—to examine the problems raised by feminist evaluations of atonement and to respond to them by attempting to rethink the doctrine with the help of a different, "unorthodox" narrative about how the life and death of Jesus can be understood to redeem human beings from evil and reconcile us to God and to one another.

In addition to feminist concerns, this book explores the insights of liberation theologies regarding atonement. The context for these theologies is a different, though not unrelated, kind of violence from sexual and domestic abuse—the violence of colonialism and neocolonialism. The very creation of the Third World by the First World—that is, the creation of a relationship of subjugation and dependence that turns the majority of the world's people and land into resources for the minority—has been supported in no small way by a Christian theology that has at its heart an interpretation of the saving work of Christ that continues to prevail today in popular First World piety. As we will see, a very particular construal of the character and function of Jesus the Christ contributed to the deification of imperial goals and the victimization and annihilation of indigenous peoples. For those who were murdered and exploited, the cross of Christianity became a symbol of domination, foreign rule, coerced religion, and cultural elitism.

In relation to the European invasion of the Americas and Africa, an invasion that has shifted in character though not in consequence over the centuries, the cross has come to symbolize an entire culture of crucifixion—an often slow and torturous death by poverty, political impotence, and ecological destruction. For more than five hundred years, the poor and the disenfranchised of Latin America, the Caribbean, and Africa have been victimized by colonialism, capitalism, and cross; they have been, and are, "crucified peoples."[5]

And yet, just as the crucifixion of Jesus of Nazareth did not lead to the utter defeat and silencing of the community that had cohered around him, so political, economic, and cultural conquest has not vanquished the spirit of the "crucified peoples" of the Third World. Resistant and defiant, they have struggled, often unto death, to maintain their lands, languages, customs, and dignity. For these men and women, Christianity is a tool not solely of submission and domination but also of liberation, while the cross symbolizes not only death but also the tenacious struggle for life in the midst of death-dealing powers. For liberation theologies, then, the cross is an unrelentingly ambiguous symbol, signifying and inspiring cruelty and compassion, domination and resistance. For them, atonement has little to do with speculative theories about a past event that purportedly abolished human evil for all time and everything to do with strategies for surviving and struggling against the human evils they encounter daily in *this* time. For them, the work of Christ is far from over, and they understand themselves to be engaged in it with every breath.

The cross, the symbol at the heart of Christianity, signifies the clash between good and evil, life and death, love and hate; it represents, finally, the event of atonement in which good and evil, justice and injustice, are paradigmatically defined for Christian peoples. The cross reminds us of the power of human evil to crush life, to punish and murder the righteous. At the same time, however, this instrument of cruel and unjust death is understood by Christian tradition to be an indispensable part of the story of redemption from human evil, of liberation from bondage. Somehow, Jesus' death on the cross bespeaks the hope of new life.

Searching for Middle Ground

By focusing on atonement, I want to point to both the brokenness and the hope at the heart of Christian theology. I want to explore the ways in which the tradition has talked *about* evil in ways that have themselves *become* evil; but I also want to argue that talk about evil is vital, for unless we are willing to recognize and attempt to understand the reality of human evil—its intractability, complexity, and subtlety—and unless we are willing, on the basis of that inquiry, to devise strategies for how to confront that evil without succumbing to its tactics, then we resign the world, and our lives within it, to destruction, to despair. A small piece of this herculean task is the Christian doctrine of atonement. My contention is that an investigation into contemporary critiques and appropriations of atonement, specifically those articulated by feminist and liberation theologies, can illumine our understanding of human evil by highlighting some of its past and present shapes and tactics and by thematizing a response to its overwhelming presence that has the potential to remake the world, piece by piece.

For me, the issue of atonement is the issue of confronting human evil. It poses the crucial question of whether, and how, human beings can be redeemed from our own evil and reconciled to God and the rest of the world. For those, like me, who theologize in a First World context, the issue of atonement confronts us with our own participation in local and global practices and systems of inequity. Whatever the evil—racism, ethnocentrism, environmental destruction, self-exaltation, or self-abrogation—atonement raises the question of complicity: How might we recognize and confront evil, our own and that of others? Reconciliation with God and one another depends upon a sober sizing up and taking on of the evil that separates us from and sets us against one another. It requires analysis and action, theory and practice, narrative and engagement.

The narrative at the center of the Christian doctrine of atonement is one of history's richest and most multivalent. Depending on who tells it, how it is told, and to whom it is told, it can yield vastly different, even conflicting, interpretations, and hence it can inspire tensive and antithetical attitudes and actions. The remainder of this introduction outlines the best-known and most influential version of this story. Many of its problematic features and implications are explored in chapters 1 through 4. There it will be argued that the dominant interpretation has, ironically, yielded domination; this revered discourse on evil has come to mirror its subject matter and hence should be rejected. In chapters 5 through 7, alternative versions of the story—ones that evoke a praxis of compassion to counter the logic of domination narrated and manifest by the popular interpretation—are presented. In the end, I offer an interpretation of the story of the life and death of Jesus as salvific, and I argue that this interpretation ought to be considered legitimate and even convincing. My intention is to look again at an ancient and largely discarded rendering of atonement, in search of a different way of understanding the life and death of Jesus as a liberating, reconciling confrontation of the powers of evil—a way that circumvents the major problems of the orthodox version while preserving its strengths, a way that can respond to both feminist critiques and liberationist appropriations of atonement. I argue that this model stakes out a small but important new territory—a genuine alternative to the two dominant schools of atonement; a middle ground that safeguards both divine grace and human activity in the event of redemption.

At the risk of sounding immodest, I am convinced that what is at stake in this endeavor is the moral authority of Christianity itself because unless we Christians can find ways of articulating for our day and age our faith in a God who liberates from evil, then we have no good news for today's world. The challenge, it seems to me, is to make this claim in a way that can account for the complexity, tenacity, and pervasiveness of human evil, on the one hand, and the miracle of grace that empowers concrete acts of resistance to evil and that yields moments of genuine transformation and hope, on the other. This has always been the task of Christian theology—to seek to understand and shed light on both the tragedy and the stubborn hope, the agony and the ecstasy, the fragility and the fullness of human existence; and to keep alive the dangerous memories of evil defied, of violence eschewed, of hardness of heart transformed, so that glimpses of redemption might open up vistas of possibility for the confrontation and transformation of evil. I understand this book to be part of this ongoing task of Christian theology. It is warranted, I believe, not merely by the constant need for contemporary articulations of ancient wisdoms, but also by the apparent failure of the innovations of the past two hundred years to alter in a substantial way popular notions of atonement that, mainstream theologians agree, are profoundly problematic.

The atonement orthodoxy that funds popular notions about the significance of Jesus' life and death is an amalgamation of claims stemming from two major models of atonement—the Anselmian and the Abelardian—often referred to as the satisfaction and moral influence models, or the objective and subjective models, respectively. While it is beyond the scope of this book to offer a comprehensive history of the development of and variations within these models, a basic familiarity with their major claims and proponents is necessary to understand what is at stake in contemporary critiques and reconfigurations of atonement.

The Anselmian Model

The Anselmian model of atonement, given classical expression by Anselm of Canterbury (1033–1109), is motivated by the question *Cur Deus Homo?* or Why did God become human? Anselm's response to this query was that God's justice demands satisfaction for human sin. According to this view, God's justice and mercy are at odds with each other because of human sin. God wants to forgive, but divine justice prohibits unrestrained mercy because it would undermine the seriousness of sin, disrupt the moral order of the universe, and debase God's honor and integrity.

By Anselm's rationale, God's justice requires that sin be punished or that compensation be given to God in order to pay the debt of sin. However, as Anselm recognized, humanity cannot pay its debt because sin against the infinitely good and righteous God is an infinite transgression, and nothing humankind could offer God would compensate for such evil. Only God *could* pay such an infinite debt, reasoned Anselm, but only humanity *should* pay the debt for which it has sole responsibility. The only solution, therefore, is the "God-man," whose voluntary sacrifice of his innocent life is of infinite worth. With this sacrifice, Jesus satisfies God's justice so that God is free to love and forgive human beings. Jesus' death, then, effects a once-and-for-all abolition of the consequences of human evil and, consequently, reconciles humanity to God.

According to the Anselmian model, human sin creates such an abominable situation of disorder and dishonor that only one who is both divine and human can restore things. But what exactly is sin? For Anselm, it centers on issues of obligation, disobedience, and dishonor. He asks, "Is sin anything else than not rendering to God what is his due? But what is God's due? It is summed up in the one word, honor."[6] Human beings owe God honor and obedience; sin is thus the debt incurred by the failure to honor and obey God. Sin creates an objective barrier between God and humanity—a barrier that necessitates the incarnation.

The Anselmian model asserts that Christ's perfect obedience to God, even unto death, ultimately gives life to human beings and effects our redemption from death and all other wages of sin. Anselm explains that "as death came upon the human race by the disobedience of man, it was fitting that by man's obedience life should be restored." Yet Jesus' obedience during his life does not erase the importance—indeed the necessity—of his death. His death is not merely the unfortunate consequence of a life of obedience but is, rather, absolutely necessary in order to make satisfaction to God and to reveal God's omnipotence.[7] Paradoxically, suffering and death, which for sinful humanity are the sign and shackles of disobedience, are for Jesus the Christ the sign of perfect obedience and the indispensable means of redemption for all creatures.

In addition to obedience, the Anselmian definition of sin brings to the fore another key concept in this model of atonement: honor. Indeed, for Anselm the issue of God's honor is the all-important catalyst that motivates and shapes his inquiry at every point. The crucial question for Anselm is not, What about sin? or How does redemption occur? Rather, his circuitous route to atonement begins with a concern for God's honor. "Why the God-man?" he asks; why did God, the most holy and righteous One, choose to become human—to enter into the lowliness of earthly existence, undergo ignoble sufferings, and die a most humiliating death? As he attempts to understand and explain the offensive fact of the incarnation, Anselm's primary concern is often to guard the dignity of God and hence to reject any idea that ascribes anything "unbecoming" to God. As a result, he not only defines sin as the "debt of honor which we owe to God," but he also argues that because of this debt, God simply cannot "cancel sin without compensation or punishment," for "this is unbecoming to God." For Anselm, God's honor circumscribes not only human sin, but divine activity as well: "God's liberty and choice and compassion . . . we ought so to interpret these things as that they may not seem to interfere with His dignity."[8]

Closely linked with God's honor, and also of great importance to Anselmian understandings of atonement, is divine justice. Just as God's freedom and love are subject to God's honor, so, too, are they confined within the parameters of the demands of justice. For Anselm, the greatest injustice of all is "that the creature should take away the honor due the Creator, and not restore what he has taken away." Consequently, "supreme justice" is what "maintains God's honor in the arrangement of things." Divine justice requires that God's slighted honor not be ignored: wrong has been done, and it must be righted. Such a settling of accounts entails either punishment or compensation, also known as satisfaction. God's justice demands that sinful humanity either pay its debt or suffer the consequences.[9]

Another focus of Anselmian interpretations of atonement is the disorder that human evil brings into the world. Humans are culpable, according to this view, because their sin disrupts the beauty and harmony of the universe, bringing ugliness and strife. Here, too, however, the importance of God's honor is tantamount, for since the world is God's creation, any harm done to it is by implication also done to the Creator: "When he [humankind] does not choose what he ought, he dishonors God . . . and he disturbs the order and beauty of the universe, as relates to himself, although he cannot injure or tarnish the power and majesty of God." And though the emphasis is different, the outcome does not change insofar as God's justice, even when confronted by disorder rather than dishonor, still demands compensation or punishment.[10]

Thus in the Anselmian model, sinful humanity comes up against the hard wall of divine justice, which holds it unremittingly accountable for its disobedience, dishonor, and disorder. Divine compassion does not eclipse or even soften the demands of divine justice and the moral order of the universe. Compassion is born of justice, not vice versa. Divine mercy is circumscribed by the demands of justice, and justice demands that debts be paid, honor be restored, order be maintained; otherwise, the gravity of sin is treated lightly, and human responsibility for evil becomes a farce. Even a merciful God, therefore, cannot forgive an unpaid debt, for "such compassion," says Anselm, "is wholly contrary to the Divine recompense of sin." Divine mercy is indeed without restrictions, claims Anselm, but only in its eschatological fullness: "I do not deny that God is merciful . . . [but] we are speaking of that exceeding pity by which he makes man happy *after this life*" (emphasis added). Human sin, the unfortunate hallmark of *this* life, puts God's justice and mercy at odds with each other, and the claim of justice, according to the Anselmian model, is absolutely nonnegotiable.[11]

This dilemma creates an impasse that can be bridged only through extraordinary means—hence the necessity of the incarnation. Jesus the Christ is both human and divine and so is capable of paying humanity's infinite debt and, in so doing, of saving human beings from punishment. This, then, is the reason for the incarnation: "The same being should be perfect God and perfect man, in order to make this atonement." The offering of Christ's life is a gift of infinite worth—it is sufficient to satisfy the demands of divine justice, to restore honor, order, and right relationship.[12]

To explain how Christ pays humanity's debt, proponents of this model often claim that his death was a "substitution" for ours because he was sinless and did not deserve to die. Christ substitutes for us, bears the suffering and shame that we should have borne, and dies in our stead. As a result, God is free to love us, and we are free to love God without fear of death.[13] In addition, a frequent argument is that because Christ's life was infinitely valuable, the offering of his life was more than sufficient to satisfy God's justice; it actually constituted a surplus payment so that the debt of sin is understood to have been paid once and for all. Furthermore, the Anselmian model often presents Christ's death as a "sacrifice" offered to "expiate" human sins, or to "propitiate" God's wrath. This sacrifice, along with the suffering it entails, is strictly voluntary, according to this model; and it is precisely as freely given that it is salvific because, insists Anselm, "nothing can be more severe or difficult for man to do for God's honor, than to suffer death voluntarily."[14] Once satisfaction is made through Christ's voluntary, sacrificial death—that is, once the demands of justice are met, God's honor restored, and the order of the universe reinstated—the barrier of sin that separates God and human beings is removed once and for all, and atonement is achieved.

Countless reformulations of Anselm's basic theory emerged in the centuries following his life, and although the central tenets remained constant, some new twists were introduced and gradually came to be viewed as normative. By the time of John Calvin in the early sixteenth century, the attention paid to God's honor was replaced by a focus on the wrath of God; concomitantly, the death of Christ was interpreted not in terms of satisfaction but as punishment for sin. According to Calvin, human sin is a dreadful curse that inevitably and rightfully incites the wrath of God because we have broken God's law and stand condemned to eternal death: "Because a deserved curse obstructs the entrance, God in his character as Judge is hostile to us." Calvin claims that "in order to interpose between us and God's anger, and satisfy his righteous judgment, it was necessary that he [Christ] should feel the weight of divine vengeance." And so "the Son of God endured the pains produced by the curse and wrath of God, the source of death."[15]

Calvin argues that God mercifully allowed Christ to bear the punishment for our sin. In his death, Christ took the place of—substituted for—sinful humanity, bearing the full brunt of divine wrath so that we do not have to. Through the necessary death of Christ, says Calvin, "we are reconciled to God, satisfaction is given to his justice, and the penalty paid." And yet it was not simply the *fact* of Christ's death, according to Calvin, that effected our righteousness; rather, what set this death apart from all others were the suffering, the fear, and the pain that he endured. Lest we imagine that Christ was "shamefully effeminate" in his salvific role, Calvin insists that he suffered not only death, as do "robbers and other malefactors," but also "the curse and wrath of God"—a supernatural agony that caused him to "sweat drops of blood."[16]

Calvin's penal, substitutionary interpretation of atonement, though different from Anselm's satisfaction theory, bears a clear family resemblance to it. This new take on the Anselmian model was embraced by Calvin's successors and was recognized as the normative understanding of atonement within Protestant Christianity for three centuries. The Anselmian model with a Reformed twist remained dominant until the early part of the nineteenth century when a series of critiques and alternative interpretations pushed it out of the theological center for a time.

Thanks to the brilliance of Karl Barth in the twentieth century, the Anselmian model of atonement was infused with new vitality. Although he uses contemporary language and categories, Barth's understanding of atonement shares many of the hallmarks of the Anselmian model, particularly its emphasis on the objective nature of sin, the universality of human culpability, the wrath of God, the costliness of redemption, and the substitutionary character of Jesus' death.

Jesus saves human beings by being *for* us, says Barth, which means that his very humanity is constituted by "the solidarity with which [Jesus] binds Himself to His fellows." And because "the humanity of Jesus is originally and totally and genuinely fellow-humanity," redemption means that "He interposes Himself for them, that He gives Himself to them, that He puts Himself in their place, that He makes their state and fate His own cause." Jesus saves them from their "state and fate as sinners fallen victim to death" by representing them—by being fully and relationally human—and by substituting for them, by taking their place at the bar of divine justice. As divine-human substitute, Jesus sacrifices his humanity, his life, so that humanity might avoid the curse of sin and death, the destruction of divine judgment. And, insists Barth, no other offering would have sufficed: "In His interposition for them the man Jesus had thus to sacrifice Himself in this cause of others. It is not merely a matter of His turning to them with some great gift, but of his giving Himself, His life, for them. It was a matter of dying for them." For Barth, then, atonement is effected by the representational, substitutional, sacrificial death of Jesus.[17]

In a departure from the Anselmian model, Barth does not view the death of Christ in terms of satisfaction or transaction because his focus is at all times on atonement as an encounter with the living Christ who is simultaneously transcendent and personal. Atonement is, in one sense, a once-and-for-all event, utterly transcendent and beyond human manipulation—*not* the inevitable working out of a historically immanent impulse, but discontinuous with all human efforts; and yet its efficacy becomes real only as it is embodied in the concrete, historical divine-human encounter. For Barth, Christ does not offer satisfaction to God but is understood, rather, as mediator, as the one who represents both divine and human and so is able to fulfill the covenant commitments of both parties and thus to mediate the distance between them caused by sin. However, while Barth replaces the Anselmian theme of satisfaction with the idea of mediation, Jesus' obedience to God, especially unto death, is the locus of his atoning power. And the divine–human encounter is designed to elicit precisely this response of obedience from human beings. In addition, because Christ took our place as sinners before God, and in that capacity acted rightly—that is, obediently did the will of God—we can experience unity with Christ in faith and hence be redeemed from sin and wrath.

In Barth's thought we find a rendering of atonement that, save for the rejection of the satisfaction theme, is a thoroughly modern account of the Anselmian model. While other, more recent theologians have espoused various construals of this model, Barth remains its most persuasive twentieth-century proponent.[18] The basic logic and conceptual framework of Anselm's formulation of atonement have proved to be amazingly resilient and continue to be viewed as relevant, and even normative, by vast numbers of Christians. Although the most widespread and enthusiastic support for this model appears to come from the more "fundamentalist" branches of Christianity, its presence is keenly felt in mainline Protestant denominations, and in Catholicism as well, because of its inclusion in creeds and hymnody and its simple and unambiguous logic.

The Abelardian Model

A mere generation after Anselm, Peter Abelard (1079–1142) suggests an interpretation of atonement that stands in stark opposition to the Anselmian model. He exhorts: "How cruel and wicked it seems that anyone should demand the blood of an innocent person as the price for anything, or that it should in any way please him that an innocent man should be slain—still less that God should consider the death of his Son so agreeable that by it he should be reconciled to the whole world!" In opposition to the Anselmian model, Abelard reasons that since human beings were incapable of paying an infinite debt to God, the purpose of the incarnation must not be the payment of anything to anyone. Rather, he understands the incarnation to be the ultimate revelation of God's love for humanity: "To us it seems that we are justified nonetheless in the blood of Christ and reconciled to God in this: that by his extraordinary grace exhibited to us, in that his son assumed our nature, and by teaching us by word and example, persevered until death, he draws us closer to himself through love."[19]

According to proponents of the Abelardian model, a crucial dimension that Anselm and his successors overlook is the importance of the actual

historical existence of Jesus the Christ. By reducing the meaning of the incarnation to the death of Christ, as the Anselmian model does, inadequate
attention is given to the question of *why* Christ had an earthly life and ministry at all—why he spent three decades on earth before he died, and why he
chose, as Abelard puts it, to endure "such numerous fastings, insults, scourg-
ings and spittings, and finally that most bitter and disgraceful death upon the
cross" in order to reconcile us to God. The only possible answer, suggests
Abelard, is love.[20]

In the Abelardian view, reconciliation between God and human
beings—that is, atonement—is brought about by love, the love of God that
Jesus the Christ perfectly embodies. This love is so potent that when human
beings encounter it, we are actually inspired to emulate it, to love God as Jesus
loved God, and to love one another as Jesus loves us. The event of atonement,
then, is an event of creative love: God created the universe out of love; God
became incarnate in Jesus out of love; and in and through the incarnation,
God elicits from human beings a responsive love. The example of divine love,
says Abelard, has this result: "That our hearts should be enkindled by such a
gift of divine grace, and true charity should not now shrink from enduring
anything for him."[21] Thus for Abelard, as Paul Fiddes puts it, "the love of God
is the means as well as the motive of redemption."[22] In his unsurpassable compassion toward human beings, which he exhibited throughout his life and
even unto death, Jesus is the perfect embodiment of God's love for humanity.
And in his unwavering devotion to God, Jesus is the perfect example of humanity's love for God. He is, therefore, the archetype of divine love—embodying in himself and exemplifying for others the fullness of God's mercy.

It is not simply the *fact* that Jesus lived and died that is redemptive, according to the Abelardian model, but the *way* in which he did these things—
the specific behaviors and attitudes that he exhibited in the process of living
and dying. In particular, his unselfish willingness to suffer for humankind's
sake, even to the point of a most terrible death, is extolled: "He suffered truly
for your salvation, on your behalf of his own free will, and by his suffering he
cures all sickness and removes all suffering." Other qualities identified as redemptive are Jesus' unwavering obedience to God, his self-sacrificial humility, and his persistence in prayer.[23]

In and through his life, claim supporters of the Abelardian model, Jesus
exemplified perfect love—love characterized by compassion and forgiveness
as well as freely chosen suffering, sacrifice, obedience, and humility. He is
thus a "moral exemplar" for human beings, a pattern that we try to emulate.
But he is also *more* than an objective ideal because he actually influences
human beings to *want* to emulate him; he awakens love, enkindles forgiveness, inspires obedience, elicits penitence.[24] Atonement occurs, then, as

human beings experience the limitless depths of the love of God and are transformed by it. The catalyst for this transformation, this awakening, is the knowledge and experience of the particularities of Jesus' life and death. When as sinners we read or hear about the astounding love that God revealed in Jesus, and the lengths that Jesus was willing to go to in order to express this love, proponents of the Abelardian model are convinced that our stony hearts will be softened, that God's amazing forgiveness will generate in us gratitude, penitence, and obedience. In a letter to his beloved Héloïse, Abelard urges her to imagine that she is a witness to Christ's passion:

> Are you not moved to tears of remorse by the only begotten Son of God who, for you and for all mankind, in his innocence was seized by the hands of impious men, dragged along and scourged, blind-folded, mocked at, buffeted, spat upon, crowned with thorns, finally hanged between thieves on the Cross, at the time so shameful a gibbet, to die a horrible and accursed form of death? Think of him always, sister, . . . Keep him in mind. Look at him going to be crucified for your sake, carrying his own cross. Be one of the crowd, one of the women who wept and lamented over him. . . . Have compassion on him who suffered willingly for your redemption.[25]

For Abelard and his successors, the story of the voluntary death of the innocent Jesus and of his horrible suffering is understood to awaken in its hearer a contrite heart, a reforming, reconciling love. The Abelardian view of atonement, then, is circumscribed not by justice but by mercy. The incarnation is a gift of divine love; it is not necessary but gratuitous; its purpose is to educate, not placate, to please rather than appease. Frederick Dillistone explains, "The establishment of justice for which [Abelard] looks is not the exacting of a *quid pro quo* nor the restoring of a tarnished honor."[26] Real justice involves, rather, the voluntary service to others that is motivated and guided by sacrificial love—the love perfectly exemplified by Jesus.

Another important deviation from the Anselmian model is evident in the Abelardian view of sin. While both models agree that certain behaviors such as disobedience and rebellion are sinful, their views diverge at the conceptual level. For Anselmians, sin is an objective barrier, an infinite wall between God and humanity that only God can surmount through the death of Christ, required to satisfy divine justice. For Abelardians, on the other hand, sin is a relative distance, a gap between where we are and where we ought to be; and all that is needed is a prompting, an awakening or moving, which is achieved in the life and death of Christ, the perfect expression of divine love.

As we have seen, Abelard introduced into discourse about atonement at least two novel emphases: the creative love of God, and the importance of the

individual human response to this love. Atonement occurs as the human subject is touched by divine love—incarnate in Jesus the Christ—and allows this
love to transform one's entire being into a Christlike pattern of obedience,
humility, and compassion.

It was not until the nineteenth century that the Abelardian model of
atonement gained popular support in theological circles. Its best-known proponent, Friedrich Schleiermacher, rejected traditional attempts to construe
atonement in terms of satisfaction, substitution, or punishment. Like
Abelard, Schleiermacher emphasizes the exemplary nature of Christ's life and
death, as well as human beings' capacity to respond to God's saving intention.
Schleiermacher insists that although humanity's original perfection has been
besmirched by the ugliness of sin, it has not been completely wiped out because we retain vestiges of our original predisposition toward God-consciousness.[27] Christ's perfect God-consciousness is both the fulfillment of
human potential—the perfection of human nature—and the in-breaking of
something novel, the definitive revelation of divine–human fellowship. Thus,
Christ originates and makes possible a completely unique communion with
God, a simultaneity of immanence and transcendence that enables all those
who follow him to move toward ever greater fellowship with God and one
another.

For Schleiermacher, atonement is the ongoing process by which human
beings—moved by the potency of God's love and empowered by communities of faith—aspire toward perfect God-consciousness as originally embodied and made possible by Jesus the Christ. The actual historical person of
Jesus of Nazareth, as well as the community that cohered around him, creates
the possibility of divine-human intimacy and mediates this possibility to all.
And the free response of human subjects transforms the possibility of perfect
God-consciousness into increasing approximations of actuality.

Regarding the necessity and efficacy of Jesus' suffering and death,
Schleiermacher asserts that "no complete assumption into vital fellowship with
Christ, such as makes redemption and reconciliation completely intelligible,
would have been possible before the suffering and death of Christ." However,
the suffering and death are understood to have salvific import not in and of
themselves, but as consequences of Jesus' fidelity to his mission—a commitment that "yielded to no opposition, not even to that which succeeded in destroying His person." We are mistaken, and deluded by "a magical caricature,
if we isolate this climax . . . and regard this giving up of Himself to suffering
for suffering's sake as the real sum-total of Christ's redemptive activity." Rather
than a voluntary self-immolation, Jesus' passion is rightly understood as "sympathy with misery," and as an outgrowth of his complete solidarity with sinful
humanity, made possible by his perfect God-consciousness.[28]

Somewhat surprisingly, Schleiermacher affirms traditional notions of Jesus the Christ as victim and sacrifice, as manifesting "perfect submission, without complaisance on the one side, or bitterness or ill-humour on the other," and yet he insists that these postures or roles are "the crown of His *active obedience*" (emphasis added). Because the suffering of sympathy "accompanied Him throughout His whole life"—because, in other words, "Christ was receptive toward everything which came to Him from the corporate life of sin"—Schleiermacher suggests that even the apparent passivity of Christ was the inevitable outgrowth of his active commitment to human beings and to God. "Looked at more closely," he says, "active and passive obedience were bound up with each other at every moment" of Jesus' life and death.[29]

In addition to reinterpreting the idea of obedience as it relates to the saving work of Christ, Schleiermacher puts a new spin on the ideas of substitution and vicarious satisfaction. Contrary to Anselm and his theological successors, Schleiermacher argues that "if we are to express ourselves with any accuracy we cannot say . . . that Christ fulfilled the divine will *in our place* or *for our advantage.*" Such assertions of substitutionary or vicarious atonement, he maintains, render humans utterly passive and hence undermine our responsibility for participation in our own salvation. As Schleiermacher insists, "Christ's highest achievement consists in this, that He so animates us that we ourselves are led to an ever more perfect fulfilment of the divine will." Jesus redeems humanity from sin and evil, then, not by "magically" acting in the stead of humanity, enduring the punishment we deserved or doing *for* us so that we no longer have to do for ourselves; neither is atonement achieved by externally injecting individuals with salvation. Rather, "in His suffering and death, occasioned by His steadfastness, there is manifested to us an absolutely self-denying love; and in this there is represented to us with perfect vividness the way in which God was in Him to reconcile the world to Himself." Through a life of "sympathy with misery" expressed in "an absolutely self-denying love," Jesus the Christ actualizes such intimacy with God, such blessedness of existence, that when we encounter this truth in our communities of faith, our hearts are enkindled with divine love, and the obstacles to our God-consciousness that were previously experienced as sin become opportunities for growth.[30]

In the twentieth century the Abelardian legacy is evident in so-called liberal theologies, such as the "social gospel" of Walter Rauschenbusch, and in process theologies.[31] Despite the substantial differences of this model from the Anselmian one, its emphasis on God's salvific, reconciling love as being decisively manifest in the life and death of Jesus—and particularly in his perfect obedience to God in humility and self-sacrifice—has merged with the Anselmian view to create the prevailing understanding of atonement. While the Anselmian model expresses the necessity and significance of Jesus' *death*, freely and actively willed so as to bear the consequence of our evil for us, the Abelardian model interprets the meaning of his *life*—embracing suffering and humiliation as expressions of love for humanity and obedience to God. Together, these models constitute an atonement orthodoxy that has withstood two centuries of scrutiny and that continues to enjoy canonical status within most Christian circles.

The latest barrage of criticism directed at this construal comes from relative newcomers to the theological scene. Feminist and liberation theologians contend that popular convictions about the saving work of Christ have had deadly consequences and therefore demand uncompromising critique. Feminist theologians in particular have directed relentless criticism toward this atonement orthodoxy, shedding light on some of its excesses and dangers and calling for its rejection. In concert with this position are concerns raised by womanist theologians about the impact of atonement doctrine on women and men of color. As Delores Williams has persuasively argued, the historical context that shapes African American women's experience of the doctrine of atonement is significantly different from that of most European American women and hence yields distinctive responses to traditional interpretations of the doctrine. Yet while the experiences and priorities of white women and African American women often diverge in important ways, feminist and womanist theologians tend to agree that traditional understandings of the redemptive efficacy of the suffering and death of Christ are problematic enough to demand careful scrutiny and, furthermore, to warrant rejection.

At the same time, however, these same theologians recognize the necessity of making moral claims; indeed, they understand their deconstructions of traditional views of atonement as moral responses, as confrontations of theological disease and abuse—and thus, the question of human evil and of God's response to it does not disappear but becomes even more urgent. The awareness of the theological bankruptcy of popular views of atonement, then, only highlights the need for alternative construals that can thematize both the reality and lethality of human evil and the hope for its transformation.

1

Surviving Traditional Notions of Sin

Traditional interpretations of atonement share, at minimum, the claim that through Jesus the Christ, God has effectively confronted the forces of sin and evil and in so doing has freed humankind *from* bondage to these forces and *for* right relationship with God. Yet this minimal claim involves complex assumptions, assertions, and arguments that often take conflicting forms; as a result, what is held in common frequently pales in comparison to the differences in interpretation on questions such as the particular content and effect of sin and evil, the specific role of Jesus in the process of their undoing, and the understanding and function of God in this equation. When viewed from a feminist perspective, however, the differences appear almost negligible, and an atonement orthodoxy emerges rather easily. This orthodoxy includes a network of assumptions and claims about the nature of sin and evil and the identity and function of God and Jesus the Christ, which it is the goal of these first three chapters to "unpack" and evaluate.

One of the primary preoccupations of feminist theology has been to emphasize the contextual character of all thoughts, ideas, and formulations. Drawing on the insights of critical social theorists such as Max Horkheimer and Jørgen Habermas into the false presumption of objectivity in most social theory, feminist theologians have extended and reshaped the critique to reveal the androcentric, or male-centered, character of traditional Christian theology.[1] Beginning with the recognition that theological doctrines and traditions have been shaped almost exclusively by men, whose ideas and interpretations have been erroneously promoted as value-free and universally applicable, feminists and other contextual theologians have further noted that these ideas and interpretations inevitably reflect the experiences and interests of their authors, who tend to be members of society's educated elite. These insights have motivated feminist theologians to expose and evaluate the disastrous history of effects that two thousand years of androcentric Christian theology have had for women, children, disenfranchised men, and the earth itself.

Feminist theologians have tried to be forthright about the contextual character of their own ideas and formulations. They have sought, on the one hand, to offer critiques of mainstream theology insofar as its doctrines and interpretations have been ignorant of, indifferent to, or exploitative of the concerns of women, children, and disenfranchised men; and, on the other hand, to propose alternative ideas and construals based on a commitment to the promotion of the full humanity of women and men, as well as the integrity and diversity of the nonhuman world. Hence a feminist hermeneutic may be understood as an interpretive posture or scheme that seeks, negatively, to confront and oppose what threatens or diminishes the physical, psychological, and/or spiritual well-being of women and other historically disenfranchised beings and, positively, to protect and promote such well-being.

Feminist analyses of traditional (male) Christian theology are multiplicitous and diverse in method and content; yet there is a shared conviction that despite the insight, wisdom, and creativity of much of the tradition, its concepts, theories, and doctrines frequently participate in a "politics of submission"—that is, they take place within, are shaped by, and contribute to the perpetuation of relations of domination among individuals, groups, and institutions.[2] More specifically, feminist theologians contend that regardless of its intentions, traditional theology has contributed to the creation and continuation of patriarchal modes of thought and practice and thus has had a deleterious impact on women, among others. Moreover, it is argued, a chief culprit in this sad process is the doctrine of atonement, which involves understandings of sin and evil, God, and Jesus the Christ that contribute to the exploitation and victimization of women and children and that, furthermore, militate against the creation of relations of mutuality, justice, and compassion.

Indeed, the very doctrine whose purpose it is to explicate the transformative truth that sin and evil have been decisively and effectively confronted through the divine agency of the person and work of Jesus the Christ has, paradoxically, become the means *par excellence* through which the sin of violence against women and the evil of patriarchy have been sanctioned by Christian theology. In response to this fact, feminist theologies focus on the doctrine of sin and evil in order to expose its subtle poison.

Out of Paradise

At the root of the doctrine of atonement is the reality of sin and evil.[3] As the story of Adam and Eve thematizes, our experience of everyday life is that it is not a paradise. Something is not right in the world, and somehow, human beings are responsible for this situation. Answers to the questions of exactly what is wrong, what caused the aberration, and what shape it takes have been thematized, defined, and symbolized in various ways throughout the history of Christian thought. Despite the diversity of interpretation, however, feminist scholars are in agreement that traditional views have tended to contribute to a politics of submission and must themselves be denounced as evil.[4]

Traditional configurations of sin and evil, with their emphases on disobedience, rebellion, willfulness, and original sin, have come under heavy fire by feminist theologians in recent years and have led to a revolution in thinking about atonement. At the forefront of feminist critiques is the unapologetic commitment to the protection and promotion of the full humanity and overall well-being of women.[5] Based on this commitment feminist theologians ask, What is the impact of atonement theories on the lived experience of women? And more specifically, What is the relationship between violence against women—whether physical, emotional, spiritual, economic, or political, whether overt or covert—and traditional understandings of sin and evil? Feminist evaluations and constructions of atonement frequently pay special attention to the alarming reality of sexual and domestic violence against women and children because there appear to be direct and indirect links between religious beliefs or theological categories—particularly those at the heart of traditional construals of atonement—and the victimization of women and children.[6]

The focus on sexual and domestic violence requires theologians and practitioners of religion to recognize that at issue in discourse about atonement, or any theological idea, are not abstract theological formulations or an innocuous play of ideas. While theological warrants, logical consistency, historical continuity, and other traditional criteria by which theologies are typically judged *are* legitimate, their significance pales in comparison to the actual impact of such ideas and criteria on the real lives of particular people. Theory and practice, feminist scholars agree, are inseparable.[7] Atonement theories should be evaluated not solely on the basis of their noble intentions or conformity to standards of orthodoxy, but also in light of their experienced effects. As Shelley Wiley asserts, "The lived-out consequences of a particular theory are, in fact, part of that theory."[8] When the lived-out consequences of the understandings of sin and evil implied by popular conceptions of atonement become the focus of attention, their untenability becomes clear. As we look again at some central themes related to traditional explications of sin and evil, this time through the lens of a feminist hermeneutic, our attention is drawn especially to the possible or actual negative consequences for the lived experiences of women and children, to the question of whether or not the theories legitimate the dehumanization, exploitation, and subjugation of some by others.

The Temptress and the Saint

The in-breaking of contemporary feminist Christian theology came with Valerie Saiving's 1960 article "The Human Situation: A Feminine View," in which she pointed out that traditional formulations of sin were based exclusively on the experience of males; not only were they inadequate in representing women's experience and different social location, she argued, but they had the result of compounding the obstacles to the healing of women's brokenness.[9] Since Saiving's watershed article, feminist criticisms of notions of sin and evil have become commonplace and share a concern for the issue of whether or not a particular construal contributes to the devaluation of women; yet the number and common focus of feminist critiques do not undermine their continued relevance, especially when so much of traditional views of atonement hinges precisely on how sin and evil are understood.

An early criticism of popular conceptions of sin and evil focused on their use of the myth of the Fall—particularly the biblical story of Eve's special culpability—to explain the origin and character of human evil. According to traditional interpretations of this myth, the curiosity, sensuality, and willfulness of the woman Eve spoiled the perfect bliss and abundance of God's creation. Woman's selfish but seductive rebellion against God's authority caused man's disobedience and, by extension, the untold suffering that thenceforth marked finite existence. Blaming Eve for human sin, claims Mary Daly, is just the beginning of a two-thousand-year history in which Christianity has scapegoated women as evil incarnate and in so doing has legitimated violence against them in never-ending forms. Eve's mythic disobedience in the garden and her subsequent seduction of Adam into her sinister plan resulted in the original breach between human beings and God. So it is that Eve is known in Christian theology as the originator of sin, as the one whose selfish deed taints all subsequent generations and, eventually, causes the horrible execution of God's beloved child Jesus, whose death finally cleanses the obedient from original sin and will, at the eschaton, restore the world to the original perfection of Eden. Although Daly admits that the intent of the story of the Fall was "to cope with the tragedy and confusion of the human condition," she insists that "since it was an exclusively male effort in a male-dominated society, it succeeded primarily in reflecting the defective social arrangements of the time" and has "reinforced sexual oppression in society."[10]

Largely as a result of this foundational narrative, Christian theology has tended to define sin in terms of disobedience, rebellion, willfulness, and sensuality, and hence the virtues it has extolled include obedience, submission to authority, selflessness, and sacrificial love. In other words, says Daly, "the qualities that Christianity idealizes, especially for women, are also those of a victim." Paradoxically, the traditional morality of Western culture has idealized precisely those qualities—obedience, passivity, meekness, humility—which its leaders eschew but which they extol for the oppressed masses. Christianity has preached submission but practiced domination; socialized women and the poor to passivity while acting with ruthless aggression to maintain its power and control at any cost; and as a result of its doublespeak on sin, "lulled/dulled to sleep" its own scapegoats so that they "forget the reality of gynocide" and instead internalize "the old embedded mechanisms of self-hatred and horizontal violence," which keep them entrapped in the cycle of victimization. Daly claims that this patriarchal definition of sin, with its scapegoating logic and projection of guilt onto women, is the *real* Fall, "the primordial lie," which signals "the 'Fall' of religion into the role of patriarchy's prostitute." The traditional view of sin and evil, then, "misnames the mystery of evil, casting it into the distorted mold of the myth of feminine evil," and in so doing "provides the setting for women's victimization by both men and women."[11]

A sad reality is that traditional definitions of sin, as well as the mind-sets and behaviors accompanying them, are often reinforced by Christian teachings and institutions, especially as they contribute to the development of young girls. Mary, the mother of Jesus, for instance, is held up to girls and women as the perfect role model. Her purity, passivity, and vulnerability are idealized in scripture, song, prayer, and passion plays and vignettes. She is depicted as uniquely suitable for being the mother of the Savior *because* of her demure innocence. Only occasionally have Christians emphasized Mary's individual agency and courage, or her marginalized status as the working-class mother of an illegitimate child. More often, her wide-eyed bewilderment and unquestioning obedience are exalted as honorable, often in conjunction with her role as perpetual mother—the woman who fulfills her gendered duty for all eternity. For Catholic girls in particular, Mary is lifted up as the model human being, the one whom all good girls should emulate. In Protestant traditions, the adulation of the innocent and obedient Mary is usually seasonal, coinciding with celebrations of the birth of Jesus; and although these traditions do not generally consider Mary to have continuing efficacy in the world, the power of the myth of the perfect, unsullied, perpetual mother continues to carry enormous theological and social weight for Catholics and Protestants alike.

The lesson for Christian girls and women is this: to avoid the evil of Eve, the willful one, we should cling to the legacy of Mary, the compliant one. In such an identity lies our hope for salvation from Eve's original sin. The irony of this designation of Mary as the premier role model for women and girls is not lost on Daly, who points out that since Mary is set apart from all women insofar as she was both virgin and mother, as well as conceived without original sin, she is literally impossible to imitate.[12] Yet women and girls are continually encouraged to identify with her purity and obedience; to do otherwise would be sinful.

The legacy of the two most renowned women in Christian history, Eve and Mary, has made itself felt in traditional thinking about sin and evil, both in terms of what is demonized and in terms of what is deified. Assumptions about the character of good and evil have been indelibly marked by the stories of these two women, and these assumptions have often translated into attitudes and behaviors that have wreaked destruction in the lives of real girls and women. In their study of female incest survivors, Annie Imbens and Ineke Jonker suggest that the religious upbringing of the girls made them "easy prey to sexual abuse in the [extended] family" and also militated against their healing from the abuse. In particular, incest survivors recalled that "the myth of the sinful woman" helped convince them that their abuse was punishment they deserved for being "bad" or evil. One survivor recalled, "Sacrificing yourself was always part of religion . . . you learned to put up with injustice and not to resist." Sin defined as disobedience and selfishness, in tandem with an emphasis on an otherworldly heaven, played a major role in the girls' victimization; as one admitted, "I was afraid to make one wrong move because then I wouldn't go to heaven"; and another recalled that "the only way to get into heaven was to be obedient enough and, above all, not to think of myself anymore."[13]

Theologies of Quietude
The constant emphasis on the sin of disobedience in the history of Christian thought has meant that resistance to or rebellion against authority is to be avoided at all costs. Such a theology of quiescence has worked to the advantage of ruling elites, abusive parents, partners, and elders, and all those whose violence depends in part on the passivity and pliability of another.[14] For those not officially schooled in the intricacies of Christian doctrine, these lessons are learned frequently through the stories, sermons, prayers, and hymns of Christian worship and discourse. In addition to the influential myth of the Fall, prayers of confession recited during Christian worship services teach participants to define sin in terms of disobedience, while freedom from sin is understood in terms of obedience. Witness this excerpt from the United Methodist liturgy:

> Merciful God,
> we confess that we have not loved you with our whole heart.

We have failed to be an obedient church.
We have not done your will,
we have broken your law,
we have rebelled against your love,
we have not loved our neighbors,
and we have not heard the cry of the needy.
Forgive us, we pray.
Free us for joyful obedience,
through Jesus Christ our Lord.[15]

Reflecting on the impact of this sort of prayer on its supplicants, Marjorie Procter-Smith reminds us that for women and children victimized by sexual and domestic violence, obedience becomes the harbinger of suffering, terror, and even death; thus, "the presuppositions of this prayer are particularly dangerous" for victims of abuse.[16] Prayers such as this one, though seemingly innocuous, inscribe their petitioners with an ideology of quietude that treats resistance to authority as a shameful transgression—a posture that plays into the hands of abusers and undermines the well-being of victims.

By defining sin and evil in terms of disobedience, willfulness, and rebellion, traditional construals have offered divine legitimacy to social, political, and economic systems of inequality and injustice as well as to individuals who seek justification for their abuse. Sin as pride brings with it undertones of guilt, blame, and self-hate for the one who dares to assert herself against authority; it also breeds a sense of powerlessness, since self-assertion is seen as problematic; and it justifies punishment of the willful. For women and children in abusive situations, the definition of sin as willfulness or pride can have devastating effects as it encourages victims of abuse not to resist, not to fight back, but to remain passive and compliant, to sacrifice their own concerns and needs for another, and then to despise their powerlessness and compound the inevitable self-loathing that results from acquiescence to violence.

In her discussion of sin and evil, Rita Nakashima Brock echoes Valerie Saiving and others in emphasizing that traditional views have so focused on sin as willfulness or pride that self-sacrifice has become "the highest form of love" within mainstream Christian theology. This is problematic for women and children, says Brock, because "it puts persons in conflict with themselves" and encourages blame, punishment, and guilt.[17] When self-love is seen as sinful, self-hate is often the result, and for women who are typically socialized to be self-effacing, as well as for children who must struggle to form their identities in an uncertain and sometimes hostile world, self-hate can be a debilitating posture that creates easy victims. Brock insists that rather than eschewing willfulness with interpretations of sin as pride, Christian theology must encourage people to resist victimization; she suggests that "nurturing willfulness" ought to be one of the fruits of theology. Reflecting on her own childhood, Brock comments, "I believe my willfulness served me well, because it made me resistant to coercion, both physically and theologically."[18] Jennifer Manlowe concurs that "'surrendering our wills' is at the core of female oppression in patriarchy." Based on her work with sexual abuse survivors, she asserts that a "survivor seeking a better sense of self must find a place where her will is not seen as the source of her problems. Her will, her power to act on her own behalf in the social world, is something she must recognize and nurture."[19]

While it may seem to many that this kind of psychological delimiting of women and children has finally ended—that these groups have been liberated from the shackles of past oppression and are now free to define their own identities and opportunities—plenty of indications remain that willfulness among women and children is still perceived as a threat to the social and moral order. The recent phenomenon of Promise Keepers, the hugely popular men's movement whose goal is to empower men to reclaim their proper role as head of the family and the church, is a dramatic example of this widespread perception. This movement is based on the conviction that men's failure to provide adequate moral and economic support has led to increased crime and social problems, and that women's audacity to leave the confines of traditional gender roles and to exert their own agency and ingenuity is chiefly responsible for unraveling the social and moral fabric of Western civilization. It is now up to men, the thinking goes, to reclaim their true masculinity; they must graciously but firmly take back from women the power and opportunity that men unwittingly relinquished and that women willfully embraced, to the woeful destruction of social and spiritual well-being. Men must promise to be generous, gentle, and fair leaders of family, church, and society, but there is no doubt that they must lead because that is what they were created to do. Women, the logic continues, are to abdicate authority and influence voluntarily, demurely, obediently. To do otherwise would be to defy natural and divine law.

In film and television, the depiction of women's agency and willfulness as a tragic flaw continues to be a popular theme. One of the most dramatic examples is the acclaimed film *Breaking the Waves* by renowned Danish director Lars von Trier. The story's heroine is Bess, whose selflessness is readily eulogized by family, friends, and pastor. Indeed, she is the paragon of Christian goodness—volunteering to scrub the church floors regularly, a sexual innocent upon her marriage to the strapping Jan, and a doting and compliant wife. Her unassuming innocence, disarming generosity, and fanciful demeanor bid the viewer to see her sympathetically, admirably.

The audience is granted access to the interior workings of Bess's celebrated morality through moments of prayer. From these intimate sessions we learn that Bess's God is a harsh master who derides her for being selfish, for not putting the needs and concerns of others before her own. More than anything, Bess is convinced that God desires her obedience to her husband; it is God's will that she show Jan the depth of her love by loving him selflessly.

When Jan is paralyzed in an accident at sea, he convinces Bess that only love can keep him alive. Since he cannot make love to her, she must have sex with other men while pretending she is with Jan, and then she must tell Jan of these exploits so that he can experience her love firsthand. Despite her horror at such sexual promiscuity and vacuous relationality, Bess summons the courage to fulfill her beloved's wish. Eventually, her actions cause her to be excommunicated from her church and rejected by her family. Yet she defiantly continues to prostitute herself, convinced that Jan's life depends upon her wholehearted obedience to his request and that God desires her wifely obedience, no matter what the cost.

What makes the story particularly pernicious is its ability to create viewers who are sympathetic to Bess's worldview. Bess's odd theology and reluctant masochism are convincingly depicted as signs of strength and courage, of angelic fidelity, faith, and goodness. Viewers are invited to see her perverse enslavement as an act of courage and commitment. Her condemnation by town, church, and family merely enhances her status as the persecuted innocent one whose transcendent morality is simply beyond the comprehension of those around her.

When the paralyzed and tormented Jan scribbles a note to Bess begging her to "Let me die. Evil in head," the viewer is allowed, for a moment, to consider Jan's request for Bess's prostitution as a moral aberration. Shortly thereafter, however, on her way to another loveless sexual encounter—this time to submit to the force of a violent man whom she had earlier fled—Bess prays to God for guidance and is affirmed in her sacrifice of love. Even when that sexual encounter turns violent and causes Bess's death, the logic of her sacrifice is upheld as Jan miraculously recovers his health. At the investigation into the cause of her death, the physician who treated both Jan and Bess proclaims that in the final analysis, Bess's death was caused by her goodness. She was simply too good for this world—too innocent, too loving, too giving, too obedient. Her violent death is cast as a courageous martyrdom, an act of transcendent love that stands as a lesson to those whose love is less than sacrificial. The film concludes with the ever-overcast sky opening up to reveal sunlight and blue sky, with heavenly bells tolling divine approval of this little angel's sacrifice.

Organizations such as Promise Keepers and films such as *Breaking the Waves* reflect the fact that the designation of women's willfulness as problem, as threat, as sin, has *not* disappeared from contemporary consciousness but is constantly being restated and recycled. They also demonstrate the deleterious impact of such an association, for whether women are being demonized as causing the "breakdown of family values" or deified as the bearers of perfect goodness through obedience, their agency and autonomy are under attack. Traditional Christian definitions of sin as pride and disobedience provide plenty of ammunition for this kind of dehumanization.

An additional problem with traditional views of sin has to do with the category of "original sin." The Augustinian legacy of a universal stain, a burden of guilt that we did not create but for which we are held responsible, *does* afford insight into the pervasive, "always already there" character of human evil, but it also contributes to a spirituality of shame that can worsen the predicament of those already shamed by the experience and stigma of sexual abuse. By depicting sin as an ahistorical quality, traditional notions make it into an abstract state separate from the particular relationships that shape human beings. The result, ironically, is that we are not required to take responsibility for the suffering we inflict. Nor are we empowered to respond to this universal burden of guilt with any kind of agency.

For survivors of sexual abuse, self-blame is a major obstacle to freedom and healing, and their sense of violation and defilement is only aggravated by notions of inherent sinfulness. Many of the abuse survivors with whom Manlowe worked, for instance, "pleaded to God not only to protect them, but also to purify them from their essential sinfulness."[20] Clearly, self-acceptance and personal power are essential for the healing of such victims, and yet sin defined as eternal and universal, or as characterized by disobedience and willfulness, actually engenders self-loathing and passivity. Too often, such feelings permit and perpetuate damaged selves and relationships.

Contextualizing Notions of Sin and Evil

Feminist critiques of popular views of sin and evil remind us that at stake in our theological conceptions is not merely scholarly reputation, intellectual coherence, or continuity with tradition but, sometimes, the very life and dignity of our fellow humans. In the face of such high stakes, it becomes clear that theological tradition has been so heavy-handed in its emphasis on sin as willfulness vis-à-vis an inscrutable authority, and on the seamless universality of human evil, that it has failed to account for the actual complexity of human destructiveness. Clearly, self-aggrandizement and prideful or indifferent self-assertion are distortions that Christian theology ought to address; egocentrism *is* a problem, and our theologies need to respond to it. The question is, Do one-sided conceptions of sin as disobedience, rebellion, and willfulness do justice to the gamut of human destructiveness? I think not. In fact, such conceptions reflect a dangerous myopia that has left entire classes of people without adequate theological resources for making sense of their experiences of the world and for accepting the gift of divine compassion as their own. At the same time, the lack of complexity in traditional thematizations of human evil has allowed certain individuals and groups to use theology to buttress their power at the expense of others. What we need is not the elimination of traditional notions of sin and evil but their contextualization and relativization. Within certain contexts, rebellion *is* demonic, pride *is* destructive, and willfulness *is* hurtful; but within other contexts, these qualities can literally save lives.

Despite their widespread discontent with traditional notions of sin, feminist theologians recognize that some such notion is indispensable to the formation and flourishing of human communities. Legitimate denunciations of the tradition's excesses and perversions regarding sin and evil should not come at the expense of any and all talk about these ideas. As Rosemary Radford Ruether argues, the rightful rejection of concepts of human evil that scapegoat women or others should not lead to neglect of "the basic theological insight that humanity has become radically alienated from its true relationship to itself, to nature, and to God."[21] The brokenness, suffering, and injustice caused daily by human attitudes and activities, both personal and institutional, must be taken seriously as aberrations of the wholeness and justice that God intends for the world.

I agree with Reinhold Niebuhr, Ruether, and others who argue that these and other aberrations come about as a result of "the distortion of the self-other relationship into the good-evil, superior-inferior dualism."[22] When the uncertainty of difference—of the irreducibility of the other—is perceived as a threat to oneself or one's gender, lifestyle, nation, race, or group, discomfort and self-doubt often turn into desperate attempts at self-securing in which the other is objectified not merely as different but as evil and hence inferior.[23] Particularly in times of crisis or when there is a perceived scarcity of goods, difference becomes the catalyst for demonization. It is simply easier to project onto the unknown or strange other my fears and insecurities; when I do this, the world seems easier to understand and negotiate because there is clarity—there are good and evil, us and them, mine and theirs. My tightly drawn social, emotional, and religious boundaries tell me whom to love and whom to hate, whom to trust and whom to fear, who will be saved and who will be damned. Within this neat conceptual and moral universe, ambiguity and complexity disappear into the stark but reassuring light of simplicity and certainty. I learn—but soon it is purely instinctive—when to clutch my purse tightly to my side and when to stride confidently down the walk without a worry in the world. As I drive through certain parts of the city, I unconsciously check to make sure the car doors are locked, for "these people" are not my people, and they probably want to hurt me or take what is mine.

Such subtle acts and thoughts populate my daily living and reflect the disability of an oversimplified morality that begins with the socially reinforced desire to divide an amazingly rich and multifaceted world into discrete, easily negotiable terms, and then to assume that the well-being of my self and group is somehow constantly under siege and in need of defense and fortification, no matter what the cost. This shift from discomfort to domination, from uncertainty to control, from ambiguity to reductionism, is the paradigm of evil, and it is at the root not only of individual indifference and cruelty but also of systemic evils such as sexism, racism, and ethnocentrism, for once the different one is thematized as "other"—the one whose very being poses a threat—then all manner of violence against the now-demonized other is justifiable.

Mary Potter Engel argues that rather than limiting our notions of sin and evil to just one model or definition, we need to expand our theological vision, keeping in mind that different contexts may require different concepts, that one size need not fit all. For example, when it comes to situations of interhuman violence and abuse, "specific behaviors that are labelled 'sin' by theologians are often *at the time of abuse* positive survival tactics for which the victims should be praised rather than faulted." Consequently, it may be helpful not "to reduce sin to a single root metaphor" such as disobedience or willfulness but to expand our conceptions and categories so as to include an expanse of destructive attitudes and actions. Thus, it is necessary to devise context-specific definitions that can account for "the ways in which victims as well as perpetrators have been tempted by evil structures."[24]

The primary goal is to make perpetrators of violence accountable, thereby stopping their violence and creating a space for the healing of their victims and the restoration of right relationship. A secondary objective is to avoid the temptation to reverse the traditional dualism (woman = evil, man = good) by asserting that women and other victims are exonerated from sin and evil. Women, like men, embody attitudes and behaviors that harm self and other, so we need categories that can recognize and respond to the different social histories and identities of women—the very real facts of women's multifaceted victimization—while also holding women accountable for the damage we do.

Engel proposes that these goals can best be met if we think of "sin" in terms of individual responsibility, and "evil" in terms of systems, structures, or patterns of oppression. Evil and sin are understood to be inextricably linked, and yet they are to be stressed differently in varying contexts: "When one is speaking of perpetrators, sin, individual responsibility, and accountability should be stressed" so there is no doubt that the perpetrator has done a horrible wrong that must be addressed; alternatively, "when one is speaking of and to victims, evil should be stressed" so that they might have an ethical framework within which to denounce the violence done to them while also recognizing the ways in which they may have been "tempted by evil structures, lured into complying with their own victimization."[25] Such a distinction allows the behavior and attitudes of both perpetrator and victim to be evaluated and criticized without "giving the impression that perpetrators (largely men) and victims (largely women) are coresponsible or equally sinful" for sexual violence. Hence the pervasiveness of human evil is recognized without allowing for an uncritical leveling that mitigates the demands of justice.

On the basis of this contextualized framework, we can evaluate the adequacy of specific definitions of sin and evil for situations of sexual and domestic violence. Sin defined as disobedience or willfulness is problematic because, as we have seen, such a view defuses rage, resentment, and other catalytic emotions, entrapping abused women and children in cycles of violence buttressed by cultural and religious assumptions of male authority and prerogative. Sin as pride or self-love is also problematic, particularly for victims recovering from abuse because, as Engel points out, "one of the enduring scars of abuse is self-blame or self-hatred"—an emotion abusers count on for their own protection.[26]

Interpretations of sin and evil that have been proposed in recent years as alternatives to traditional definitions should also be evaluated according to this bifocal standard. One definition that has been suggested as a feminist alternative is sin as moral callousness or hardening of heart.[27] Because this definition places the onus of responsibility squarely on the shoulders of the perpetrator of abuse rather than suggesting that the victim somehow brought it on herself through insubordination, it is an improvement over traditional views. And yet, as Engel indicates, this construal also has its weaknesses, for while it may be helpful in dealing with the sin of perpetrators and colluders, it is problematic when applied to the victims of sexual and domestic abuse as well as many other kinds of violence. In situations of violence, "the numbing of the self, the dissociation" that would fit under the category of "hardening of heart," can be a "necessary survival technique" used by victims "in order to distance themselves sufficiently from the abuse in order to bear it until such a time as they are able to escape or alter the situation."[28] Sin defined as moral callousness may be helpful in some circumstances and harmful in others.

Similarly, viewing sin as "betrayal or lack of trust" also effects a useful shift away from disobedience and toward a focus on a different kind of relationship between persons, "for it acknowledges that we exist together primarily not in an external system of rules but in dynamic relationships of trust, fidelity, and mutual obligation."[29] According to this way of understanding, sin is the shattering of the covenant of mutuality, "the breaking of the bond by the perpetrator through betrayal of trust, not the brokenness itself, in which victims cannot help participating."[30] And yet this definition, too, could be used by abusers to convince their victims that to resist the violence, or to expose it to others, would be to betray the covenant partner and hence to sin.[31]

Sin as alienation has been a popular notion in recent decades and is helpful insofar as it shifts attention away from disobedience, self-love, and anger. However, when applied to situations of personal violence, it is so broad and vague as to be almost useless. In addition, Engel notes, it "does not do justice to the active exploitative structures of a society built for the strong against the vulnerable." It does not take seriously enough the fact that violence against women, children, and others, though often individual, has structural support and systemic manifestations that must be addressed. Further, the definition of sin as alienation usually implies that the desired state is one of reconciliation, which can be problematic because it "suggests that any victim who is struggling to create a separate identity for herself is wrong." Finally, because this definition implies that "all participation in the condition of alienation is wrong, it casts blame equally on perpetrator and victim" and should not be employed uncritically but only in conjunction with other views that can account for the injustice of sexual violence.[32]

Another long-standing definition is that of sin as concupiscence. As Sallie McFague has shown, this view of sin can yield much fruit from a feminist perspective when it is broadly construed.[33] However, according to Engel, because of the tendency of those who have traditionally espoused this view to associate sin with sexuality and to focus on sin "individualistically rather than relationally," sin as concupiscence can "contribute to blaming the victim by identifying women as conspirators with the powers of this 'lower realm' and exonerating men as helpless victims of uncontrollable impulses."[34]

Another definition considered by Engel, and the one that appears to have the fewest weaknesses from the perspective of concern for the liberation of the vulnerable from sexual and domestic violence, is "sin as distortion of the self's boundaries." This view is an improvement over construals of sin in terms of disobedience or self-love because it implies a recognition of the fact that "powerlessness as well as power corrupts." Perpetrators are held accountable for their violation of the other's emotions, privacy, body, and/or will; while victims, especially women, are encouraged not "to lose [themselves] in others" but instead "to develop a sense of power as action and a strong sense of themselves as responsible individuals and to learn appropriate ways to love themselves."[35] As Valerie Saiving insisted in 1960, violence against others and violence to the self, both transgression and diffusion, are problems that any understanding of sin ought to account for. At the same time, this view of sin as distortion of the self's boundaries should not be used to imply that the responsibility of perpetrator and victim is equal. This definition needs to be complemented by and placed within a framework of an understanding of evil as systemic; otherwise, its narrow focus on the personal and interhuman spheres limits its applicability and usefulness.

Searching for Balance

This discussion of the destructive consequences of popular notions of sin and evil reveals a troubling paradox. On the one hand, traditional views permit the conflation of the Divine and the human, so that human rulers—whether parents, priests, CEOs, or presidents—can use notions of sin as disobedience or rebellion to shore up their own power at the expense of the less powerful. The practical consequence of this kind of identity of human authority and divine authority is injustice and abuse, as situations of sexual violence bring into sharp focus. At a theological level, the result is that the transcendence of God—the qualitative difference between divine and human that grounds human morality and stands in judgment of its perversions—is lost. God becomes a tool of the human will to power. God's *Godness*, the Wholly Other that can never be captured or controlled by finite minds or actions and that summons human individuals and communities toward self-overcoming renewal and transformation, is sacrificed on the altar of the human will to power.

On the other hand, however, these same definitions of sin and evil can be interpreted to focus so exclusively on divine-human relations that they establish human morality solely or even primarily in relation to a transcendent Other, with the result that the interhuman sphere is practically ignored. When sin is defined exclusively or primarily as humanity's insubordination to or alienation from *God*, our inhumanity to one another becomes an ancillary concern. Nel Noddings suggests, "The religious tradition has ratified evil by distracting us from each other and leading us to believe that our salvation rests in our relation only to God."[36] In this scenario, then, the overwhelming *transcendence* of God distracts us from our responsibilities to one another.

In both renderings of sin and evil, it seems to me, the breadth of human experience and brokenness is ignored and the character of divine activity delimited. At the root of this troubling paradox is a facile rendering of divine transcendence and immanence. According to traditional formulations, divine transcendence is understood to imply and even require domination; it signifies an absolutely unilateral relationship, a power-over that disempowers all others. Immanence, on the other hand, is thought to imply an undifferentiating relationship of identity—a collapsing of the Divine and the human that is at best amoral and at worst idolatrous. These definitions of divine being and activity stem from and reflect the problems of a *patriarchal* framework

with its assumption of inequality and so are actually perversions of sound theological insights. In opposition to this distortion, I argue that a logic of antithesis—of a strict either/or—is *not* necessary to achieve differentiation.
Divine transcendence does not require the infantalization or powerlessness of
human beings, and neither must divine immanence undermine human
morality. Rather, transcendence and immanence can be seen as complementary, organically related qualities of divine reality and activity that ground and
stand in judgment of human actions, attitudes, and institutions, even while
they are mediated through the contingencies of human history and ideas.[37]

Within such a framework, divine authority can be understood to be
based not in a logic of domination but in a logic of compassion, of the concern of the Creator for the well-being of all creation. Thus, God's authority
and power are understood to intend and enhance human flourishing within
the larger community of life, exemplifying power as power-in-and-toward-
community. Sin, then, is not disobedience qua authority; it is not rebellion
against God seen as isolated from the world, but rebellion against God's care
for the world, against the world as God's manifestation of creative love,
against the world as God's body.[38]

The challenge from a feminist perspective, in the final analysis, is to reject construals of sin and evil that do not safeguard the full humanity and
agency of women, children, and disenfranchised others, including the nonhuman world, precisely because in not protecting those who have been historically marginalized and exploited, Christian construals of sin and evil enslave
rather than redeem or liberate. Indeed, insofar as it is the function of the doctrine to name, thematize, and denounce the attitudes, behaviors, and patterns
that result in the diminishment of life, growth, opportunity, and community
of and for *all*, the Christian doctrine of sin and evil undermines its own viability when it fails to do these things. From a feminist perspective, it is clear
that given our knowledge of the horrors and unjust dynamics of sexual and
domestic violence, it is no longer possible to define sin and evil in terms of disobedience, self-love, or willfulness unless and until the patriarchal framework
within which these definitions are understood to function is replaced.

Beyond Patriarchy

The ramifications of this recognition for traditional interpretations of atonement are enormous. The atonement orthodoxy claiming popular support
today has at its core the conviction that human pride and rebellion against
God's authority are solely to blame for the suffering, strife, and alienation in
the world and for the disruption of the divine–human relationship. As a result
of this conviction, the people and movements that defy convention, circumvent authority, or otherwise vary from social norms are experienced as threats

to a sacred order, fallen angels whose deviant ideas and ways are to be vigorously resisted. This fact is clearest in what we have identified as the Anselmian model of atonement, although since the Abelardian model defines sin primarily in terms of disobedience and/or willfulness, it is similarly problematic.

According to the Anselmian model, human sin is understood in terms of disobedience and dishonor. By refusing to grant God the honor deserved/demanded by the Divine, human beings display a willfulness that will not be tolerated. Disobeying the rules of relationship in which the honor of a superior is always to be recognized in an appropriate fashion is a serious act with serious consequences. If humankind had only paid proper homage to the rules of convention, the logic goes, the entire christological drama would have been unnecessary. Mutuality, reciprocity, a healthy balance between being-for-self and being-for-others—these are not the goals of divine-human relationship, at least not the relationship implied by conceptions of sin and evil based on disobedience and/or dishonor. Rather, this view contributes to a politics of submission of cosmic proportions. In addition, the sin committed by human beings is usually understood to be a universal, ahistorical act for which all are equally responsible; there is no room here for distinctions between victim and victimizer, for nuances in determining degrees of culpability and expectations for repentance or rehabilitation. Furthermore, the Anselmian model includes a purely juridical notion of justice, one untempered by love or compassion; indeed, as a result of the original rebellion, obedience becomes the prerequisite of love.

From a feminist perspective, the implications of the Anselmian view of sin and evil are profoundly problematic. The implied model of relationship based on the unilateral power of one over another not only mirrors situations of systemic violence and personal abuse, but also offers them divine sanction. The sharp dichotomy of love and justice that is implied creates the false impression that these two are mutually exclusive rather than organically related so that the claims of each impact the exercise of the other. In both Anselmian and Abelardian traditions, the focus on disobedience includes a definition of love in terms of obedience, which is problematic for all those who need or want to resist the prevailing order. Although the Abelardian model avoids the love-justice dichotomy, it still exhibits the problems associated with viewing sin in terms of disobedience or willfulness.

The main difference between these two traditions, it seems to me, is that the Anselmian model not only reflects but actually *requires* a theological paradigm of domination; it is preconditioned by unequal power relations and cannot exist in their absence. God's power and authority are grounded in an absolute transcendence that requires the powerlessness of human beings—a state enforced by the constant threat of punishment. It is a model easily co-opted by power-hungry mortals because it assumes and reinforces inequalities of power.

The Abelardian model, by contrast, does not appear to be irrevocably wed to such a paradigm. Its primary focus is on love, not punishment; on transformation instead of the reinstatement of a relationship of inequality. Thus, the classic emphases on love as obedience and self-sacrifice, and on sin as disobedience and willfulness, reflect the shape of the Abelardian model within a patriarchal paradigm but may not exhaust its possible meanings. Indeed, extracted from this paradigm these emphases point to important insights into human pathologies and possibilities. Once the assumption of unequal power is rejected, new definitions of love and sin become possible. In the final chapter of this book, such a depatriarchalized version of the Abelardian conviction that God is love will be affirmed within the context of a reconstruction of the patristic model of atonement. For now, however, we turn our attention to the understandings of God implied by traditional models of atonement.

2

Wrestling with God

Metaphors intended to characterize God have a dual directedness. On the one hand, they point toward the absolutely indescribable—God, the infinite, ultimate reality, the ground of being. At the same time, they direct attention toward the finite, for it is only in and through the language and conceptualities of finite beings that any God-talk at all is possible. The problem with traditional notions of God, then, is not that they are metaphorical, since theological language is inevitably so. Rather, the problem is that they draw on and reflect only a small segment of reality and experience, granting it unlimited, universal, and exclusive relevance and authority.

When only certain groups' experiences, or certain roles, are permitted to "figure" the Divine, these experiences and roles begin to be seen as theonomous—as elevated into the realm of the holy—so that the areas from which they come attain special power and authority. When these valued realms happen to be inhabited and defined by those who enjoy social, economic, and political power, and who have historically used this power to shore up their authority and wealth at the often considerable expense of others, religious symbols become tools for perpetuating the status quo; theological metaphors provide divine sanction for injustice and oppression. Indeed, God-talk becomes demonic.[1]

Sallie McFague notes that when one metaphor or model for the Divine excludes other images and loses its contingent dimension—when its hypothetical character is forgotten and "what ought to be seen as *one* way to understand our relationship with God has become identified as *the* way"—it has become an idol.[2] Feminist theologies contend that this is precisely what has happened to the patriarchal model of God; whatever its original intention or function may have been, it has become an idol that gives legitimacy to a way of life that privileges wealth and power and that contributes to patterns of victimization and abuse. Thus, interpretations of atonement that depend upon this model hinder the full humanity of women, children, and disenfranchised men as well as the integrity and diversity of the nonhuman world.

A Theology of Control

In the Anselmian strand of atonement thinking, God's sovereignty is of the utmost importance. God is like the medieval king or feudal overlord of Anselm's day: in control of his affairs and quick to confront, and usually punish, any who challenge or threaten his authority or status. Hierarchy is the hallmark of order, and God is at the top of the hierarchy. Sin, defined as disobedience, dishonors God and disrupts the order of the universe; it is punishable by death. Undergirding this conception of God is a theology of control.

Feminist criticisms of the sovereignty metaphor are numerous. They take issue with its hierarchical character, its assumption of unbreachable distance between God and world, its valorization of power as domination, and its apparent obsession with order and authority. The conception of God as divine king or ruler pictures God as separate from the world, ruling it from above, and portrays human beings, by implication, as rebellious subjects in need of control. Thus, the Anselmian view of atonement infantalizes human beings insofar as it portrays us as disobedient *and* helpless. We are to blame for an infinite transgression, but we are powerless to mend the situation. If God is all-powerful king, then we are abject subjects, completely helpless and utterly dependent. God's power requires our powerlessness.

Paradoxically, then, the model of God as sovereign encourages two antithetical but equally dangerous self-perceptions among humans: either we associate ourselves too closely with God's power, imagining ourselves to be superior to and in control of the world around us; or else we view ourselves as so different from God that we have no real power at all, and we become easy victims for those who embrace the former conceptuality. Either way, a healthy sense of self as both limited and powerful is obscured.

At the heart of the sovereignty metaphor is a logic of subordination that can offer sacred sanction to interhuman hierarchy and injustice because it relies on and supports an understanding of power as domination. It also feeds a sense of despair, fatalism, and passivity among those who assume that because God has all the power, we humans should abdicate responsibility for the world. In addition, images of a transcendent, heavenly God remind us that the earth is only of ancillary importance, so how we treat the nonhuman environment is not a primary concern.[3]

Taken together, feminist critiques reveal that the metaphor of divine sovereignty has become a central piece in a theology of quietude. Like traditional views of sin and evil, normative construals of God are dangerously amenable to power politics because they provide religious examples of and justification for systems and relationships of sustained inequality. The injustice of such social and political arrangements is hidden behind the language and legitimacy of theology. The human will to power is seen as an inevitable or natural reflection of the divine will, and patterns of victimization become part and parcel of "the way things are." As Sharon Welch has argued, "The concept of an omnipotent or providential deity serves to subvert rebellion and remove the imperative of responsibility for social change," a dynamic that "insures the survival of the social system by eliciting accommodation to it."[4]

Such status quo theologies, with God's sovereignty as their foundation, express a fear of change and an obsession with security that have characterized much of Christian thought through the centuries. As Welch points out, they reflect an almost pathological demand for universal or absolute truth at the expense of critical thinking, diversity of perspective, and a healthy recognition of fallibility. Despite the fact that models of divine sovereignty are intended to stand as a limit to and correction of the human will to power, they make this point at the price of valorizing absolute power. The assumption "that absolute power can be a good," says Welch, obscures the fact that it requires domination and submission, that it legitimates and necessitates relationships of inequality and alienation. Ironically, then, "the claim of relativization, of submission to the greatest power, legitimates domination of others."[5]

The Deification of Power

The emphasis in traditional models of atonement on divine omnipotence often defines and valorizes power *as* absolute, as noncontingent, solidary, unitary—in other words, as devoid of mutuality, relationality, plurality, or partiality. According to this view, to be powerful is to be totally independent and unaffected by others. To be powerful is to *have* power, a mentality making power a commodity that one competes to attain and accumulate. To be powerful is always a relative accomplishment since it depends upon *having more* power than one's peers, colleagues, friends, or competitors. At the root of traditional construals of atonement is the divinization of unilateral power—that is, as Rita Nakashima Brock articulates it, power that is "hierarchical and is demonstrated by dominance, by status, by authority, and by control over people, nature, and things."[6] Such power feeds on and requires a complementary, but equally problematic, kind of power: power as compliance, as self-sacrifice and submission. Clearly, both power-as-control and power-as-compliance are two sides of the same coin, for both create and perpetuate relations of domination and submission.

To predicate the divine-human relationship on this model is to sacralize inequality, to ordain exploitation. It is also to posit a terrifying, immoral deity whose greatness depends upon the abasement of others. In situations of child abuse, say researchers Annie Imbens and Ineke Jonker, "the crucial element is the offender's unilateral position of power, which limits the child's freedom and her options."[7] In these and other contexts in which power becomes a tool of violence, it is difficult to deny that people who use power to dominate others benefit from a theology that portrays divine power as control. In their glorification of God's absolute power, traditional Christian theologies wield a dangerous weapon whose easy accommodation to human violence renders it morally reprehensible.

Even while models of divine power are used to buttress and legitimate the earthly power of the powerful, these same models render the masses of human beings power*less*. As a result of the constant emphasis on power as domination and submission, most Christians become infantalized and are at the complete mercy of another to save us. Our sense of powerlessness in the face of an all-powerful one becomes a self-fulfilling prophecy that compounds our helplessness and passivity. For those who are victimized by patterns and systems of social, economic, and political exclusivity or injustice, or by interpersonal abuse, this disempowering cycle can be especially acute because it undermines the will to resist or protest dehumanization and thus perpetuates and entrenches the victimization. As one incest survivor recalls: "In their (the church's) religion, you had to sacrifice your own self completely. You [weren't] allowed to offer any resistance. So you couldn't stand up for yourself. God created people. People exist to serve God."[8] Here the debilitating effects of divine sovereignty and absolute power come into sharp focus.

To many Christians, the insight that we humans are, ontologically or theologically, completely powerless and hence absolutely dependent on someone else to save us, is precisely the truth at the heart of Christian wisdom and is absolutely indispensable. Nonetheless, it seems to me that in today's world, our knowledge of the reality and pervasiveness of personal and institutional abuse and oppression brings with it a responsibility to reconfigure theological convictions and doctrines so that they no longer contribute to patterns of evil. Such reconfigurations need not be seen as a threat to Christian identity or community but should, instead, be understood as responses of faith, as attempts to create theologies that reflect the experience and hope that God desires the freedom and flourishing of all creatures. Emphases on human separation from God and on our profound need for saving grace and power must not come at the expense of human dignity and agency. Whether we like it or not, the history of effects of an infantalizing theology is violence and injustice on earth. Rather than clinging doggedly to past formulations of divine power, insisting that the solution is simply to embrace them more passionately, we must be willing to risk tradition and legacy, to think new thoughts, to let the winds of the Spirit breathe transformation into our theological constructions and spiritual lives. Without such daring, our faith becomes an empty and idolatrous mantra, a lifeless collection of dogma.

A Good Model Gone Bad

When divine sovereignty and omnipotence are combined with the model of God as father, as they are in most Anselmian and Abelardian strands of atonement thought, the abusive potential of these ideas becomes incontrovertible. Regardless of the original intentions and adequacy of the model of divine fatherhood, feminist theologians agree that because it has been interpreted to exclude the viability of alternative models, it has lost its transformative power and become an idol. In patriarchal cultures, the model of God as father essentially divinizes fatherhood and destroys its potential to function metaphorically. The result, says McFague, is that "'father' becomes God's 'name' and patriarchy becomes the proper description of governing relationships at many levels."[9] The sad result is that the model of divine fatherhood is absolutized and granted hegemonic status, while the richness and complexity of the divine-human relationship are ignored.

Ultimately, the problem is not with fatherhood per se or with parental models of God.[10] Family relationships are some of the most powerful influences in our lives, and healthy, loving parenting can become a meaningful example of divine love and care, manifesting dimensions of the divine–human relationship that cannot be otherwise expressed. Yet within the context of the patriarchal family, "fatherhood" too often connotes control, domination, the seat of power and authority, the sole arbiter of justice, and the dispenser of punishment; and God the Father is then understood to embody and legitimate these characteristics. Notions of father as provider, partner, lover, caretaker, and protector are eclipsed by the overwhelming emphasis on patriarchal power and authority.

The focus by many feminist theologians on the issue of family and sexual violence is one piece of a much larger puzzle in which patriarchal relations—that is, relations of domination—govern patterns of individual, group, and institutional interactions and hence pervade personal relationships as well as economic and social policies and practices. Sexual and domestic abuse can be viewed as a microcosm of societal violence funded by a patriarchal culture. When we direct our attention to this terrible phenomenon, we see that images of God the Father are often accompanied in the experiences of survivors of abuse with "imperatives to obey" and to keep silent about the violence. Susan Brooks Thistlethwaite notes, "The divine anchor for the power of the father in God the Father is a powerful tool for keeping the silence." This insight finds support in the work of Imbens and Jonker with incest survivors. Their study leads them to conclude that "the power of the father and the male members of the (extended) family [is] the most important factor contributing to the sexual abuse of girls."[11]

For some survivors of sexual violence, the image of God as the ideal father stands in stark contrast to their own father's violence and thus becomes a source of resistance to abuse; but more often, God is identified with the woman's own father. Survivors recall that "Father wanted to be worshiped, too," and that "Father was a kind of god." Another commonality among survivors is the image of God the Father as "easily offended" and "jealous," as one who "demands obedience and conformity."[12] Resisting abuse, even through tears, is often interpreted as rebellion, not only against the perpetrator of violence, but against God. In some cases, the connection between God the Father and the male or parent abuser is made explicit, as when perpetrators make reference to God to rationalize their abusive behavior.

One of the main problems with Christian understandings of God as father is that they tend to conflate and confuse feelings of fear, respect, and love in ways that both infantalize battered women/believers and bind them to their batterer/God. Anne Marie Hunter's work on this poisonous dynamic is instructive. Hunter contends that in most families and communities, there exists a confusion among love, respect, and fear, and this confusion carries over into the way we think about and relate to God. In typical patriarchal households, the family or home is an ambivalent place for children. On the one hand, it is a place for "togetherness and solidarity, a base for ethical training and understanding, and a familiar constant in the midst of immense cultural upheaval and transition"; on the other hand, however, it is often "rigidly hierarchical, and [demands] the self-sacrifice and obedience of the individuals who [fall] within its domain." The tension between these emotional trajectories is kept in play by a blending of the ideas of love, respect, and fear. Love is expressed by showing respect, by exhibiting an attitude of deference and obedience toward elders or the family unit as an entity; and "where love alone [is] inadequate to secure the respect" deemed appropriate, fear enters the equation as the subtext that wards off rebellion and chaos and keeps the whole "fragile equilibrium" intact.[13] Love within the patriarchal family, then, occurs within the context of particular assumptions about power. Children learn that love occurs in the midst of, and often as a result of, fear and respect.

When the complex conjunction of fear, respect, and love that characterizes much of family life is combined with religious injunctions requiring children to honor their parents and love God, the sad result is that "children are faced with a tormenter they love, not one they hate."[14] In this scenario, religious ideas and convictions aggravate and support familial dysfunction and abuse. For Christians, the directive to love and respect/fear our earthly parents is intimately tied to our image of and relationship to God the Father, our heavenly parent. When the believer is seen as the "child of God" and God is understood as divine father, the divine–human relationship mirrors the parent-child one, and thus "in the relationship between the child-believer and the father–God, we normalize and legitimate, indeed, we sacralize, the fear/respect/love construct that characterizes the relationship of the child to the parent."[15] So family violence is "reflected, sanctioned, and justified on a divine level."[16]

Hunter further contends that the continuum of fear, respect, and love functions not only in child–parent and believer–God relationships, but in adult male–female relationships in general, and in abusive male-female relationships in particular. In these relationships, the woman is infantalized by the batterer, who "often sets himself up as the parent (or father) who has the right to punish (abuse) the child-woman." The fear/respect/love dynamic also helps explain why some women remain in abusive situations; many stay for socio-economic reasons, yet there are emotional reasons that are often more difficult to recognize. Just as "deep-seated connections among fear, love, and respect bind together families, communities, and relationships between the child-believer and the father-God," so can such complex emotions bind an abused woman to her abuser. Like many others in a patriarchal culture, battered women find themselves with "a tormenter they love, not one they hate."[17]

To begin to dissolve the fear/respect/love combination that is responsible for the latent violence of most all relationships—divine-human and interhuman—within a patriarchal culture, Hunter urges that "we need to undermine not only the 'poisonous pedagogy' that confounds fear/respect/love in our children, but also the *imago dei* that sanctifies this pedagogy." In other words, family violence will not end until its theological support is terminated. The implication of this insight for the doctrine of atonement is that traditional views that model the divine-human relationship in terms of the fear/respect/ love continuum of control ought to be rejected. Furthermore, insofar as traditional views assume a father-God who infantalizes us into children-believers who owe "him" respect and obedience—out of either love or fear—then, as Hunter concludes, "we are all in danger of being emotionally bound in destructive relationships, and, ultimately, of creating a God who has become 'a tormenter we love, not one we hate.'"[18]

Despite the recent attitude of backlash against victims of family and sexual violence, there is overwhelming evidence to indict families, schools, churches, and government agencies—in other words, the social institutions most directly responsible for the protection of children and other vulnerable populations—for turning deaf or insensitive ears to the problem of abuse.[19] As

the complicity of Christian people, rituals, and institutions is gradually transformed into genuine support for victims, as well as rehabilitative efforts toward
perpetrators, theological doctrine must also be transformed or reconstructed.
Construals of atonement claiming that redemption from sin and evil occurs
through the absolute power of the sovereign father-God—whether imaged as
offended overlord, wrathful judge, or loving parent—are no longer acceptable.

Nowhere to Hide

In addition to calling into question the legitimacy of metaphors of divine sovereignty, omnipotence, and fatherhood, theologies concerned about ending
violence against women and children must be critical of traditional images of
God that assume that God is all-knowing and all-seeing. When placed
within a context of power-as-control, traditional claims of divine omniscience
can increase the destructive impact of the patriarchal model of God. Battered
women and abused children frequently exist under the pervasive surveillance
of their abusers. Male batterers typically attempt to circumscribe the activities and curtail the freedom of their victims; some even go so far as to mon-
itor phone calls and confine their victims to the home, although more subtle
controlling tactics are more common. The jealousy of the batterer, combined
with his need to control his victim and to deter her from revealing the abuse
to others, can create situations of virtual imprisonment for the woman involved. For children, the abuser often concocts an elaborate world of secrecy
and make-believe in which special "love" games are played but never, ever dis-
closed. To refuse to play the game, or to disclose its existence, is to reject all
relationship with the abuser, usually a parent, relative, or respected adult, who
insists that any such rebellion will be known to the abuser, who will then be
forced to punish the child either physically or, more insidiously, emotionally.

The victim's predicament can be likened to the one described by
philosopher Michel Foucault in *Discipline and Punish*, in which the panopticon design of prisons allows guards to see every cell at every moment.
Foucault argues that this pervasive surveillance becomes, over time, a normative gaze that is eventually internalized by the individual prisoners, who become the object of their own subjection, policing themselves voluntarily because of their interiorization of the power situation. The constant situation of
surveillance renders external surveillance unnecessary because the inmates
become "caught up in a power situation of which they themselves are the
bearers."[20]

Similarly, in a patriarchal society, the white and male gaze is so pervasive that it is normative and hence invisible; individuals learn to see themselves through the lens of the normalizing gaze of men, thus internalizing
this gaze and becoming self-policing subjects. The situation of battered

women and abused children is compounded by the explicit surveillance they often undergo from abusers. In addition, the Judeo-Christian God, who is described as, among other things, jealous, all-seeing, ever watchful, and omniscient, can extend the normative male gaze into realms where no human eye can see. Even private rebellions or mental insurrections are seen and known—and so the self-policing must extend into the most private regions of heart and mind.

According to one survivor of child sexual abuse, God's omniscience and omnipresence highlighted the injustice of God's silence/ passivity in the face of abuse: "I had to be really careful because He saw everything. I didn't understand His almightiness, because He didn't intervene and left me to fend for myself for so long." In addition, the notion that God was "domineering and jealous" caused abuse victims to fear God: "Religion was being scared to death. It seemed to me that women were always to blame." The inconsistency between views of God as all-seeing, good, just, almighty, and protective, on the one hand, and the recognition, on the other, that despite all this knowledge and ability God permitted the abuse, causes many victims to doubt their experience and instincts and to obey God's inexplicable ethic of submissiveness and self-hatred out of fear and confusion. Imbens and Jonker observe: "They were afraid of God's almightiness in combination with the divine all-seeing eye. They recognized these characteristics in their own fathers who committed incest." Finally, they point to the connection between God's power and omniscience: "Power can only be maintained by constantly keeping an eye on everything. That is what the powerful do, and God does that, too. He is all-seeing."[21]

Among the church fathers, Augustine was certainly aware of the self-policing potential of an all-seeing God. He made frequent use of the rhetoric of God's surveillance in order to admonish both men and women to avoid shameful behavior, as in this bit of counsel: "It is necessary to be as fearful in private as in public. You are seen whether you are inside or outside. The light burns: he sees you. The light is extinguished: he sees you. Inside your bedchamber, he sees you. Thus fear him whose care it is to see you, and this fear will make you chaste."[22] In our day, this fear-based theology sacralizes a normative male gaze that can reach into the deepest recesses of life and mind, watching, listening, objectifying, and delimiting the lives of those who lack the cultural power or maturity to avert it. This "big brother" God empowers abusers and confuses, terrifies, and terrorizes their victims.

The Shame of It

A final point of focus is the problematic issue of God's honor. Anselmian explanations of atonement emphasize that human sin takes one of three forms:

disobedience, disorder, and/or dishonor. Disobedience and disorder are quelled by images of God as all-powerful sovereign and father—images whose devastating history of effects stands as an indictment of both Anselmian and Abelardian models of atonement insofar as these models rely on such metaphors. But what about honor? Is it an equally objectionable emphasis, or does it manage to avoid the pitfalls of the other images? For many contemporary women and men, the concept of honor is a vague or irrelevant one, and the claim that it is a primary attribute of the Divine may be confusing. But in Anselm's day, honor was a central value around which social convention revolved. Today it is the idea of shame that is found in the titles and subtitles of self-help guides and recovery bestsellers, is heard frequently from podiums and pulpit and, according to Donald Capps and others who work in the counseling field, is one of "the most common experiences of torment caused by religious ideals."[23]

It may be instructive to look again at the notion of honor, in contradistinction to which shame is often understood, and to explore the implications of the Anselmian emphasis on it, keeping in mind such questions as: What is at stake for God, according to the Anselmian view of atonement? Why is honor such a crucial dimension of the Anselmian conception of the Divine? Or, to put it differently, who benefits from an emphasis on divine honor? Are there negative consequences to an emphasis on God's honor, similar to those we have explored in relation to the metaphors of divine sovereignty, omnipotence, and fatherhood?

To gain insight into the assumptions and expectations that may have cohered to the idea of honor during times when it was a critical cultural concept, we turn to the discipline of cultural anthropology, which employs the subdisciplines of archaeology, linguistic anthropology, and ethnology in an attempt to describe and explain human behavior. Cultural anthropology can inform our understandings of Christian theology by shedding light on the context in which its sacred texts emerged—a context that influenced Anselm's theology and continues to impact contemporary cultures.

In the mid-1960s, anthropologists concluded from their fieldwork in Mediterranean villages that the value system in the Mediterranean area can be best evaluated in terms of two complementary categories, honor and shame. It was argued that these categories embody the social ideals that shape and integrate the lives of small communities by providing a scale of social worth in terms of which individual behavior can be measured and understood and social relations between individuals and groups can be mediated. As such, honor and shame were proposed as cultural archetypes of the Mediterranean value system.[24]

According to these studies, honor involves both self-regard and social esteem. It is one's estimation of one's own worth as well as the social assessment or recognition of that worth. Thus, one's peers function as arbiters of one's worth. Honor is a corporate value in another sense as well—it derives from individual conduct, but it also has consequences for those who share in the collective honor of the individual; so the honor-status of individuals reflects and influences the honor-status afforded their (extended) families. To allow oneself to be dishonored is to shame not only oneself but one's family as well. As a result of one's inherited family or societal rank, one is understood to have *ascribed* honor—an honor-status into which one is born. In addition, one can gain *acquired* honor as a result of social interaction, particularly as one participates in the dialectic of challenge and response. This dialectic occurs constantly between equals as they speak, give gifts, insult, and compliment each other in day-to-day activities. This dialectic characterizes interaction between people in the public sphere. A particular conversation or gift, for example, is a challenge to its recipient, who must then respond in an appropriate fashion, which means that the response should be reciprocal "and then some"—it should be basically in kind, in other words, a similar gift or comment, but with an added degree of generosity so that the response becomes a challenge to which the other must now respond in an appropriate fashion. In this way, daily business and personal exchanges occur in a natural to and fro manner.[25]

A crucial component of the challenge-response dynamic, however, is that it occurs between equals, that is, between those of equal status. A faux pas occurs when an inferior challenges a superior, for the challenge implies equality, and one who misjudges one's status is dishonored or shamed. When such a blunder takes place, the offended superior can shame the pretentious challenger by not responding or by pointing out the presumption of the challenge; or the offended one can choose to respond in kind, which increases his own status because of his generosity toward an inferior *and* increases the status of the challenger, whose risky challenge has been recognized as worthy of response. In such a situation, the honor and status of the superior are maintained, for he is in a "win-win situation." In these common, everyday exchanges between persons, says Pierre Bourdieu, honor is won and lost, defended and stolen: "It is the challenge, in fact, which gives one the sense of existing fully as a man, which demonstrates one's manliness to others and to oneself." The crucial importance of all this is aptly described by Bourdieu when he remarks that "existence and honor are one."[26]

The flip side of honor is designated as shame, which is loosely understood to refer to one's sensitivity to maintaining one's honor. To have one's claim to honor rejected by one's peer(s) is to be dishonored or shamed. Also implied, though not always explicitly articulated, is the functional connection between honor and shame and the sexual and gendered division of male and female. Almost without exception, "honor" refers to male honor, while shame is its foil and thus often refers to women. Honor is a public value; it is won and lost, says Bourdieu, in "the open world of the public square, reserved for men." Its complementary but opposing principle is shame, which is associated with "the intimate life, and more precisely, the feminine world, the world of the secret, enclosed space of the household."[27] Along with this gendered division of space comes the demarcation of all reality, based, apparently, on the perceived differences between men and women.

While men do indeed win and lose acquired honor, as males they nevertheless have ascribed honor. Relative to women, then, men have honor, but relative to other men, they can acquire both honor and shame. In contrast, women have ascribed shame and are understood as intrinsically shameful. Sheila Delaney explains, "Women . . . are, by their created nature, already ashamed. The recognition of their constitutional inferiority constitutes the feeling of shame." And yet, as shamed individuals women can *acquire* honor insofar as they do not cause the men in their lives—fathers, husbands, brothers, and sons—to be shamed vis-à-vis the public world of men. Delaney continues, "Shame is an inevitable part of being a female; a woman is honorable if she remains cognizant of this fact and its implications for behavior, and she is shameless if she forgets it."[28]

Honor and shame were important social values during the first centuries of Christianity. Karen Jo Torjesen argues that when women in early Christianity overstepped the confines of the household and ventured into the public realm to teach and minister, they came into conflict with the gender-based idiom of the honor-shame dialectic; as a result, they were denounced as shameless; their lack of concern for their reputation caused them to be dishonored. Since "maleness itself functioned as a cultural symbol for honor," the socially appropriate role of a woman was to do everything possible to safeguard what shards of honor she acquired as a result of her relationship to men; thus, "the cultural value of shame prescribed the feminine personality as discreet, shy, restrained, and timid." Shame, then, "was indicated by passivity, subordination, and seclusion in the household." Torjesen argues that the value placed on female shame, and the concomitant commodification of female sexuality and sexual ontologization of women's being, is a common feature of patriarchal societies. To be "feminine" is to depend upon men for one's identity and status; it is to obey cultural norms; it is also to be appropriately shameful about issues of sexuality.[29]

The indisputable touchstone of appropriate female shame is the maintenance of sexual purity, since male honor depends upon it. In early Christianity, a "woman's honor was her good reputation, and this had always to be a reputation of chastity."[30] Based on her fieldwork in twentieth-century Spain, Jane Collier concurs: "A man's honor was a function of his mother's, sister's, and wife's sexual chastity. A family's reputation depended on the sexual shame of its women and on the readiness of its men to defend, with violence if need be, its women's purity."[31]

In a world in which "honor and existence are one," an honorable man is one whose own legitimacy is ensured by a chaste mother, whose progeny's legitimacy is ensured by a chaste wife, and whose family reputation is upheld by a virginal sister. Within such a cultural milieu based on the idealization of virginity and fidelity, the very being of girls and women, as well as the foundation of the entire social fabric, depends upon and is reduced to male control of female bodies. Sexual violence committed against a woman, such as rape or incest, is understood to reflect her lack of appropriate shame, and so the victim is held responsible for her victimization, and men are encouraged to use any means necessary to circumscribe women's behavior. Women and girls have as their *raison d'être* their status as "actual or potential rape victims," for it is their violability upon which male honor and power—and indeed the entire honor/shame archetype that orders individual identity and social interaction—depend.[32] Delaney explains why the stakes are so high in the honor/shame game in which women's sexuality is an indispensable pawn:

> At the most reduced level, the boundary of a woman is her hymen.
> It is reserved for and is the possession of the husband. In breaking
> it, he possesses the woman. Once broken, he can come and go as he
> pleases, as he, but no one else, may enter his fields with ease. If the
> boundary of what is his has been penetrated or broken by someone
> else, he is put in the position of a woman and is therefore shamed.
> Thus male honor is vulnerable through women.[33]

Various criticisms of the honor/shame "archetype" have been elaborated, and yet even the most outspoken critics recognize the tenacious efficacy of the categories of honor and shame for evaluating human behavior.[34] For our purposes, the value of cultural anthropology's study of honor and shame is the possibility that it might shed some light on the role of honor in the Anselmian model of atonement. The claim is not a historical one—that, for instance, there is a traceable causal connection between Mediterranean norms and those of medieval Europe or contemporary United States[35]—but a much more modest one, a hermeneutic one—that perhaps reading the Anselmian account of honor through the lens of the honor/shame dialectic will yield interpretive fruit; that perhaps such a grid or lens will enable some insight into the logic of the Anselmian God, for whom honor is a defining characteristic.

When we revisit Anselm's explanation of atonement, this time with the honor/shame dialectic in mind, some clarity does indeed emerge. The fact that ignites the fateful chain of events is that the challenge of human sin offends God's honor.[36] By presuming equality with God, humankind has committed a social blunder that, because of God's inestimable status, brings infinite dishonor, or shame, to humankind. Furthermore, because God is sovereign of the world, and because of the corporate dimension of honor, this faux pas has cosmic consequences; indeed, it disrupts the order of the universe. In societies whose stability depends upon the maintenance of strict hierarchies and status distinctions, attempts at upward mobility are serious threats to the status quo and hence to the entire social fabric. To seek to be on a par with one of superior rank is to disobey social convention, to rebel against prevailing norms.[37] Within this context, human sin becomes an earth-shattering act of presumption.

Now God, as the offended party, has three choices: (1) "he" can ignore the challenge altogether and convey the message that this challenge by an inferior is not worthy of response, in which case the challenger, the human being, might either "break even" in the honor game or lose a modicum of honor, depending on the interpretation of the public;[38] (2) God can choose to be generous and respond to the challenge *as if* it came from an equal, and in so doing increase the honor of the human being; or (3) God can shame the challenger by pointing out the audacious assumption that equality with a clear superior is even considered by one of such inferior rank, and demand that the insult be redressed. Regardless of God's response, divine honor is not diminished, for as Anselm reminds us, "it is impossible for God to lose honor; for either the sinner pays his debt of his own accord, or, if he refuse, God takes it from him."[39] An alternative reading might go like this: it is impossible for God to lose honor, for either the challenger voluntarily abdicates his honor and compensates God for the affront, or God shames the challenger and takes his honor from him anyway.

In his assessment of the situation, Anselm rejects the possibility that God would respond to the challenge of human sin with equanimity or generosity, for to "cancel sin without compensation or punishment . . . is unbecoming to God." Indeed, "God's liberty and choice and compassion . . . may not seem to interfere with His dignity." Mercy and justice are seen as mutually exclusive, and the former is eclipsed by the latter. Neither does Anselm allow for the possibility that the human being could admit to the error in judgment, apologize for the affront, and graciously back down, for the greatest injustice of all would be if "the creature should take away the honor due the Creator, and not restore what he has taken away." The only option remaining, according to Anselm's logic, is for the presumptuous challenger to repair God's offended honor; and of course, this is the one thing that cannot be done because God's honor is infinite. Here we have, then, the necessity of the incarnation.[40] And yet the caveat, which Anselm recognizes but dismisses, is that the divine honor is never actually affected by the challenge of human sin in the first place. The demand for compensation, or satisfaction, is utterly arbitrary. Even within the honor/shame framework, God *could* choose to respond with generosity and compassion, but God instead chooses to present the uppity challenger with the "damned if you do, damned if you don't" choice of either punishment or shame.

In the final analysis, Anselm's successors were probably wise to deemphasize the honor component of the original model of atonement because the God it depicts is capricious at best, and cruel at worst. From a feminist perspective, this dimension of the model fares no better than the implications of divine sovereignty and omnipotence upon which the model depends; all portray God as a status-paranoid power-monger who deliberately humiliates and infantalizes human beings under the guise of justice. What the honor/shame dialectic clarifies, in addition to this paternalizing dynamic, is the gender idiom that is implied in the dynamic, for in relation to a God whose sovereignty and power ascribe unto him infinite honor, the disobedient human being is dishonored, shamed, *feminized.* Human sin, in effect, blurs the carefully maintained boundary between superior and inferior, patron and client, male and female, upon which the social order depends. To challenge God, then, is to sin; and to sin is *to become female,* which, in a patriarchal society, is to be rendered powerless. The religious injunction not to sin, therefore, is an admonishment not to be feminized, not to allow oneself to be dominated; domination becomes, consequently, a holy task, a sacred posture.

Within this context, the biblical commandment to "honor thy father and thy mother" appears in a new, sinister light. One survivor of family violence offers this account: "My father often said the commandment: Honor thy father and thy mother, and: Thou shalt love thy neighbor as thyself. . . . I was completely abandoned to his will because I obeyed those commandments." Another recalls: "Father was always walking around quoting proverbs. His favorite was, 'Honor thy father and thy mother,' and: 'Work is no disgrace.' You just had to be strong and do what you were told. Later on, when you went to heaven, comfort and happiness would be your rewards."[41] For these women, "to honor" means to obey, to revere, to fear. Resistance to the will of a parent, especially a father, is a challenge to his honor—to the family's honor, indeed, to the "family values" upon which societal order depends—and will indubitably be met with either punishment or shame. Appropriate behavior for women and children is subordination, compliance, and passivity. And once the boundary of sexuality is penetrated, the damage is inestimable; it is not merely a physical intrusion but an ontological stain. So resistance is pointless. Shame is eternal.

The Task at Hand

This chapter has demonstrated that feminist criticisms of traditional under-standings of atonement require a fundamental rethinking of the models of God implied in such understandings. When certain models gain hegemony and lose their metaphorical character, they lose their transformative potential and become signs and tools of the status quo. Thus, God becomes "a good old boy," or a domineering father, an abusive parent or partner, or an arbitrary and merciless tyrant. Because of the ultimate character of the Divine—because for most people "God" connotes what is the greatest and the best, what one should aspire toward—the influence wielded by models of God is enormous. Such influence demands of theologians and practitioners of religion that we take seriously the implications of our God-talk and that we reconfigure our metaphors and concepts when necessary.

Feminist critiques of metaphors of divine sovereignty, omnipotence, fa-therhood, and honor demonstrate that their negative effects make such a re-configuration necessary—now. One small piece of this task has to do with the doctrine of atonement. The challenge is clear: to configure atonement in such a way that avoids the metaphors and related problems of divine sovereignty, omnipotence, honor, and fatherhood as traditionally construed; to ask whether it is possible to claim that in Jesus the Christ, God has acted to con-front sin and evil in a definitive manner.

3

Saved by the Divine Victim?

The most basic claim of the Christian doctrine of atonement is that *in and through Jesus the Christ, God has acted to confront and confound the powers of sin and evil* that enslave human beings, and in so doing, God has opened up for humanity the possibility of right relationship with the Divine and with other creatures. But what is it *about* this figure Jesus, whom Christians recognize as the Christ, "the anointed one," the Messiah, that is salvific? What does redemption mean, and in what way is Jesus the locus of it? The doctrine of atonement attempts to get at these questions by recognizing that, at minimum, to be saved, to be redeemed, is somehow to be extricated from the hold of sin and evil. Whatever else it may be, salvation is freedom *from* sin and evil; and this liberation is the necessary precondition of right relationship with God, with self, and with others. The doctrine of atonement recognizes that for healing to occur, the disease must be stymied, the virus attacked and destroyed, or at minimum, the cancer identified, contained, and reduced so that the possibility of life continues.

There is, then, an organic connection between notions of sin and evil and construals of redemption; that is, the shape and content of salvation depend upon the specific character of sin and evil as well as assumptions about the nature of divine activity. Atonement is the necessary first moment of the process of redemption; it is the moment in which the destructive hold of sin and evil is exposed and loosened, making fullness of life possible. The claim of Christianity is that this confrontation with the powers that bind is embodied in a decisive manner in the person and work of Jesus, who incarnates or embodies divine presence and activity in the world.

Salvation and Victimization

The claim that "Jesus saves" stands at the very heart of Christian theology, but how Jesus does this and what Jesus saves from and for are questions that have a variety of interpretations. The Anselmian tradition, for instance, focuses exclusively on human sin and claims that the voluntary death of the innocent Jesus, the God-man, satisfies the debt created by human sin and "takes away" our sin, allowing us to stand in right relationship to God once again. Jesus' death "atones" for, or pays the debt of, human sin. By contrast, the Abelardian model suggests that humans are moved by the story of the life and death of Jesus—particularly the virtues of humility, obedience, and self-sacrifice he embodies in the face of immense hardship and suffering—to reject sin, understood primarily in terms of pride and disobedience to God, and to mold our lives on the model of Jesus.

Feminist and liberation theologies argue that both these approaches are too narrowly concerned with the individual and/or the human soul. The overwhelming emphasis of theological tradition on personal sin and guilt, and on salvation as freedom from individual sin, ignores or discounts the historical, corporate, and sociopolitical context of all events and activities. In so doing, it fails to account not only for the interpersonal and institutional manifestations of sin and evil but also for the meaning and shape of redemption in relation to these extra-individual spheres of existence.

Feminist and liberation theologians attempt to counter the narrow focus of the tradition by defining salvation primarily in terms of "liberation." This shift in terminology signifies also a shift in emphasis, an attempt to broaden the scope of the Christian idea of redemption and to enrich its meaning to reflect both the complexity of biblical accounts of redemptive activity and the indisputably contextual nature of human existence. According to this broader framework, salvation is understood to include the liberation not only of individual human souls or spirits, but also of relationships, communities, and institutions. Salvation is understood to be the process of being freed *from* situations of enslavement and oppression *for* situations of freedom, wholeness, and equality. Redemption, then, involves a dual transformation in which persons and communities move out of relationships and systems characterized by alienation, exploitation, and injustice and into relationships and systems characterized by mutuality, compassion, and justice.

Within this framework, it is crucial that the two movements or transformations be consonant. In other words, the means and content of the negative dimension of salvation—the event or process in which the bonds of oppression are loosed—must not conflict with the means and content of the positive dimension—the event or process of moving into healing and freedom of self and community. The means of atonement, insofar as atonement is understood to refer to what we are calling the negative dimension or first moment of salvation, must be consistent with the vision of wholeness, mutuality, and compassion that the positive dimension or second moment of redemption connotes. The very *process* of atonement must reflect the meaning of salvation, the particular character of redeemed existence. The means and the end should not be contradictory but complementary, so that the *way* in which redemption is understood to occur does not conflict with the meaning of redemption itself.

Feminist critiques reveal that when traditional models of atonement are measured by the standards of salvation, the former are found to be in clear and often radical conflict with the latter. If salvation is understood to include, among other things, the full personhood of women, children, and the poor, as well as the opportunity for full participation in communities, programs, and institutions intended to reflect the justice, compassion, and inclusivity of the *basileia*—of the reign or dominion of God—then models of atonement that assume, encourage, or result in relationships of systemic inequality or exploitation are themselves evil and must be rejected. An adequate construal of atonement is one that contributes to salvation from violence, not one that encourages victimization.

For feminists, the christological component of traditional views of atonement is most problematic for women and children within a patriarchal society. At the root of the problem, suggests Elizabeth Johnson, is "the fact that Christology in its story, symbol, and doctrine has been assimilated to the patriarchal world view, with the result that its liberating dynamic has been twisted into justification for domination."[1] The most important strand in this theological twist is the doctrine of atonement, with its central symbol of the cross. This symbol has become for many feminists a nearly insurmountable theological stumbling block.

Necrophilic Theologies

Jesus' death on the cross signaled the apparent defeat of his mission and of God's incarnate presence and activity. However, Christians gradually interpreted this death to be the revelatory moment *par excellence* of the meaning of the incarnation, of divine triumph over sin and evil, and of subsequent Christian identity. Therefore, what appeared as a scandal of incomprehensible proportions became the basis for theological transformation and Christian community.

What made this dramatic reinterpretation of the meaning of Jesus' death necessary and relevant was the context of the early followers of Jesus. This context, argues Elisabeth Schüssler Fiorenza, was characterized by "the historical 'fact' of unjust oppression." The earliest interpretations of the theological meaning of Jesus' death emerged from the experience of struggle and persecution. Likewise, feminist interpretations of the meaning of the cross emerge from a context of oppression; thus, feminist critiques of the cross should be viewed as a theological discourse whose motivation stems from the concrete experience of violence. The task of critically assessing atonement theories from the perspective of those struggling for freedom from religious and sociopolitical violence is not, then, necessarily discontinuous with Christian tradition. Indeed, it can claim the earliest decades of Christian history as its precedent.[2]

One of the most problematic characteristics of atonement orthodoxy is its tendency to make the death of Jesus *the* defining event of the incarnation and of God's reconciling work. For Anselm, the death of the God-man, and nothing else, satisfies God's justice and honor because only the offering of an infinite payment on behalf of the finite transgressor is sufficient to cancel the infinite indebtedness to the Divine. According to this logic, the incarnation itself is understood to have its *raison d'être* in the voluntary death of the innocent Jesus. The net result of this line of reasoning is the idea that Jesus lived so that he could die. The actual historical *life* of this death-wish Savior is important only insofar as it attests to his innocence, sinlessness, perfection—in other words, insofar as it witnesses to his unique suitability for an atoning death.[3]

The Abelardian model had its origin precisely in the rejection of this sort of theological obsession with death, for as Abelard pointed out, it renders the actual life of Jesus theologically dispensable and cannot account for the thirty-three years that Jesus spent as a living, walking, talking person. However, Abelard went on to stress the crucial significance of Jesus' death as the perfect example of the depth of divine love; our hearing about Jesus' willingness to suffer unto death for the cause of love awakens our hearts toward similar love. For both the Anselmian and the Abelardian traditions, the death of Jesus either exclusively or most completely effects atonement. The death of Jesus saves human beings from bondage to sin.

From a feminist perspective, this theological exaltation of death is profoundly problematic. Mary Daly, for instance, calls this theology "necrophilic" because it focuses on Jesus' death as necessary for salvation, indeed as the primary event that frees humanity *from* death as punishment for sin and *for* eternal life with God.[4] This emphasis runs the risk of exalting death, of spiritualizing and romanticizing it, which can undermine individual and communal outrage at the countless deaths caused by neglect, violence, greed, and ignorance. To glorify death is to domesticate it, to soften its tragedy, to render it acceptable, which in a world characterized by wrongful deaths by the millions is simply unacceptable.

According to Francis Fiorenza, the tendency in much of Christian theology to understand atonement primarily in terms of the salvific death of Jesus represents a departure from the earliest attempts within Christian circles to understand the redemptive efficacy of the figure Jesus. For Paul, John, and the authors of the synoptic Gospels, the death of Jesus is only one of many categories or events used to interpret salvation. The narrowing that occurred in subsequent theological tradition, argues Fiorenza, is "short-sighted" in that it fails to ask what position toward death the historical Jesus may have taken; furthermore, it fails to take into account the efficacy of Jesus' life. In addition, traditional views have focused so narrowly on the meaning of Jesus' death and on the need to make theological sense of death itself that they have ignored the equally necessary task of articulating a theology of life, of thematizing the ultimate and sacred dimensions of life itself.[5]

The harmful ramifications of traditional notions of atonement as being effected primarily, if not exclusively, through the redemptive death of Jesus become disturbingly clear when evaluated from the standpoint of the concrete experiences of violence against women and children. Romantic visions of a martyred Savior function in many cases to keep victims of abuse in their death-dealing situations. The sacralization of death stymies outrage against death and the attitudes, actions, and systems that create it. It can also be used as a weapon of control by abusers who play on the religious sensitivities of their victims. When Jesus' death, interpreted as a salvific martyrdom, is combined with social prescriptions of women's sexual purity, the result can be fatal for victims of sexual violence. Even when this combination is not apparent, however, Jesus' death becomes the example of perfect self-sacrifice that believers ought to emulate; and as we have seen, this kind of theological idealization of self-sacrifice can perpetuate cycles of victimization.

Imitating the Divine Victim

When the life of Jesus *is* treated as an important theological datum for understanding atonement, traditional models tend to emphasize and idealize events and qualities of Jesus' life and person that are just as objectionable as the exaltation of his death. The Anselmian model accords salvific import to the life of Jesus only insofar as that life reveals him to be without sin; because of this sinless life, Jesus is seen as "the perfect sacrifice" whose voluntary offering of his innocent life suffices to mollify God's offended honor or unrelenting justice, or to repair the cosmic disorder created by human sin. According to this model, Jesus' life of purity and self-sacrifice, when offered as satisfaction to God, wipes the slate clean between God and human beings, taking away the debt of sin and allowing for the restoration of the proper divine-human relationship based on human deference and obedience to God.

Despite their marked differences, the Abelardian model shares with this Anselmian one the conviction that what is most important about the life of Jesus—what has redemptive efficacy—is a constellation of qualities at whose center are humility, self-sacrifice, and obedience. For the Abelardian tradition, the great hardship and suffering that Jesus willingly endured out of love for human beings perfectly expressed his obedience to God; and the great suffering has the power to move human beings to embrace these same qualities in our lives and, in so doing, to be set free from sin as pride and disobedience. Jesus' endurance of pain and cruelty is understood by the Abelardian model to have positive moral consequences; his suffering becomes a means of moral persuasion, moving human hearts toward God.

Taken together, the salvific values of suffering, self-sacrifice, and obedience are too easily distorted into a theological tool of subjugation. Removed from a context that values and attempts to safeguard the health and fulfillment of all beings, these values can be emphasized to a pathological degree, contributing to the suffering and exploitation of the vulnerable and hence demeaning the humanity of oppressor and oppressed alike. As Mary Daly first pointed out, the qualities extolled in Jesus by traditional theology—such as obedience, selflessness, and sacrificial love—are those of a victim. Christians are encouraged to emulate the Divine Victim by mirroring the qualities that theology has emphasized as salvific. The impact of this victim theology on those already victimized by patriarchal social norms can be, as we saw in chapter 1, positively baneful. In addition, obedience to authority is given divine sanction by the assumption that Jesus' obedience to God is part of his atoning activity. Within Christian tradition, obedience to earthly authorities becomes part of one's Christian duty and is deemed a virtue. For many women, such emphases only strengthen their dependency and increase their likelihood of victimization. In a cultural context in which violence against women is the norm rather than the exception, powerlessness and compliance are the last things we need to be taught to model.

One of the most offensive components of classical theologies of the cross from the standpoint of those concerned about the relationship between theological violence and "real" violence is the notion that Jesus endured his suffering and death willingly; that is, the idea that what is redemptive about Jesus' life is his *freely chosen* obedience and self-sacrificial love. "On the night before he gave himself up for us," reads a popular liturgy, which implies that Jesus' sacrifice of himself is fully voluntary.[6] According to this logic, Jesus *chooses* to be a victim, and to do likewise is to be Christlike. Based on her experience in the battered women's movement, Sarah Bentley notes that "many a battered woman will persist in returning to increasingly dangerous relationships, citing . . . the model of Christian love as 'turning the other cheek' or 'following Jesus' example.'" The result of such reasoning and action is that, "far from improving the situation, her refusal to protect herself has the opposite effect on her partner, encouraging continued and often more serious abuse."[7]

According to Elisabeth Schüssler Fiorenza, admonitions to imitate the Divine Victim through voluntary suffering "are not isolated aberrations in the Christian Testament but go to the heart of Christian faith: trust in God the Father and belief in redemption through the suffering and death of Christ."[8] Yet such a belief is not necessarily problematic; indeed, as I will argue in a later chapter, Christian theology *must* find ways of coming to terms with this suffering and death, of incorporating even tragedy into its scope. But it must do so in ways that do not romanticize, eternalize, or otherwise endorse or enhance suffering. This task of finding sophisticated, responsible ways of understanding the theological significance of Jesus' suffering and death has been at the fore of theological undertakings at various times during the past two hundred years, and under the weight of feminist criticism it has come center stage once again. Through the lens of a feminist hermeneutic, old and new excesses, perversions, and problems with traditional notions of atonement are brought into sharp focus. Not all these problems were central features in past theological construals, yet they have found their way into the everyday imagination and religious practices of vast numbers of Christian men and women and so must be confronted as they actually exist.

In her analysis of liturgical language used during Christian worship, Marjorie Procter-Smith points out that in many worship traditions, the death of Jesus is interpreted primarily in terms of the Suffering Servant literature within the Hebrew Scriptures, as in this example read at the Good Friday service in mainline Christian denominations:

> He was oppressed, and he was afflicted,
>> yet he did not open his mouth;
> like a lamb that is led to the slaughter,
>> and like a sheep that before its shearers is silent,
>> so he did not open his mouth. (Isa. 53:7)

"Certainly the model of a suffering servant is problematic to women who are socially constructed to be suffering servants," remarks Carol Adams, and yet Christian liturgical practices inscribe participants with the image of Jesus as the suffering lamb, going obediently to his slaughter.[9] As a prayer in the United Church of Christ *Book of Worship* claims:

> In the fullness of time
> you came to us
> and received our nature

in the person of Jesus,
who, in obedience to you,
by suffering on the cross,
and being raised from the dead,
delivered us from the way of sin and death.

In a similar theological mode, the Episcopal/Anglican Book of Common Prayer contains this assertion about the salvific import of Jesus' perfect obedience and selflessness:

He stretched out his arms upon the cross,
and offered himself, in obedience to your will,
a perfect sacrifice for the whole world.[10]

The pernicious result of this sort of reasoning is that it presents self-sacrifice as normative for Christians, which, argues Christine Gudorf, "functions to resign victims to their suffering."[11] Certainly, self-sacrifice is at times a healthy and appropriate posture, particularly for those who reap the benefits of gender, class, or race privilege, or for those whose sense of self-importance has become exaggerated; but it is not *always* a good thing, and this caveat calls for rethinking notions of salvation. The last thing contemporary Christians need to embrace is a theology that lures us into acquiescing to suffering and death, for so much of it is caused by human greed, cruelty, and indifference; so much of it is the result of our own evil. What needs theological expression or awakening is, rather, the *resistance* to unnecessary suffering and to evil that is also a major theme in the Jewish and Christian traditions. In chapter 7 of this book I attempt to reinvigorate one important tradition of struggle or resistance that is usually ignored or maligned by Christian theologians but has enormous potential to reconfigure the meaning of Jesus' death in ways that neither glorify suffering nor ignore the necessity of incorporating it into Christian theology and practice.

Another problematic mainstay of traditional Christian thought is the idea that suffering builds character—that because of its pedagogical potential, suffering should not be resisted but passively endured. This concept of suffering as "soul making," says Nel Noddings, is "deeply flawed" because "instead of concentrating on the alleviation and possible elimination of suffering, Christians are urged to find meaning in it."[12] Gudorf concurs: "It is certainly dangerous—and also cruel—to assume that suffering inevitably leads to real life, to joy, to meaning, to wholeness. For suffering destroys. It kills, it maims the body and the spirit, it produces despair and evil."[13] Evidence of this theologically powered fatalism is offered by Jennifer Manlowe's work with battered women: "I heard women reflect on their own abuse in ways that divinized their suffering: 'Like Jesus, I must suffer for my husband to come to Christianity.'"[14] From a feminist perspective concerned about combating violence in its many forms, assertions about the salvific effect of suffering are extremely disturbing. Consequently, feminists recognize the cross, the central signifier in traditional affirmations of the redemptive effect of Jesus' suffering and death, as a "theologically and ethically dangerous" symbol that "has functioned as an instrument of violence—spiritual, psychological, physical—from the first century onward."[15] And yet, as I argue in a subsequent chapter, the recognition of the real and potential problems with theologies of the cross does not mean that all attempts to make theological sense of the suffering and death of Jesus should be abandoned, but only that the problems with which any such attempt has to contend should not be underestimated.

In addition to numbing the conscience of the perpetrators of violence, the romanticization of suffering supports victims' internalization of their oppression by making suffering a good, a virtue. In so doing, it merely compounds their victimization. Such romanticizing tendencies, it seems, have no ideological boundaries; they occur on political Right and Left. For those of a conservative bent, the perpetuation of the status quo is often a top priority, primarily because "the way things are" is to their social and economic benefit. Poverty and inequality are rationalized as necessary evils of what is seen as a basically good system. By contrast, liberals often recognize and denounce the injustices of the status quo, but their strategies for halting oppression frequently depend upon the patronizing caricaturization of oppressed groups. Ironically, argues Christine Gudorf, the idealization of the suffering of victims that is typical of doctrines of atonement is a tool used frequently by "the religious left" in misguided attempts to put an end to just such suffering. To convince those in power to stop victimization, the Left tends to project romantic portrayals of victims as people whose very ability to endure extreme pain and suffering should warrant "awed admiration"—the extent of their suffering, their powerlessness against dehumanizing systems and policies, is assumed to be the mark of worthy character. Those who suffer the most are most likely to receive attention, so victims get back-door encouragement to enhance their own victimization.[16]

Furthermore, claims Gudorf, in a culture marked by increasing desensitization—that is, in a culture in which "constant exposure to violence of all kinds desensitizes our ability to feel"—the evocation of compassion toward those who suffer requires increasingly dramatic displays of horror and pain. And so once again, "the Christian left falls prey to romanticizing victims," for "those who want us to care about their suffering victims are tempted to focus more and more on the suffering, in order to capture our attention. . . . The greater the suffering of victims, the more they seem to deserve our attention; the more they suffer, the more courageous, strong, and virtuous they seem."

In this way, the very people and groups that seek actively to put an end to the reality of unjust or radical suffering can unwittingly aggravate such suffering by romanticizing victimization. Gudorf's intention, as I understand it, is not to suggest that the horrors caused by individual, communal, and societal violence should go unaddressed, but that in our attempts to combat such violence we need to take care that our strategies are consistent with the ends toward which we work. Gudorf insists, "Those who suffer unjustly should not need to *deserve* our attention" (emphasis added). Her insights make it clear that within the contemporary context, at least, romanticizations of Jesus' suffering add theological fuel to the fire of victimization.[17]

Perhaps the insistence on attributing redemptive meaning to Jesus' suffering and death stems from Christians' desire to situate everything within an essentially comic framework—that is, to assume that even undeserved, unjust, dehumanizing suffering must have a positive purpose, or else the goodness of God will be somehow compromised. Increasingly, however, theologians are suggesting that such assumptions go against the grain of human experience, that they take the reality of human evil too lightly, and that they delimit God by dictating that God function within a human moral system that is at least as much the product of wishful thinking as it may be of revealed truth. Wendy Farley asserts that traditional Christian theologies tend to ignore the reality and illogic of what she calls radical suffering, "a kind of crippling of the human spirit by contingent and external forces." To suggest that radical suffering has some redemptive meaning, says Farley, ignores the essentially tragic character of human existence and ignores the unredeemable cruelty and dehumanization of suffering. Farley agrees with Rebecca Chopp that "massive suffering cannot be resolved into any meaning."[18] Insofar as traditional understandings of Jesus' suffering reduce outrage and resistance toward suffering—by either romanticizing it or implying that one person's suffering has magically wiped away the suffering of others—they run the risk of compounding the misery of those already victimized by radical suffering.

A further point of contention raised by some feminists is the claim implied by traditional understandings of atonement that Jesus' suffering was the outgrowth of his obedience to his Father's will. Such a theology, it is argued, constitutes "divine child abuse" insofar as God the Father is thought to require the suffering and death of his beloved child to compensate for the lack of respect/honor/obeisance he (God) receives from others (humanity); and Jesus, like a typical child victim for whom love is identified with obedience to the adult's authority, obliges.[19] Such a scenario is surely a distortion of most theological treatments of atonement, and yet it has made an indelible impression on significant numbers of Christian women and men. Imbens and Jonker report that "the combination of the way [the incest survivors] often experienced Jesus (as loving, good, close by, and providing security) with this torturous death (often explained as God's will in order to redeem the sins of humankind) gave these survivors a terrifying image of God: the image of a sadistic father, someone hungry for power."[20]

Atonement orthodoxy tends to depict Jesus as the Savior child whose obedience to his Father's will, or whose desire to please his Father, knew no limits. Consequently, his voluntary sacrifice of self is held up as the model of true Christian identity and action. To love is to relinquish self, this orthodoxy implies, for that is what Jesus did. The impact of this pedagogy on those who lack personal or social power can be devastating indeed.

Scapegoats and Surrogates

Another plank in the atonement orthodoxy platform is the conviction that Jesus bore the punishment that was due human beings, so that his victimization took the place of, or substituted, for ours. Like an older sibling who chooses to bear a parent's abuse in hopes that younger ones will be spared, Jesus willingly accepts the punishment meant for others and thus saves us from the wrath of the Father. This image of a Divine Victim impels those who wish to imitate Christ to live "sacrificially." One survivor of incest remarked, "Sacrificing yourself was always part of religion. . . . You learned to put up with injustice and not to resist."[21] This lesson, however, seems to be taught most often to those who already lack cultural power. Daly suggests that for those whose social status and/or role prescribes acquisitiveness rather than sacrifice, for those with relative social power, the image of Jesus as victim has the effect of evoking intolerance: "That is, rather than being enabled to imitate the sacrifice of Jesus, they feel guilt and transfer this to 'the Other,'" who is then compelled to "imitate" Jesus in the role of scapegoat.[22]

Traditional theological interpretations of Jesus as the Divine Scapegoat have prompted womanist theologian Delores Williams to raise unsettling questions about "the tendency within Christian societies to scapegoat 'non-mainstream' peoples." In the United States, African Americans have been the "national scapegoats," blamed for everything from crime to welfare to high illiteracy rates, says Williams; and the religious image of the salvific scapegoat condones and even promotes the creation of such "victims" because it implies that scapegoating is "a normal and natural process in social living." Williams asks, "If the Christian image of salvation is an innocent person suffering for the errors and sins of another person or group, how can races that have been the underclass in such a system hope to achieve social justice in Christian nations?" Doesn't the belief in the "salvific power of the blood of others"— implied by traditional construals of atonement when they assert the salvific effect of Jesus' suffering and death—have as its precondition the existence of the victim? Concludes Williams, "We African American Christians may be participating in our own victimization as a people when we express such a belief." Williams's study suggests that claims about redemptive suffering and/or death implied in both Abelardian and Anselmian models of atonement may unwittingly teach traditionally marginalized people to accept their status as scapegoats. In addition, they may allow persons in power to legitimate their creation of scapegoats and surrogates by imagining that God has done likewise.[23]

The End of Innocence

According to popular understandings of atonement, the innocence and purity of the Savior-child are indispensable. Only a perfect victim can reconcile sinners with God, and so the life of Jesus is important as evidence of his innocence. In addition to being humble, self-sacrificial, and obedient, those who would be Christlike must be pure.

While women, children, and the poor have historically been romanticized as naturally good and innocent, Gudorf notes "that what was really being idealized was their powerlessness, which for ruling elites is, of course, their virtue."[24] Similarly, Rita Nakashima Brock argues that innocence can be an immobilizing quality that entraps women in false notions of an eternal feminine nature, which is essentially good and pure. Within this scenario, it becomes impossible to view women as both good and evil—they are in some sense inherently good, and yet that goodness depends upon "an innocence of choice and a passive acceptance of this female nature." For victims of violence, however, survival can depend upon the nurturing of willfulness. When innocence and passivity are associated with goodness, and knowledge and action are considered evil or impure, "innocence makes for passive scapegoats."[25]

Brock echoes Gudorf's critique of the religious Left's romanticization of the suffering of victims by pointing out that the granting of high moral ground to *innocent* victims, which is a hallmark of U.S. society and its social justice structures, can have problematic consequences. While the concern for innocent victims has had commendable results insofar as it has allowed various marginalized groups to demand justice, the dangerous implications of this type of moral logic should not be ignored. Brock explains, "If a victimized group can be proven to lack innocence, the implication is that the group no longer deserves justice. Any hint of moral ambiguity, or the possession of power and agency, throws a shadow across one's moral spotlight." The result of this reasoning is that "maintaining one's status as victim becomes crucial for being acknowledged and given credibility." Hence victimization is actually encouraged by the requirement that victims be innocent.[26]

The expectation that victims are innocent can be an enormous obstacle in efforts to combat violence because victims can never live up to such nostalgic visions. Their very brokenness often comes as a shock to those who seek to become allies of the oppressed, resulting in a demystification of the victims' goodness and the subsequent disillusionment on the part of potential allies. When innocence is a requirement of justice, justice becomes practically impossible.

In addition, as Brock points out, this logic of innocence, which hides the fact that "most of us are not just victims," prevents the development of a critical awareness among victims about the dangers of reactionary energy—that is, energy that imitates the power it opposes. An adequate moral framework must include, on the one hand, an understanding of the complexity of oppression and abuse—as well as the willingness, made possible by such an understanding, to condemn abuses of power—*and,* on the other hand, "an understanding of the ambiguities within which people live their lives," which includes the awareness that generalities about guilt and innocence are rarely accurate and often compound abusive patterns of relating. Ultimately, says Brock, "this tendency to identify with innocent victims, and to avoid discussions of the moral ambiguities of life continues to place responsibility for abuse on the victims of the system." We need to recognize that "abuse is wrong not because victims are innocent, but because abuse, even by good people for good causes, dehumanizes the abuser and abused."[27]

For survivors of sexual abuse, the dictum of innocence implied by traditional construals of atonement is a unique source of theological torture, for their innocence has been taken from them in a clear and irreversible way. The disabling guilt often experienced by such survivors is frequently caused by their sense of self-betrayal when their bodies are involuntarily aroused by the sexual contact, or when their need for affection causes them to confuse exploitation with genuine intimacy.

Despite the poisonous effects of the theological emphasis on innocence, however, its importance is conveyed to young girls again and again through stories not only of the unblemished Lamb, Jesus, but also of girls and women whose commitment to sexual purity brought them everlasting life. Imbens and Jonker report that the incest survivors they interviewed had been influenced by the female role models they were encouraged to emulate by their Christian upbringing. The premium placed on sexual purity by the popular stories of the virgin Mary, Maria Goretti, and Saint Lidwina of Schiedam, for instance, encourages young believers to go to any length, even death, to protect their chastity and to bear their sufferings.[28] The lesson to be learned from such morality stories is that sexual purity is the girl's or woman's responsibility and should be safeguarded, no matter what the cost.

Kathleen Zuanich Young explains that within Roman Catholicism, virgin martyrs are frequently held up as examples of a feminine Christian ideal. The stories of these young women, "who 'gave' their lives because of a spiritual commitment to the preservation of the hymen," reflect the premium placed on the control of women's sexuality. This premium finds expression in assertions—implicit and explicit—that "the physical fact of virginity indicates spiritual valor" and that "the inappropriate loss of the hymen diminishes the chances for eternal salvation." Girls who hear the story of "Saint" Maria, of how this twelve-year-old girl valiantly chose death by stabbing rather than the loss of her virginity; or of Saint Agnes, who "was beheaded rather than sacrifice her virginity"; or of Saint Agatha, who endured "various tortures, most notably tearing off her breasts," learn that sexual purity is a prerequisite of spiritual purity and, concomitantly, that sexual defilement is a fate worse than death. For female survivors of sexual violence, the message is clear: since they are still alive, they must be bad girls. One survivor remembers her shame at allowing herself to be defiled: "I was no longer 'immaculate,' as they called it, no longer a virgin. I'd ruined it."[29]

Obsessions with female sexual purity, and the theological emphasis on the merits of Christian innocence and self-sacrifice that fund them, are by no means limited to Catholicism. Andy Smith states that for evangelical Christians, sexuality is frequently viewed in terms of purity; in other words, "sex is pure only within marriage." This association, claims Smith, "compounds issues of sexual violence" because in their concern with "the question of 'the right organ in the right orifice with the right person,'" Christians pay little attention "to the context of power, consent, and choice regarding what happens to one's bodily self in a sexual relationship." Consequently, "when an evangelical woman is raped, she assumes she has 'sinned' by having sex because she has never been told how rape is different from sex." While Protestant women may never have heard of Saint Maria Goretti, they *have* heard of the innocent Jesus, and their desire to emulate him contributes to their victimization in dramatic ways. Smith recalls, "I have heard evangelical women say they would kill themselves if they were raped because it would mean that they were no longer 'pure.'" In such ways, stories of virgin martyrs and sacrificial innocents become significant means of social control of women's physical and spiritual lives, inscribing them with a sexual morality that deifies purity, innocence, and self-sacrifice and that figures survivors of sexual abuse as ontologically stained since they chose life over chastity.[30]

Superhero Christologies

Another component of classical formulations of atonement is the assumption that through his life and death, Jesus the Christ unilaterally frees humanity from bondage to sin and evil. In this scenario, Jesus is seen as a spiritual hero-warrior who single-handedly conquers evil. According to feminist theologians such as Schüssler Fiorenza and Brock, the representation of Jesus as the Divine Hero on whom humans are totally dependent for salvation is a problem for at least three reasons.

First, such an account decontextualizes Jesus, implying that he was in his life somehow unconnected to and unaffected by the events, people, and issues around him. This ahistorical view of Jesus leads to a spiritualization of the Savior and salvation, which can contribute to the devaluation of the concrete problems and concerns of real, historical people. For those concerned about the very real existence of violence against women and children, the spiritualization of salvation can undermine efforts to work for justice and compassion in *this* world. A second reason that feminist theologians are critical of a hero christology focuses on the model of humanity it implies. Since Christians understand Jesus to be fully human and to reveal or reflect the fullness of humanity, the message sent by the model of Jesus as hero-Savior is that full humanity can be embodied in an individual and that, by implication, relationships to others are purely ancillary. Autonomy or separateness, then, is the essence of humanity, while mutuality and responsibility to others are secondary. Such an anthropology lends itself to patriarchal notions of the disconnected self and of unilateral or hierarchical power that contribute to the creation and justification of unjust relations. Finally, by assuming that salvation occurs unilaterally and that Jesus is the sole locus of redemptive activity, a hero christology renders humans powerless and dependent upon an external power for salvation. We learn to abdicate responsibility to those who have the power we think we lack. This one-way relationship between hero and victim ensconces hierarchical relationships, unilateral power, and the adulation of authority and undermines social accountability—all of which are hallmarks of abuse and violence.

Seventy Times Seven

In addition to emphasizing the salvific import of Jesus' death, suffering, obedience, self-sacrifice, innocence, surrogacy, and heroism, traditional models of atonement tend to present forgiveness as a redemptive activity to be emulated by Christians, who are told to "bear with one another and, if anyone has a complaint against another, forgive each other; just as the Lord has forgiven you, so you also must forgive" (Col. 3:13). Jesus' forgiveness of the sins of others, even the most despised and/or impure, may appear to offer hope to victims of violence, and some *do* find solace here. However, the admonition to forgive often results in a leveling of sins that undermines efforts to achieve justice.

Too often, victims of abuse are encouraged to forgive their tormentors in a one-way act of selfless compassion, an expression of divine "unconditional love." Their pain and outrage are frequently left unaddressed, as is the abuser's responsibility for his behavior. The obligation to forgive makes the victim responsible not only for her own healing but for her abuser's as well. The emphasis placed by traditional christologies on the "virtue" of forgiveness, and the anguish caused by this moral dictate, is voiced by this survivor of incest: "That was the worst. I had to forgive him 'seventy times seven.'" Another had this recollection: "I always had to ask God's forgiveness for defying my father."[31]

As Young points out regarding Saint Maria Goretti, one of Maria's most admired actions was her prompt and selfless forgiveness of her attacker, Alessandro Serenelli: "Maria Goretti forgave her attacker before she died. Because Maria forgave him, her mother forgave him. Because Maria and her mother could forgive him, Alessandro Serenelli could forgive himself and expect society to do likewise. Thus, the rape victim, the sexually abused girl, and the battered wife are given the message by the Catholic Church to take responsibility for their abusers, to forgive them, and by forgiving them, redeem them."[32] When forgiveness is upheld as the Christlike or saintly response to wrongdoing, victims may learn that they have no right to their outrage and that justice should be subsumed by love.

For abusers, forgiveness can become a means of avoiding accountability through cheap grace. Andy Smith notes that "evangelical churches often see the sin of the rapist as being overcome by lust, not that he perpetrated an action of violence against another person." As a result, the assumption is that "all he needs to do to 'atone' is to pray for forgiveness from God (which is immediately granted); it is not necessary for him to seek forgiveness from the survivor, or be held accountable in a larger context, in the community and in the church." Such sanguine interpretations of forgiveness contribute to the notion "that one's relationship with God is separate from one's relationship with the community"—a claim summarily rejected by feminist and liberation theologies because it legitimates a double-standard morality that can justify all manner of abuse.[33]

When forgiveness is heralded as a salvific good—perfectly embodied by the Savior Jesus—and when Christian men, women, and children are encouraged to forgive their enemies, even at the risk of eschewing the need for justice, theology becomes a tool of oppression rather than liberation. In this context, Jesus the Divine Victim whose final words are of forgiveness for his oppressors becomes a theological symbol that perpetuates violence and undermines efforts to create justice.

Rethinking Jesus

We do well to remember that feminist objections to traditional understandings of christology and soteriology are based not on the assumption that every problematic possibility always, or even necessarily, becomes an actuality. Probably most dimensions of classical soteriology were formulated with the best of intentions; moreover, they likely once functioned as appropriate and intelligible explanations of an ultimately mysterious event. Nevertheless, in the context of today's world, their potential to inflict harm and to provide crucial ideological support for unjust attitudes, actions, and systems undermines their legitimacy and makes them incredible bearers of transformative truth. Taken together, the oppressive weight of traditional assumptions and claims about the salvific character and action of Jesus is impossible to ignore. Surely we are in need of better, healthier, more just ways of thinking about the event of redemption and Jesus' role within it.

If we take seriously the claims discussed here, then there can be little doubt that traditional construals of atonement actually perpetuate evil. For victims of abuse, even those not raised in an intentionally Christian environment, attempts to assimilate what they are experiencing, to make sense of it within their understanding of the world, often depend upon Christian images, assumptions, rules, and expectations embedded in their meaning-making milieu. Particularly when considering these people, it is difficult to deny that resistance to and recovery from relational abuse are significantly hampered by the typically espoused Christian "virtues" of suffering, self-sacrifice, innocence, and forgiveness—all of which have roots in christological formulations characteristic of traditional models of atonement.

The most disturbing point about these norms is that they can claim religious justification, theological rationale. Their power comes in large part from certain interpretations of the character and significance of the life of Jesus, whom Christians recognize as the Christ or Messiah. As the embodiment of authentic divinity and humanity, Jesus the Christ is understood, on the one hand, to incarnate God's presence, activity, and intentions in the world and, on the other, to reflect and reveal the essential or God-given nature of human existence. In the person and work of Jesus the Christ, then, Christians recognize both God and themselves as they *really* are. The claim of the doctrine of atonement is that particular attributes or activities of this Messiah set humans free from things that distort our true nature and, hence, open up the possibility for us to be who we were created or intended to be—creatures in the image of God. According to atonement orthodoxy, christic attributes or activities that have redemptive efficacy include suffering, obedience, self-sacrifice, innocence, forgiveness, and death.

However, far from embodying the Christic or salvific, these "virtues" actually enslave many women and children in abusive relationships, entrap them within self-effacing identities, and confine them within the prison of a patriarchal theology and culture based on the denial of their full personhood. A feminist hermeneutic reveals what Brock calls the "brokenheartedness" at the center of atonement orthodoxy—its (mis-)representation of Jesus the Christ as the Divine Victim whom Christians, especially women, children, and the poor, are called to imitate. This theology clearly reflects the interests of the powerful and works to the severe disadvantage of those who lack sexual, economic, and cultural power. It is, in the final analysis, a theology ideally suited for perpetrators of violence whose identity and influence depend upon the creation and manipulation of passive and complicit victims.

4

Cross and Sword

Why not simply get rid of the doctrine of atonement? If traditional interpretations of the saving work of Christ have in practice imprisoned, alienated, and dehumanized, then why bother? The force of feminist critiques makes it impossible to ignore the fact that at the heart of Christian belief lies a doctrine whose poison threatens to infect the entire body of faith. The crucial question now is, How should one respond to this knowledge? As expected, the diagnosis differs depending on the assessment of the damage done. According to some, the dis-ease is so widespread and so lethal that the Christian religion itself must be abandoned in its entirety—destroyed as quickly as possible, or at least quarantined until an antidote is discovered. According to others, amputation is necessary; if we could just get rid of that part about Jesus on the cross, the thinking goes, Christianity would be okay. Still others choose to live in denial, as if ignoring the sickness will make it go away.

A fourth response, and the one I find most intriguing, is to opt for reconstructive surgery, so to speak. This option begins with a sober recognition of the problem—the doctrine of atonement *has* had disastrous consequences—but it also includes an appreciation of the important place and function of the doctrine in the theological body. The same organ that has diminished the well-being of some has enabled the very survival of others. To opt for amputation without considering the life-saving function of the organ is perhaps too hasty a move.

If we turn our gaze away from the so-called First World to look at how the doctrine of atonement has been an energizing, empowering, transformative part of religious belief and experience for women and men in the so-called Third World, then we cannot simply dismiss the doctrine as hopelessly oppressive. Interpretations of atonement articulated by Third World theologians are by no means monolithic, and yet they tend to reflect a set of shared commitments as well as several common claims regarding sin, God, and salvation. These commitments and claims constitute a remaking of Christian theology. Weaving the old and the new together, these theologies re-create the doctrine of atonement, challenging the ways in which past construals have fed injustice, while cautioning Christian feminists not to be too quick or myopic in their rejection.

The Liberation of Theology

Liberation theology was born in Latin America in the 1960s but soon spread to other regions of the world, including Africa, Asia, and pockets of North America.[1] The contexts within which this theology arose had at least one thing in common: massive historical suffering caused primarily by the predatory economic and political practices of First World governments and institutions, in collusion with the ruling elites in Third World countries.

Like feminist theologians, liberationists begin with a hermeneutics of suspicion; that is, their encounter with traditional Christian claims and construals leads them to the grave realization that much of what has been proclaimed as true, natural, and right reflects the limited perspective of those First World-educated elites who have had the privilege and power to promulgate their own ideas, experiences, and interests. Social location, then, is a crucial component in the meaning-making process. The questions we bring to a text or situation, and the answers we glean from the encounter, are profoundly shaped by our social and political context. To a large extent, meaning is in the eye of the beholder. Thus, one of the foundational claims of liberation theologies is that all theology is *interested* theology, that all theology is necessarily interpretive and inevitably limited and biased. There is simply no such thing as a universal or objective rendering of Christian experience or truth. Even biblical narratives are interpretations.

Furthermore, the interpretations of Christian theory and practice that have held sway for hundreds, even thousands, of years have in many cases functioned to the distinct disadvantage of the masses of people—working people, poor people, uneducated people; indeed, the very conditions that have created and sustained unfair labor practices, poverty, and illiteracy on a global scale have found support in traditional articulations and practices of Christianity. Under the guise of neutrality and universality, Christian theology has been used to support such evils as slavery, colonialism, genocide, ecological devastation, global banking and trading arrangements designed to perpetuate North-South inequalities, racist immigration policies, and so on. On behalf of the victims of such practices, liberation theologies insist that neutrality is a convenient myth promoted by the privileged. In a world of exploitation and injustice, neutrality is simply not possible.

All theology implies a taking of sides, a set of choices about who is human and who is not, who God is and what God intends for the world. And as Gustavo Gutiérrez suggests, liberation theologies have as their primary focus an entirely new subject: "A goodly part of contemporary theology seems to take its start from the challenge of the *nonbeliever*. . . . In a continent like Latin America, however, the main challenge does not come from the nonbeliever, but from the *nonhuman*—i.e., the human being who is not recognized as such by the prevailing social order." When the nonperson rather than the nonbeliever is the subject of theology, completely different questions, problems, and priorities come to the fore. Gutiérrez continues: "These nonhumans do not call into question our religious world so much as they call into question our *economic, social, political, and cultural world.*"[2] The motivation for doing theology is not primarily the individual search for personal self-fulfillment or immortality but the desire for a transformed world.

From the standpoint of the Third World masses in whose interest liberation theologians claim to do their work, the paramount task of theology is to confront suffering and to develop strategies for understanding and combating it. If Christianity is a religion of soteriology—a religion whose main concern is salvation, healing, reconciliation, transformation toward peace and justice—and if it gives witness to the salvific reality of the God of love and life in this world, then any and all interpretations of this religion and this God that contribute to oppression, injustice, and suffering are to be rejected. Given the complicity of Christian beliefs, practices, and institutions in the suffering of Third World peoples, liberation theologians call for the *liberation of theology* from unholy alliances with political and economic systems that require victims.

What makes liberation theologies *theological* and *Christian* is their commitment to the Christian claim of a just and loving God whose intention for the world is its transformation toward communities of justice and compassion. However, this very rendering of "the Christian claim" is clearly shaped by an interest in such transformation; while liberation theologians reject the idea of an objectively true theology, they are nevertheless convinced that their interpretation of Christian truths is not only legitimate but in fact represents a more accurate and comprehensive articulation of biblical witnesses to, and ongoing experiences of, divine presence than do traditional construals. They make the audacious, but eminently sensible, claim that "the view from below" is more comprehensive, and hence more accurate, than "the view from above."

Those at the base of the sociopolitical hierarchy are forced to learn to play by the rules of the rulers, but they also know the consequences of such a game; they learn through experience the shortcomings of the prevailing order, and they survive their misery by imagining and working toward alternative configurations. Because their experience includes both majority and minority knowledges, their vision of reality is more expansive, more complete, than the self-serving perspective of most of the privileged. The context out of which liberation theologies emerge, and in response to which they are continually shaped, is partial and biased, as all are, and yet theology done from "the underside of history" affords a truer view of reality than those promulgated from seats of power.

Insisting that orthopraxy, or right action, is at least as important as orthodoxy, or right belief, liberation theologians point out that many traditional theologies *say* one thing but *do* another—they analyze and proclaim a God of mercy and healing, a God whose affection cannot be earned or manipulated through worldly wisdom or wealth, a God whose love extends to the ends of the earth and beyond, and yet the writers and practitioners of this theology shamelessly promote their own self-interest at the obvious expense of others. In response, liberationists affirm "a theology committed to seeking liberation from those evils for which Christianity itself is co-responsible and for which it expresses repentance."[3] By pointing out and denouncing such profound hypocrisy and discontinuity, and by calling Christian persons and communities to conversion to faithful living in response to the God of love and life, liberation theologies take on the role of the prophets of old.

In addition to the prophetic call for the liberation of theology from ideologies of domination is the proclamation of a liberating God. When the Bible is read "with Third World eyes," the God who is seen there is not primarily one who saves only the individual soul but a God of the people, a God who accompanies the downtrodden and who acts on behalf of the poor, a God who empowers the powerless and who indicts the oppressors of crimes against humanity and against God. Along with the story of the Exodus, in which the enslaved Israelites are led by God out of bondage into freedom, the biblical accounts of the Hebrew prophets are frequently cited by liberation theologians as examples of God's character and intentions for the world.[4] In the Christian Scriptures, liberation theologians also find ample evidence that God is a God of love and life. In the words and actions of Jesus, especially as recounted in the Synoptic Gospels, the dominion of God is announced and embodied as a new way of being based on compassion and mutuality. Those who are deemed unacceptable by conventional social groupings and purity codes are the very ones whom Jesus befriends, touches, learns from, and loves. And those whose concern for status or ritual overrides their concern for mercy and justice are defied by the lowly One from Galilee who dares to go to the very seat of power, Jerusalem, to uncover its abuses and to manifest a different kind of power, a liberating power that eschews domination and affirms mutuality, no matter what the cost to his personal well-being.

These and other biblical passages and traditions are said to reflect a "preferential option for the poor." The Bible, argue liberation theologians, gives witness to God's special concern for the poor and the outcast and admonishes persons to care particularly for "widows and orphans," for "the least of these," for one's neighbor—the one who in a moment of need was passed by unmercifully by religious and political leaders and institutions. "To know God is to do justice," insisted the prophet Jeremiah, and in a world characterized by structural inequalities along lines of race, class, gender, and ethnicity, doing justice requires that we make an "option" on behalf of those who have been cast into life's highways and byways by the forces of greed, selfishness, and indifference. This is, after all, what God has done. Yet as Robert McAfee Brown explains, such a preferential option "doesn't mean an *exclusive* option for the poor—as though God only loved the poor and hated the rich." Rather, liberation theologies affirm that God loves *all* people; however, "because in God's world the poor get a decidedly unfair share of the world's goods (due chiefly to human greed), the fact that God does love *all* means that there must be food, shelter, jobs, and humane living conditions for all and not just for some."[5] To make an option on behalf of the marginalized is, in the broad scheme of things, to choose the well-being of all, for all are implicated in and dehumanized by systems of exploitation. Paradoxically, in caring especially for the downtrodden, God manifests divine equanimity and inclusivity.

To affirm a theology of liberation is to make an epistemological break—to entertain a new possibility of interpreting reality, a new way of thinking about God and everything connected to God. Within this situation of novelty and transformation, liberation is not merely one characteristic or emphasis among others; rather, it is the horizon against which everything else looks different from before. It is a new perspective from which all else is understood and analyzed. It requires the liberation of theology from self-serving illusions of neutrality and universality, the recognition that "the view from below" affords a legitimate and expansive vision of reality, and the affirmation that God is a God of love and life who cares especially for the poor and outcast and who desires that we do the same.

Which Christ?

The central claim of Christian theologies of all stripes is that God, the Ultimate, the Sacred, became incarnate in the human person Jesus and thus has been made known to the world in a decisive and salvific way. Liberation theologies do not claim exception to this assertion. However, they are faced with a dilemma, for historically, christology has been a highly ambiguous and dangerous component of Third World Christianity. It was introduced in almost every case as a weapon of conquest, a tool of oppression; and yet somehow, it was gradually refashioned by the oppressed themselves into a locus of struggle, of resistance, and of hope. In this chapter we look at ways in which christology, and especially certain understandings of Jesus' suffering and death as salvific, has contributed to Third World oppression, while in the following chapter we explore the ways in which liberation theologies are reinterpreting the doctrine of atonement to reflect their encounter with God's saving presence in a world racked by suffering and injustice.

For Latin American liberation theologians, the foundational context for doing theology is colonialism, past and present. During the sixteenth-century European expansion into Latin America, Christianity was brought to the continent to provide religious sanction for political, economic, and cultural conquest. The two symbols of this process were the sword and the cross— signifiers of crown and church—which were understood to work hand in hand to serve the same end of European hegemony. Pablo Richard notes, "The Spanish sword which attacked and murdered the bodies of Indians by day at night became the cross which attacked the Indian soul."[6] Within only 150 years after the conquest began, the 70 to 90 million indigenous inhabitants of Latin America were reduced to a mere 3.5 million.[7] In this genocide, the complicity of the Christian church is well documented.

Referring to his adventures of exploration and exploitation, for instance, Christopher Columbus, known as a dedicated Christian, wrote to Isabella and Ferdinand of Spain: "I set out in the name of the Holy Trinity, in whom I place my hope of victory."[8] It is reported that upon his arrival on the shores of the New World, one of his first acts was to plant a cross. In addition, he emphasized the etymology of his name: Christopher, meaning "Christ-bearer," and the Spanish version of his surname, Colon, meaning "one who peoples anew."[9] So it was that Christopher Columbus—Christianizing Colonizer— represented the marriage between politics and religion, greed and God, that was characteristic of European encounters with Latin America. According to Saúl Trinidad, Columbus thought it was his God-given vocation to evangelize the New World in order to fulfill prophecies from the Hebrew Scriptures.[10] As a result of this sort of logic, says José Miguez Bonino, "the ancient dream of a 'Catholic kingdom,' a unified political and religious structure ruled by Catholic teaching down to its last details—the dream that could never be realized in Europe—was transported to Latin America."[11]

In this process of conquest it was necessary to establish military and political rule, cultural hegemony, and religious unity; other gods or strange forms of worship were not tolerated. Religions that included various forms of sacrifice were especially condemned as "primitive" and "savage." Christ's sacrifice was the full and sufficient one—all others were inferior, unnecessary, misguided, blasphemous. Ironically, however, "millions of human beings were sacrificed on the altar of gold and silver." Despite the lip-service paid to God and Christ by the colonizing Christians, "gold and silver became [their] 'new gods.'"[12]

Once colonization ended and political independence from Spain was achieved in the nineteenth century, the violence merely changed its appearance as Latin American countries became economically dependent upon other "Christian" nations of the North such as Great Britain and the United States. Promises of development, democracy, and prosperity enticed Third World leaders to make the rich resources of their lands and labor available for exploitation by industrialized nations of the North. In return, northern-controlled institutions such as the International Monetary Fund and the World Bank were encouraged to make enormous loans to Third World countries for development projects; much of this money never made it past the pockets of corrupt local dictators. Today, as massive tracts of land and human labor continue to be converted from subsistence crops to luxury crops—no longer feeding the Latin American masses but instead feeding the desire of First World consumers for fresh cantaloupes and strawberries all year round—as rain forests are demolished to make room for grazing cattle to meet First World appetites for beef; and as the interest on the development loans is itself exorbitant enough to disable most southern economies, the relationship of dependence between First and Third World has been invigorated and institutionalized in new and complex ways. Colonialism has given way to neocolonialism. Gold and silver, it seems, are still the reigning gods.

Christianity in Latin America was the child of violence, and the abuse has not let up. The cross, used to symbolize Christ's triumph over sin and death, brought even more death. Leonardo Boff and Virgilio Elizondo note, "12 October 1492 was the beginning of a long and bloody Good Friday for Latin America and the Caribbean. It is still Good Friday, and there is no sign of Easter Day."[13] Liberation theologians find that only the most dramatic language can denote the horror of colonialism's impact on Latin America's people and land: "In 1492 death came to this continent: the death of human beings, the death of the environment, death of the spirit, of indigenous religion and culture." Again and again, these Christian theologians call their religion to account: "The genocide and the massacre . . . would not have been possible without an appropriate theology. The historical violence was accompanied by theological violence."[14] The expansion of the gospel that accompanied and sanctioned the conquest of the Indies was justified by the claim that

Christ was being brought to the barbarians and pagans who were "caught up in the power of Satan." Maximiliano Salinas explains the prevailing logic: "The colonial equation, God/Europe: Satan/Indies, formed the basis for the evangelization of the imperial churches on the new continent."[15] Just as the conquistador's sword formed a cross at its base, the cross of Christ became a weapon of exploitation and control.

In this way, an "anthropology of domination" emerged to undergird Western expansion and to signal the birth of the "modern" period. This anthropology, argues Johann Baptist Metz, was "overlaid by many religious and cultural symbols."[16] The christological images found in Latin America cohere around two main models—the Christ of Conquest and the Christ of Liberation—both of which are funded by particular interpretations of atonement. The former model, say liberation theologians, was imported by the conquistadors and forced upon the indigenous peoples, and this model continues to have great influence in Latin America among both the elite and the masses. The reason for its longevity and appeal is its two-sided nature. On the one hand, Christ is the Conquering One; the One whose power and might are emulated by those in positions of power; the One who sanctions their power. On the other hand, Christ is the Conquered One; the One who was falsely accused, brutally beaten, and tortured to death; the One with whom the poor and marginalized can identify; the One who sanctions their powerlessness. The former christology ignores the suffering and death of Jesus as unpalatable or inconvenient, while the latter embraces it so closely that suffocation seems inevitable. Together, these two sides of the same christological coin feed the violence of the few and the passivity of the many.

As for the few, the image of Christ as resurrected Lord—conqueror of fear, evil spirits, sin, and death—was for the colonizers a boon to their self-understanding. It validated their mission, buoyed their spirits during trying times, and inspired them with a sense of holy vocation. In their theology, Christ was portrayed as celestial monarch, controlling the world from his heavenly throne. His viceroys were the terrestrial kings and their deputies, whose mission was to establish the New World as a holy kingdom. Georges Casalis suggests, "If Christ is the heavenly Ferdinand, the earthly Ferdinand thereby becomes the authentic royal lieutenant of his eternal warrant."[17] This understanding is evident in Columbus's letter to Ferdinand and Isabella in 1493: "Thus, as our Redeemer has given our Most Illustrious King and Queen this victory and kingdoms of such high estate . . . may it likewise please our Lord to grant them long life and to further this so noble undertaking, in which it seems to me that our Lord receives much service, Spain much grandeur, and Christians much consolation and pleasure, seeing that thus the name of our Lord spreads through every land."[18]

Jesus, the itinerant preacher from Galilee, becomes within this christology the heavenly possessor of power and glory whose might and authority are manifest on earth in a chosen few who are given absolute dominion over people and land. The result of the conquerors' logic, insists Casalis, is that Christ "is demoted to the rank of minister of propaganda in governments that govern by authoritarianism and torture."[19] Though the names and faces have changed since the fifteenth century, the logic remains the same today. The Conquering Christ continues to legitimize the powerful and to sacramentalize systems of domination in Latin America and in other parts of the Third World.[20] Christ is the Conqueror as a result of his victory over death; furthermore, his death is not seen as a threat to his glory, for it was an entirely voluntary sacrifice, part of the well-orchestrated offensive against Satan that, as his resurrection reveals, he won handily. Clearly, this understanding of the character and function of Jesus the Christ is ideally suited for those in power; it is no wonder they have embraced it zealously and jealously.

Among the masses in Latin America, both past and present, the prevailing christology centers on the Conquered Christ, the One who was humiliated and vanquished by the powerful of his day and who resignedly accepted his fate. Popular piety often includes an emphasis on the tortured or dead Christ—"his eyes rolled up in their sockets, his face turned down to the earth, and his whole body exhibiting the havoc wreaked upon it by the blows of his torturers."[21] This image is found in the prayers and religious festivals of the faithful as well as on crucifixes in churches, shops, schools, homes, and museums of sacred art. According to Brazilian theologian João Dias de Araújo, it is an image that "exalts Christ's death and his sufferings on the cross" and has created "in the mind of the people the image of a Christ who is dead, nailed to wood, rendered incapable of reacting, wasted by the forces of evil." This defeated Christ, insists Araújo, "has been a great generator of the fatalism and conformism that are so deeply rooted among the people of Brazil today."[22] Followers of this "Christ of Calvary alone," concur Saúl Trinidad and Juan Stam, respond with "resignation and passivity in the face of injustice and outrage" because they have been told that Christ endured his suffering and humiliation without resistance.[23]

Casalis articulates the subtle power of such theological, artistic, and liturgical representations: "When the faithful people pray before these images and venerate them, when their spirit is seared all through life by a pedagogy of submission and passivity, evidently it is their own destiny that they encounter here—and worship, and accept with masochistic resignation. Indeed, this Abject Jesus is nothing but the image of the conquered Amerindian, the poorest of the poor, for whom nothing has changed."[24] Just as the earthly Ferdinands see their experiences and destiny in Christ, so do the marginalized. Both embrace a Christ in their own image—opposites, but inextricably interwoven.

The difference, of course, is that Christ was brought and taught *to* the people of Latin America *by* the foreign invaders; the latter imposed the Christ of Conquest at sword point. And during centuries of occupation and domination, the imposed theology gradually wore down the edges of resistance; it became so familiar that even to its victims it eventually appeared natural, God-given.

The impact of the Conquered Christ on Third World women is particularly insidious as class, ethnic, and gender oppression is reinforced by a theology that glorifies victimization. Virginia Fabella recounts that in the Philippines, an Asian country that has suffered a history of colonial occupation akin to Latin American countries, most Christian women "look upon the passion and death of Jesus as ends in themselves and actually relish being victims." The focus of their religiosity is "the suffering or crucified Jesus who understands their own suffering which they passively and resignedly endure."[25] For these women, interpretations of Jesus' suffering and death as redemptive have a direct, negative impact on their well-being.

The vast majority of women and men in Latin America have been taught a christology that encourages them to find happiness in their suffering. Thus, theology is used to reinforce fatalism, to fashion a social world and a group identity in which change is largely unimaginable. The impotence of Christ is interiorized by the oppressed so that, as Hugo Assmann notes, "defeat is not perceived as a temporary reversal to be overcome in struggle . . . [but] appears as an inevitable necessity, as a condition of the privilege of living."[26]

When he is not presented to the common people as a defeated or dead Christ, suggests Trinidad, he is depicted as an innocent child. This inoffensive, sweet baby Jesus "wears a perpetual smile, for he is indifferent to what transpires around him." Happy to leave things as they are, "he seeks to settle in his 'protectors' laps, with as little inconvenience as possible." Like a "dutiful adopted child," he learns to speak the language of his patrons and even "to speak on their behalf."[27]

Clearly, these two dimensions of the Conquered Christ are intended to undermine the agency of those who follow him. Rather than resist their oppression, they are offered divine encouragement to stay quiet, lie low, accept what comes their way; they are even taught to welcome their own subordination, since to do so is Christlike.[28] As Trinidad and other liberation theologians note, this Conquered Christ is a far cry from the Jesus of the Gospel narratives, for this Christ is historicized in only two ways: "as the helpless and harmless child, and as the humiliated and defeated victim. He was born, he died. But he never lived."[29]

Taken together, the Conquering Christ and the Conquered Christ can be properly understood only as organically related, indeed as requiring each other. Assmann insists, "Christs of established power (who have no need to struggle, because they already dominate), and Christs of established impotence (who are too dominated to be able to struggle) are the two faces of oppressor christologies."[30] Similarly, Trinidad asks, "What, then, has been the function of christology in Latin America? The first thing that stands out is its role in baptizing, sacralizing, the *conquista* and the resulting oppression, as well as making a virtue out of suffering."[31] The continued presence of this christology in liturgy, hymns, sermons, and popular religious celebrations indicates its prevalence among the common people of Latin America. What was once imposed externally has become internalized.

A Double-Edged Sword

Throughout the history of Christianity in the Third World, the suffering and death of Jesus have captured the imagination of the oppressed. The idea that his humiliation, torture, and crucifixion have redemptive importance has signified to millions of men and women that *their* suffering, too, is meaningful, and that therefore, they should not resist it. It would seem, then, that feminist critiques of atonement are perfectly reinforced, for the attribution of salvific import to the suffering and death of Jesus is the linchpin in a theology of violence that has played a crucial role in the perpetuation of misery in the Third World.

The question now is: How *should* the suffering and death of Jesus be understood? Must all attempts at interpreting them as part of God's saving activity be rejected as self-immolating delusions? While many First World feminist theologians answer this second question in the affirmative, rarely, if ever, is such a response made by Third World theologians, male or female. While feminist theologians are likely to reject any understanding of Jesus' suffering and death as salvific, Third World theologians almost never do. This disjuncture between two theological "camps," which have so much in common and which so badly need the support of each other, is striking. Why this discrepancy, given their common awareness of the dangers of theologies that encourage passivity in oppressive situations as well as their shared commitment to the role of religion in transforming the world toward justice and compassion? The difference, it would seem, lies in the fact that Third World people and theologians have found not only problems and dangers in the doctrine of atonement, but enormous hope and empowerment as well.

Perhaps the situations of massive suffering and apparent hopelessness experienced on a daily basis by the majority of Third World people cast the doctrine of atonement in a different light. Whatever the reason, it does seem to be the case that liberation theologies make a dramatic departure from feminist theologies when it comes to atonement. These two theologies, which have literally re-created Christian theology during the past three decades and which seem to share the same basic commitments and to be confronted by the same or similar problems—these two theologies, which, it would seem, will ultimately either sink or swim together—find themselves at an impasse over what to do about the suffering and death of Jesus. As the previous discussion demonstrates, liberationists are by no means unaware of or uncritical toward the victimizing function of certain interpretations of Jesus' suffering and death. Their affirmation of the doctrine, then, is not uninformed or unenlightened; rather, as we will see, it is the product of careful consideration of Christian tradition and contemporary experience.

From a liberation perspective, one possible response to feminist theologians' tendency to dismiss atonement as theologically perverse or dispensable is to ask whether a genuine alternative actually exists. Many Third World theologians hearken back to Martin Luther's distinction between a theology of glory and a theology of the cross in order to articulate the alternatives and to explain why they find it necessary, in full knowledge of the drawbacks involved, to find meaning in Jesus' suffering and death. Leonardo Boff, for instance, reminds us that the apostle Paul seems to have encountered Christians whose theology was so focused on the resurrected Christ, and so dismissive of the theological import of the crucifixion, that their theology had become "an opium"—a drug that induced such feelings of ecstasy and power that its users became convinced that they could actually save themselves, that their earthly power and status were reflections of their blessedness.[32] Paul's response, meant to shake these people from their selfish stupor, is to remind them that the cross shows the fallacy of such hubris, for it reveals in no uncertain terms the depths of human evil, the bankruptcy of all schemes of salvation, the surprising wisdom and activity of the God who cannot be manipulated, who saves not through acts of power and might but through weakness, through powerlessness.

Boff says, "Christ, with his death and his cross, is the crisis, in the original sense of the word, of all human undertakings: their judgment, their moment of truth. They all come to an end on the cross."[33] David Batstone uses the biblical story of "doubting Thomas" to explain the necessity of a theology of the cross. He suggests that the historical context of liberation theologians has provided them with "a set of suspicions regarding Christology which are perhaps akin to those held by Thomas after the death of Jesus."[34] Like Thomas, who insisted that he would not believe that the resurrected Jesus was indeed the Christ unless he could see and touch the scars of crucifixion, "liberation theologians are equally suspect of any claim of Christ's presence if they cannot recognize in that figure of proclamation the 'scars' of the crucified Jesus. For they are convinced that it is his cross which calls into question all knowledge about God."[35]

To do away with the doctrine of atonement is to do away with any theology of the cross; it is to ignore the fact that there *is* meaning in the suffering and death of Jesus, that here we learn something genuinely new about God, and something devastatingly ancient about human nature. The alternative is a theology of glory, which sees God in power, in happiness and prestige. Such a theology, insist liberationists, may ring true in the First World, where power, prestige, and progress are seen as real possibilities, but amidst the poverty, illiteracy, and violence of daily life in the Third World, this theology looks suspiciously like colonizing Christianity with its Conquering Christ. Black South African theologian Takatso Mofokeng articulates this sense of suspicion and betrayal. He claims that under the influence of imperial Christianity, "the cross was emasculated and lost its power to bring crisis to reality and transform it. Emphasis shifted to the resurrection as the event in which God is present. He disappeared from the cross. And his disappearance from it is nothing but a betrayal of the poor and the oppressed, a betrayal of those people in the world who are hanging on the cross and crying out for liberation."[36]

In their constructive proposals, liberation theologians attempt to walk a fine and potentially dangerous line—to do a theology of the cross that does not glorify, and therefore perpetuate, suffering and death. In taking up this challenge, they stand in a long line of Christian thinkers; indeed, most all the great theologians of the tradition have attempted to strike such a balance. What is novel here is the social location of liberation theologians, for whom concerns about suffering and death take on a distinctive urgency, as well as a politicized dimension, given the massive and unjust imposition of suffering and death that marks their daily existence. Simon Maimela warns, "The theology of the cross is a double-edged sword that could be either a blessing or a curse. It all depends on who is talking about the theology of the cross, to whom it is addressed, and whose interests it intends serving." In South Africa, says Maimela, where "the cross and suffering are experienced daily" by black people who are victims of "a long 'Good Friday' of racial oppression and domination at the hands of white Christian settlers," white Christians have abused the theology of the cross "by encouraging their black victims to carry their cross of suffering with dignity and without complaint as Jesus Christ carried his." And yet, he insists, a theology of the cross "could be a source of solace . . . an expression of power over one's own suffering."[37] This latter possibility, in tandem with a recognition of the devastating consequences of theologies of glory, motivates liberation theologians to work to maintain and reconfigure the doctrine of atonement. Not all succeed in this endeavor, but those who do, offer an account of atonement that merits serious consideration by all theologians, feminists included.

5

Atonement from the Underside

The question of how God works in the world to confront evil is *the* question at the heart of this book. The Christian approach to this query, referred to as the doctrine of atonement, focuses on the figure of Jesus the Christ and claims that in the life and death of this figure, God's response to evil was made manifest in a definitive manner. For nearly two millennia, interpretations of the saving work of Christ have been formulated in countless attempts to make sense of both the tragedy of his death and the conviction that his death did not render his cause a failure. How is it, Christians have asked through the ages, that a murdered God can save us? And from what do we need to be saved? Each generation has come up with its own ideas, making use of the intellectual, cultural, and political categories at hand, and putting them into conversation with previous interpretations, including those articulated in the Bible.

According to many feminist theologians, we need to be saved *from* the doctrine of atonement, from any claim that suffering or death—whether God's or humans'—is meaningful. To make meaning out of suffering and death, it is argued, merely perpetuates them, and any religion or belief that does such a thing is demonic. God is a God of life, not death; God is life-giving, not death-dealing.

Liberation theologians agree wholeheartedly that God is a God of life; that God desires not only life, but also fullness of life, for all. Therefore, God is a God of justice: if all are to live fully, then none should be oppressed. On these things, feminists and liberationists agree. However, for liberation theologians, to affirm that God is a God of life does not mean that God is not also a God of death, for as their daily experience reflects, death *is* a part of life. To claim that God is not somehow a God of death is to exclude God from the full gamut of life; it is to diminish God, to make God unreal, to consign God only to the happy times, to the times of growth and prosperity. But as we know, life is not only—perhaps not even primarily—happiness or growth. To claim that God is really a God of life, our notion of life must include death as well as suffering, disappointment, loss, decay, tragedy. God's experience must somehow include these realities, for they *are* real. In the Third World, they are entirely too real.

Liberation interpretations of atonement attempt to bring together two convictions. The first is that God *is* a God of life and justice. God desires fullness of being for all; indeed, God is the very source and pulse of life; God is, in other words, Being itself. At the same time, however, God's affirmation of life can and does occur even in death, even in experiences of suffering and injustice. God is understood to be present and active not only in Jesus' life but also in his suffering and death. To affirm both convictions in a way that contradicts neither is the challenge of liberation construals of atonement.

Atonement from Below

One of the earliest insights of liberation theologies that is germane to our discussion of atonement has to do with definitions of sin and salvation. Traditional Christian theology's tendency to define salvation as freedom from personal sin and guilt is criticized as too narrow in scope. Such an understanding, it is argued, myopically depicts individuals as isolated from families and communities and as unrelated to cultural, political, and economic systems and institutions. As a result, salvation is seen as an individual event whose effect is primarily interior and personal. Liberation theologians insist that such a definition serves the interests of those in power by discouraging analysis and transformation of existing social and political structures.

By contrast, liberation theologies propose that to broaden the scope of salvation to include not merely the individual but the social as well, we need to think in terms of liberation. In addition, they suggest that since the focus has for so long been on the individual alone—to the great detriment of millions of people enslaved not only by personal sin and guilt but also, and perhaps primarily, by social, political, and economic systems—the emphasis now should be on the social. Gustavo Gutiérrez explains, "In the liberation approach sin is not considered as an individual, private, or merely interior reality"; rather, "sin is regarded as a social, historical fact, the absence of fellowship and love in relationships among persons, the breach of friendship with God and with other persons."[1] Thus, salvation is understood in terms of liberation, and sin is understood to include not simply the personal but the structural as well.

Sin, claims Jon Sobrino, is "that which deals death"—the human attitudes, actions, and policies that enforce death upon others, that "demand victims."[2] Put differently, sin is "the rejection of God's kingdom," the denial of God's intention that justice, peace, and mercy define reality. Sin is people's inordinate self-exaltation that "leads them to assert their own power in two negative ways": to "secure themselves against God" and "to oppress others."[3] When nationalism, consumerism, racism, or worldly success, for instance, defines one's reality, God has been replaced by lesser gods, by what is not ultimate. Such idols are demonic displays of power; from them liberation is needed. The price we pay for such idolatry is the oppression of others as well as our own dehumanization; sin against God is at the same time sin against our neighbor. Sobrino emphasizes, "Divine filiation is broken because human brotherhood is broken."[4]

Because sin is "enslaving," because it captures both oppressor and oppressed in cycles of victimization that become self-perpetuating, "its defeat is formally liberation"—freedom from slavery.[5] Sin, says Sobrino, "is not just something that must be pardoned; it must be *taken away*, eradicated."[6] Furthermore, because sin is both personal and social, liberation from it must likewise include both the individual and the structural. Commenting on these two dimensions, Ignacio Ellacuria suggests that "to think that the Church should restrict its activity to personal conversion, that this will eventually lead to structural change, is to fail to recognize that structures objectify and condition personal, individual behavior. . . . At the same time, however, the journey towards new structures will not be a Christian journey if it is not plotted out and trodden by human beings who have undergone personal conversion."[7] The biblical message of liberation, he reminds us, is broad and inclusive; it "talks about liberation from personal faults and their inner consequences for the individual. It talks about liberation from the objective forms of oppression that stem from the sins of human beings: sickness, premature death, poverty, devastation, and so forth. It talks about liberation from those in power on this earth who oppress and exploit the poor unjustly."[8]

Salvation as liberation, then, is all-encompassing. However, liberation is not only freedom *from*—its primary aim is not destruction but the creation of "a new kind of liberty and a new earth."[9] Liberation is freedom *for* fullness of life, for relationships of love and mutuality, for institutions whose aim is to enhance the well-being of *all* God's creatures.

How does liberation from sin and for right relationship take place? And what is the role of Jesus the Christ in this liberation? In addition to interpreting sin and salvation as personal and social, a central insight of liberation theologies is that to know and understand Christ's person and work, we have to begin with the historical Jesus. Unlike the conquistadors and their contemporary successors, who base their theology almost entirely on the resurrected and triumphant Christ, Third World theologians argue that the resurrection of Christ can be properly understood only in conjunction with the life and passion of Jesus of Nazareth. They affirm a christology, and an atonement, from below—an understanding of the person and work of Christ that begins with the actual life and teachings of the historical Jesus. Liberation theologies demonstrate that when the actual historical mission of Jesus is taken seriously, a theology of glory becomes impossible. Jesus is neither the Conquering Christ nor the Conquered Christ but the One who liberates through resistance to evil and compassion for the suffering.

Liberation theologians emphasize, contrary to much of theological tradition, that Jesus' suffering and death cannot be understood apart from his life. The cross is inseparable from the incarnation. Jesus' death was the consequence of the life he lived, not the result of a death wish, of some cosmic deal between God and Satan, or of God's demand for bloody satisfaction. Atonement—God's confrontation of evil and reconciliation of the world to the Divine Self—cannot be narrowed to the moment of Jesus' death or even to the passion, for it is a process that includes life, death, and resurrection. And yet, liberation theologians insist that we cannot overlook the redemptive significance of Jesus' suffering and death, for it is here that God is revealed in an unexpected and scandalous way. Without the experience and knowledge of this crucified God, liberation from sin and reconciliation with self and other are impossible.

In general, liberation interpretations of atonement share several emphases or priorities. They insist that the cross of Christ tells us something crucial not only about humanity and salvation, but about God as well. Indeed, only by way of the theology of the cross can we know the true God. The death of Jesus represents a crisis of religion, for it calls all understandings of God as the omnipotent, impassible, transcendent One into question. If saving knowledge is made known on the cross, it is the knowledge that God saves not through expected or conventional ways, not through power and might, but through weakness, through suffering and death.

In addition, liberation theologies tend to make human suffering a major theological category. Writing in the second half of the bloodiest century in history, they are keenly aware of massive human suffering and attempt to make theological sense of it. In this effort, they recognize that to exempt God from suffering—to conceptualize God as wholly transcendent and impassible—is to render God irrelevant to human experience. It is, more important, to ignore the fact of the cross. In and through suffering, suggest liberationists, the essence of God is revealed; by entering into the suffering of humanity, God shares the burden of human sin, takes it into the Divine Self and trans-

forms it into love, into com-passion: feeling-with. We are reconciled to God
through God's gift of love to us, manifest on the cross in God's willingness to
endure the suffering of human existence.

Finally, liberation construals of atonement insist that reconciliation between God and humanity includes or requires the reconciliation of humans
to one another. As a result of God's accompaniment with us in our suffering,
we are empowered to accept rejection by the world and to open ourselves to
the humanizing practice of love. Interhuman reconciliation becomes the
manifestation and validation of God's redemptive, reconciling love.

While these are the hallmarks of what liberation theologies tend to affirm in their thinking about atonement, other characteristics have consistently plagued liberationist proposals, creating conflicts and tensions with
these affirmations. The major problem has been the tendency, typical of
Christian theological tradition in general, to romanticize, dehistoricize, and
eternalize the suffering and death of Jesus. The central liberationist claim that
in the passion of Jesus, God is revealed as a suffering God, is not immediately
problematic. It begins to have troubling implications, however, when it is extended to include the claim that in and through God's suffering, salvation occurs. And it becomes of even greater concern when Jesus' death on the cross
is understood as an intertrinitarian event, as the struggle of "God against
God," or "Father against Son."[10] One problem with this interpretation is that
it dehistoricizes the suffering and death of Jesus, positing them as an internal
divine event; as a result, the commitments and struggles of the historical Jesus
become secondary—the real action occurs not on earth but in God's being.
This speculative understanding of the death of Jesus, then, means that atonement—the confrontation of evil and the reconciliation of God and world—
becomes primarily a heavenly affair. "Jesus against the Pharisees" or "Jesus
against greed" is universalized and theologized into "God against God." In a
world that stands in dire need of *historical* solutions to historical evils, the emphasis on atonement as an intertrinitarian event runs the risk of removing evil
and redemption from the historical realm in which Jesus, and all other humans, encounter it; it pushes to the side the task of addressing the suffering
and death caused daily by human actions and institutions.

A related problem plaguing many liberation interpretations has to do
with the claim that God's suffering or pain is salvific, that God redeems evil
by embracing it, by bringing it into God's own being. The danger of this position is that it tends to eternalize suffering, to offer it a theological back door
to acceptability, and that, therefore, it may undermine human resistance to
unjust suffering. If *the* locus of redemption is God's suffering and death—un-
hinged from the historical circumstances and choices that brought them
on—then suffering and death can be interpreted as salvific *in themselves*.

Passive acceptance of suffering and death is only one step away. When Kazoh Kitamori, one of the earliest influences on the development of liberation thought, argues that pain is the very essence of God, and that the way to know God, to be reconciled to God, is to transform our pain into a sacrament of God's pain, the motivation for denouncing unjust suffering, for struggling against it, is lost.[11] Another theologian of enormous import when it comes to the emergence of liberation theology, particularly its understanding of atonement, is German theologian Jürgen Moltmann. Moltmann's insistence that divine suffering is the result of divine love is a marked improvement over Kitamori's mysticism of pain, and yet Moltmann's claim that "suffering is overcome by suffering" merely resituates the problem; for him, the suffering of God saves us from solitary suffering and thus from "the torment of hell," but is that sufficient? Is accompaniment in suffering *redemption?* If the ultimate meaning of the cross is "perseverance," then the conditions that create and perpetuate suffering and injustice are left uncontested.

Although many liberation theologians follow Moltmann in seeing solidarity in suffering as the ultimate expression of God's salvific love, we will see that others recognize that this claim does not go far enough. Redemption from evil must mean more than suffering through it together, as vital as that may be. If salvation is to be a world-transforming affair, rather than a personal or even interpersonal amelioration, then it must include *resistance* to evil, struggle against its causes, concrete efforts to undo it. Liberation theologians are moving away from a sole emphasis on "suffering with" to a dual emphasis on solidarity in suffering *in the struggle to end suffering.*

A final weakness of many liberation interpretations of atonement is their claim, based on Moltmann's thought, that in the suffering and death of Jesus, God accepts radical negativity into God's being and thereby redeems it. This conviction, though comforting, affirms a conceptual neatness that belies the ambiguity of actual existence. As Johann Baptist Metz, Dorothee Sölle, Wendy Farley, and other theologians have argued, taking up the ancient position of Job, some evil simply cannot be conceptualized or theologized away. The evils of radical suffering and of dehumanizing injustice, for instance, defy logic. Their intractability and mystery elude conceptuality. The only possible "solution" to evil is not conceptual but praxic—specific, historical acts of resistance to its particular manifestations, and active compassion for and solidarity with those who are its victims.

Increasingly, liberation theologians are careful in their interpretations of the saving work of Christ to avoid the weaknesses of earlier views, especially the dehistoricization of Jesus' suffering and death; the eternalization of suffering; and the temptation to "solve" the problem of evil. They tend instead to embrace a different set of emphases, including (1) the interpretation of the entire life of Jesus, culminating in his tragic death, as the locus of atonement; (2) the insistence that his suffering may be understood as redemptive only insofar as it was a suffering in the service of the struggle against suffering; and (3) the development of specific strategies for how to resist evil on a daily basis rather than concepts for "theologizing evil away." In the remainder of this chapter I focus on the specific ways in which three liberation theologians— Leonardo Boff, Jon Sobrino, and Virgilio Elizondo—have proposed to deal with the theological meaning of the death of Jesus the Christ. Their construals of atonement bring together an Abelardian emphasis on the theological importance of Jesus' life and mission with an essentially Anselmian commitment to the continued relevance of and need for theologies of the cross that can account for the gravity and scope of human evil while proclaiming the reality of God's gracious, salvific response to that evil.

Incarnating Solidarity

Brazilian theologian Leonardo Boff interprets atonement as the work of Jesus whose constant "being-for-others" opened a new and salvific way of existence based on solidarity with others, suffering as the fruit of love and resistance to evil, power understood as service, and forgiveness toward one's oppressor. While he sees the cross as the pivotal event in the struggle against evil, he insists that it cannot be separated from the life-praxis of the man Jesus. Boff is clearly indebted to theological tradition and to Moltmann's contributions to the discussion of the significance of the death of Christ, but he is also highly critical of certain claims and implications made by both. His work, then, represents liberation theology's position of both continuity and critique with regard to traditional construals of atonement.

The cross, says Boff, is a site of conflict, both physical and ideological. Physically, it is "an instrument of atrocious punishment," a cruel device used by the Roman government of Jesus' time to publicly humiliate and torture traitors, rebellious slaves, and political dissidents. It was a form of physical punishment and an ideological tool of social control, a dramatic reminder to the masses that stepping out of line could have fatal consequences. At the same time, however, the cross is one of Christianity's "mightiest symbols— the graphic embodiment of Christ's redemption."[12] As such, it signifies the tenacity of life, the paradox of the struggle for love and justice in a violent world. Hence the cross is an "indictment of the wickedness of the persons who caused [Jesus'] death" *and* "the symbol of love stronger than death." It is "essentially ambiguous"—symbol of "inhuman-being" and of love/new-being—and this ambiguity must be maintained if the cross is to preserve its critical and its transformative dimensions.[13] For Boff, as for many liberation theologians, the cross is not simply about injustice or liberation; rather, it symbolizes the struggle between the two. It "demonstrates the conflict-ridden nature of every process of liberation undertaken when the structure of injustice has gained the upper hand."[14] The cross of Christ, the central symbol of Christianity, is for liberation theologies a sober reminder of the reality of evil in the world and of the divine mandate to resist evil to the end.

Boff and others are profoundly aware that the struggle against evil did not end with Jesus' death or resurrection. The cross was not a one-time event; many were its victims before Jesus, and many after. Despite the fact that Jesus' life, death, and resurrection did not do away with all evil, however, Boff is convinced that in and through him, God *has* revealed God's definitive response to evil. This response has set forth for all time the way of liberation from the powers of sin and evil and, consequently, the way of reconciliation with God and neighbor.

Boff places his interpretation of atonement in clear contrast to traditional understandings. He is critical of the tendency of past construals to confine redemption to only two points, the incarnation and the passion. Such a narrow focus leads to an abstract understanding of redemption because it omits Jesus' earthly life—"the salvific value of all his words, attitudes, actions, and reactions."[15] The effect of this omission, says Boff, is that it removes redemption from the realm of actual human historicity, concentrating so narrowly on a personal, interior process that the social dimensions of existence are ignored. Redemption is restricted to a time past and thus supports the unjust status quo.

Even though traditional models of atonement seem to offer multiple variations on the saving work of Christ, Boff criticizes the fact that each one depicts human beings as helpless to satisfy the demands of divine justice. Liberation is understood to consist in "Jesus Christ's substitution for human beings—Jesus Christ's effectuation of what human beings ought to have done." To avoid this infantilizing dynamic, Boff tries to maintain both the saving significance of Christ's work *and* the necessity of human participation in redemption. He insists that the genuine crux of redemption and liberation is not to be found in "abstract, formal models that shred the unity of the life of Jesus Christ." Rather, "redemption is basically a praxis, a historical process, verified in the turbulent reality of a concrete situation."[16]

Boff reminds us that "Jesus did not die in bed"; he was "violently eliminated" in an act of "judicial murder."[17] To understand the meaning of his death, we must view it within the context of a life lived in such a way as to provoke institutional furor: "Jesus' death can be understood only from the point of departure in his historical praxis, in his message, in the demands he makes and the conflicts he arouses."[18] Like other liberation theologians, Boff insists that Jesus' life and death are inseparable. Jesus' death was the consequence of the commitments that shaped his life; they include "his criticism of

repressive regimes and situations, his focus on individual and corporate liberation, his courage to confront the religious, social, and political authorities
and traditions of his day." Such commitments incited the fear and wrath of
those whose power depended on the prevailing order of reality. Clearly, then,
Jesus' message, life, and death "form a radical unity."[19]

Boff insists that the death of Jesus was not necessary for redemption. It
was inevitable, given Jesus' fidelity to the in-breaking of God's dominion, but
not necessary. "Death and the cross," he argues, "are not directly willed or
loved by God"; in fact, "of themselves they represent a cancellation of [God's]
project of life." What God willed, and what Jesus lived, was fidelity to compassion and justice. Jesus' death was a crime inflicted through abusive power,
and yet it can also be viewed as "a *historical* necessity": "Given the conditions
of nonconversion and rejection by which he was surrounded, if Jesus were to
be faithful to his Father, to himself, and to the human beings in whom he had
aroused such radical hopes of the Reign of God, he would have to reckon
with the inevitability of persecution and a violent end." Death and the cross
should not be seen as "implementations of a suprahistorical drama"; they were
not desired by Jesus or by God—quite the opposite, for they "emerge as a
consequence of a committed effort to remove death and the cross from the
shoulders of the crucified."[20]

Hence Jesus' suffering and death do not save. Rather, his whole life is redemptive, especially, says Boff, his "proexistence":

> Properly speaking, our redemption in Jesus Christ is found neither
> in the cross, nor in his blood, nor in his death. Instead, we are re-
> deemed by Jesus' attitude of love, surrender, and forgiveness. But it
> was not only his death that was loving, surrendering, and forgiving.
> It was his whole life. Jesus' entire existence was a "proexistence"—
> an existence of service to others. . . . His death is the crystallization
> and maximal expression of his life as service and love to the end.[21]

Jesus' "being-for-others" is the "christic structure" of his existence. His
"proexistence," his living on the side of life, is redemptive. This way of being
human thenceforth becomes a possibility for all humans, and this, maintains
Boff, "is the basis of our radical dignity and ultimate sacredness."[22]

The emphasis in Boff's interpretation of atonement, therefore, is not on
orthodoxy (right belief) but on orthopraxy (right practice); nor is it on a single past event to which we must give only intellectual or emotional assent in
the present. Rather, "reconciliation, new life, and salvation happen whenever
this way of existing and living, Jesus Christ's way, is imitated and lived by
human beings."[23] With Jesus, a new way is actualized, made objective; but its
continued actualization depends on our taking up the way anew.

On the cross, this way of being-for-others finds dramatic expression, for there it is confronted with the powers of evil at their most brutal. The cross, asserts Boff, is the culmination of the conflict between Jesus' use of power-as-service and the will to power of the religious and political authorities. In this fateful event, the logic of love comes face-to-face with the logic of violence. Throughout his life, Jesus refused to establish a dominion of power, choosing to serve others rather than to dominate them: "Jesus' insistence on the character of power as service, and on the last being first, . . . is an attempt to do away with the ruler-slave relationship, power structured in terms of blind submission, a structure of privileges. Jesus preaches not *hierarchia*—sacred power—but *hierodoulia:* sacred service . . . service in function of the community."[24] As a result of his refusal to give up on an ethic of compassion, Jesus suffers at the hand of an ethic of control.

On the question of the redemptive significance of suffering, Boff maintains that, on the one hand, suffering has no meaning. To suggest, as Moltmann does, that suffering and death are intrinsic to the divine identity, that suffering is an expression of God's essence, is to eternalize suffering. If, Boff argues, Jesus "takes on suffering *for the sake of suffering,* because suffering is God—because God, too, suffers, . . . then there is no way to overcome suffering." If we are to have any hope of putting an end to suffering, then we must understand unjust suffering as an affront to God. According to this reasoning, God *is* affected by suffering—God suffers—but only as a result of love: "God assumes the cross in order to be-in-solidarity with those who suffer—not to sublimate and eternalize the cross," but to be with the suffering in order to put an end to all crucifixions.[25]

Jesus' suffering *is* redemptive, but only because it is the result of the struggle *against* suffering. Suffering should not be thought of as a good, as an end in itself, insists Boff; but when it is "the fruit of courageous freedom," when it is "for the sake of a just cause," *then* it is meaningful, then it "nourishes human beings, making them stronger than all historical cynicism or spirit of resignation." From Jesus' suffering we learn that the way to respond to evil and suffering is to struggle against them, not to endure them passively. Christians are not stoics; on the contrary, "Christians rebel against evil, bending all their efforts to overcome it." Boff can affirm that "God is not a sadist" because "God favors our struggle against suffering."[26]

In Jesus' suffering and death, we see a confirmation of the being-with and being-for that characterized his life. His entire existence was an incarnation of God. His life conveyed the message "God with us" at every step. Boff remarks, "God's incarnation manifests all of his empathy with, and sympathy for, this twisted humanity." God's solidarity with the world is the meaning of Jesus' life. It is also the meaning of his death, says Boff, for despite the fact that the cross is always a crime, a manifestation of humanity's inhumanity, we learn from Jesus' death that "a conversion of meaning" is possible—that when injustice and death are accepted "out of love and solidarity . . . with the crucified of our history," they become not only crimes of violence but also signs of protest *against* violence. Without dehistoricizing the causes that led to Jesus' death, we can see how, "despite these causes, indeed immersed in these causes, God the Son accepted his condemnation as a way of entering into solidarity with the condemned of history." Moreover, this same fierce acceptance of the cost of compassion, when undertaken by Jesus' followers, "will always demonstrate the superabundance of a love that simply cannot be overcome by the mechanisms of hatred that pervade our history."[27]

Love's resiliency against all odds is the meaning of the resurrection. Jesus is resurrected, says Boff, whenever his being-for-others is manifest amid institutions and systems of greed and division, wherever life appears in the midst of death, wherever love confronts violence:

> Wherever people seek the good, justice, humanitarian love, solidarity, communion, and understanding between people, wherever they dedicate themselves to overcoming their own egoism, making this world more human and fraternal, and opening themselves to the normative Transcendent for their lives, there we can say, with all certainty, that the resurrected one is present, because the cause for which he lived, suffered, was tried and executed is being carried forward.[28]

To live as Jesus lived, suggests Boff, involves a mysticism of life based, ultimately, in the mystery of "a life generated where death appears, of love amid hatred."[29]

The final dimension of Boff's understanding of atonement is forgiveness. Once evil has been confronted with fierce compassion and resolute love in solidarity with the victims of evil, reconciliation with the enemy is necessary. Only then will evil truly be confounded, for it will then be transformed into communion. Forgiveness occurs when, despite the violence directed at us, we find a way to offer love to "the very ones who have perpetrated this horrible evil" against us. To "never leave off loving, cost what it may," was Jesus' way on the cross, and we are called to this kind of stubborn "proexistence." Boff insists that such an offer of love does not render the violence legitimate; but now, he asserts, "the crime fails to murder meaning" because it is put in service of reconciliation, of potential transformation.[30] For Boff, to oppose evil with love is the only chance we have to defeat it. The effort itself is our redemption and our reconciliation.

Have Mercy

Jon Sobrino, a native of Spain who has lived and worked in El Salvador for the past twenty years, shares with Boff many claims regarding the work of Christ.[31] However, he also has several distinctive insights that merit our attention. For Sobrino, the conflicts implied in Jesus' life come to a head on the cross. There the evil of power is confronted with the power of love in a definitive and salvific way. There God's presence is mediated through suffering and death, and God's identification with the victims of history is brought into clear focus.

Like other liberationists, Sobrino emphasizes that the saving work of Christ cannot be limited to his death because his death was the consequence of a particular life. Sobrino is critical of traditional construals of atonement that, because of their "thoughtless reiteration" of the mantra that we have been saved through Jesus' cross, create "a more or less magical conception of redemption" that eliminates "the element of scandal in the historical cross of Jesus." In addition, he argues, because of their obsession with Jesus' death, traditional interpretations have led to a "mystique of the cross," or a "mystique of sorrow and suffering," so that Christianity has been portrayed as a religion "obsessed with suffering" and indifferent to either joy or the necessity of transforming the world.[32]

When Jesus' death is understood as the outcome of his life, says Sobrino, this kind of mystification and romanticization becomes impossible. Throughout his life, and also at his death, Jesus preached about and lived in response to the in-breaking of the dominion of God. His "kingdom logic" of love of God and neighbor inevitably provoked conflict with those who eschewed such commitments. In his life and death, according to Sobrino, Jesus brought to the fore the conflict between two antithetical conceptions of power: power-as-domination and power-as-mercy. His existence can therefore be understood as a questioning search "for the true essence of power."[33]

Throughout Jesus' life, claims Sobrino, the power of mercy stood in conflict with the power of control. Jesus' condemnations of abusive power produced "a clear-cut division between those who [held] power (the oppressors) and those who [suffered] from its use (the oppressed)," and his constant choice to identify with and care for the oppressed demarcated the way of salvation.[34] Again and again, Jesus challenged the truth and power of religious and political idols, whose "ultimate evil lies in the fact that they demand victims in order to exist."[35] In the final analysis, says Sobrino, his life and death became for the world "a choice between two deities: either a God wielding oppressive power or a God offering and effecting liberation," with Jesus "appearing as a witness on one side and those in power as witnesses on the other side."[36]

By refusing to succumb to the temptation to "fight fire with fire," to use oppressive power to win the fight, Jesus chose instead to carve out a different path—the way of nonviolent resistance to evil. In his death, Jesus remained faithful to the way of mercy, bearing witness to God "in a situation where people really wanted a very different type of God." Jesus' life implies that the only thing that can oppose abusive power is "the power of love, of service, of truth."[37] Like Boff, Sobrino claims that the power of service, of being-for-others, liberates us from evil and reconciles us with God and one another. In the parable of the good Samaritan, suggests Sobrino, the principle of mercy is identified by Jesus as *the* criterion of human existence. According to the parable, "the ideal, the total human being, is represented as the one who has seen someone else lying wounded in the ditch along the road, has re-acted, and has helped the victim in every possible way."[38] For Sobrino, merciful living saves us from sin and evil and connects us with God. Rather than an analogy of pain or suffering, Sobrino's theology implies an analogy of mercy. Our salvation and the salvation of the world depend upon our concrete embodiment of the principle of mercy.

Atonement takes place, according to Sobrino's theology, when we "[take] on the sin of the world as Jesus did"—struggling against idols of power and domination, "not just standing idly by looking at it from the outside." So we must fight against evil by "denouncing it, giving voice to the victims' cry," unmasking the brutalities of abusive power. And "we must not only hate the sin but eradicate it." Active confrontation and liberation are required. The shape of this struggle, its criterion, is the principle of mercy by which we react to suffering by shouldering it ourselves in acts of solidarity and compassion. Our responsibility, admonishes Sobrino, is to reproduce in our lives the structure of Jesus' life—"a structure of *incarnation*, of becoming real flesh, real history" in concrete efforts to serve the cause of mercy and proclaim the good news of God's dominion.[39]

Struggle at the Crossroad

According to Mexican American theologian Virgilio Elizondo, Jesus' crucifixion can be understood as the culminating act of his struggle against the powers of evil. For Elizondo, Jesus' struggle is characterized especially by his confrontation of unjust authorities and systems; his conviction that only absolute dependence upon the one God can break our enslavement to idols and open us to authentic, just relationships; and his courage to "speak truth to power" at all costs. These commitments of the historical Jesus, argues Elizondo, have been ignored by most of Christian theology, which has become a tool of conquest and domination rather than a harbinger of the good news of liberation. To take seriously the life of Jesus requires the liberation of theology from its enslavement to idols of power and influence, and the affirmation of what Elizondo and other Hispanic theologians term a "*mestizo* Christianity."

Mestizo, meaning "mixed" or "hybrid," designates the reality of all Latin American peoples, for they are the offspring of two distinctive groups—the indigenous peoples of the Indies and the European conquerors. For Hispanic Americans, this hybrid identity has marked them as "other," the ones who are neither Latin nor American, the ones who fit nowhere, the ones who are eschewed as either "illegal aliens" or "ethnic traitors." As Elizondo says, rejected by both parents, "the *mestizo* is someone who is *not.*"[40] From this standpoint of "nowhere," the life and death of Jesus, as well as notions of their saving significance, take on a distinctive meaning.

A *mestizo* Christianity stands courageously with Jesus at the crossroad of good and evil, of love and hate, of nonviolence and violence, struggling to defeat the latter with the former. Its dialectical "nowhere-ness" becomes a critical principle, a self-overcoming liminality with which to call into question the stasis of the center, the idols of the powerful and the powerless alike. Its hybrid character becomes a constant challenge to totalizing identities and self-securing ideologies.

Like that of many liberation theologians, Elizondo's understanding of the significance of Jesus' life and death has been profoundly shaped by popular piety. In Latin America, Africa, and Asia, the crucifixion of the poor man from Galilee stands at the center of religious identity. While for First World Christians Easter, the feast of the resurrection, is the highest of holy days and the focal point of ecclesial celebrations, in the Third World Good Friday and the *payson,* or way of the cross, are most influential. It is the suffering Jesus, the One who was arrested in the night, beaten, and humiliated by the powerful, with whom the masses can identify. We have seen that liberation theologians express wariness toward this crucifixion piety—aware of its potential for reinforcing a religion of perpetual powerlessness—and yet they are increasingly realizing that in many cases, its function has been to unify, sensitize, and empower the poor and the marginalized.[41] As Elizondo points out, popular piety is not always a dreary or pitiful affair. Its focus on Jesus' passion reveals God to be One who knows and shares their troubles and pain—One whose presence enables dignity and survival. More than that, "the cross reveals the face of injustice." The story of Jesus' passion brings into view his struggle against dehumanization and oppressive power and authority, thus helping "the people see that Jesus' march to the cross was *active.*"[42] In the religious rituals and celebrations of the people is a nascent doctrine of atonement based on the symbols of suffering, death, and struggle.

It is in the life of Jesus, says Elizondo, that the specific character of this crossroad struggle, which culminates on the cross, takes shape. And for *mestizo* Christians, Jesus' Galilean roots are particularly powerful symbols of his mission and fate. Elizondo explains that Galilee was a place of "natural mestizaje"—"a crossroads of cultures and people," a place where those from "all centers of belonging" interacted peacefully. However, precisely because of its hybrid nature, Galilee was deemed an unacceptable, "impure" place by the Jewish leaders of Jerusalem, the center of power, purity, and proper religiosity. For God to become incarnate in a Galilean, notes Elizondo, was scandalous indeed: "That God chose to become a Galilean underscores the great paradox of the incarnation, in which God becomes the despised and lowly of the world." From the incarnation we learn that "what the world rejects, God chooses as his very own."[43]

Throughout his life, suggests Elizondo, Jesus' words and actions reflected his Galilean roots, his *mestizo* identity. He invited all, especially the poor and outcast, to participate in the dominion of God. In defiance of the purity codes of the Judaism of his day, he transgressed the standard categories of clean/unclean and righteous/sinner and declared that "shared intimacy with God is the basis for a new vision of all persons and therefore of new social structures."[44] In contradiction to popular expectations that the Messiah would come as a victorious warrior or king to restore the religio-political kingdom of Israel, Jesus announced a dominion based on love, forgiveness, and mutual service. From his position at the margins of acceptability, at the outskirts of power, Jesus was keenly aware of the need to transform the status quo, to challenge its dehumanizing logic and offer alternative ways of being and relating. Through Jesus, God experiences the rejection of the world's nonpersons. God shares their suffering, insists Elizondo, but God also affirms their struggle against such suffering.

In Jesus' way of being, says Elizondo, is revealed "a new anthropology: dignity, confidence, security, docility, and self-respect based on freely chosen dependence on the one absolute God." Because of his unwavering consciousness of God's love and his total commitment to God's dominion, Jesus is free "from all other humanly made absolutes or dependencies"—free to love without limit, to relate to whomever he pleases. The only legitimate authority is God's justice and mercy. By claiming this authority as his own, Jesus "exhibits the authority of absolute freedom." In doing so, he relativizes "not only the Sabbath but the entire law" on the premise that "every institutionalized human practice is meant to serve human needs," so those that hinder humanization and community are without authority. With words and actions, Jesus proclaims that the basis for belonging is no longer status or cultic observance, but acceptance of the common parenthood of God. Within the family of God, all are related as equals—equally beloved by God. And it is, says Elizondo, "the new relationship through a third person—God-*Abba*—that allows us to break through the exploiter-exploited dialectic and form a new partnership." Jesus' life announces "a restructuring from a bipolar to a tripolar model of relationship" so that the dialectic of domination that characterizes a culture of violence is decentered and transformed into mutuality.[45]

Tragically, "such a change is a threat to all those who have built their own personal security and prestige on the basis of an 'I versus you' or 'we versus they' polarization." The final result is the cross. According to Elizondo, the only way to understand how the suffering and death of Jesus are salvific is to view them as continuous with the commitments of Jesus' life—commitments that meet their ultimate challenge in "the Galilean crisis" in which Galilee and Jerusalem come head-to-head. Elizondo suggests that the Jerusalem authorities endorsed a theology that had become misguided by the idea that God could actually be "manipulated or coerced by rituals and observances." Their religion, maintains Elizondo, had become an idol, and the Jerusalem Temple was its primary symbol. Through the reification and commodification of ritual and doctrine, the leaders of official Judaism had built a religion for the learned and privileged on the backs of the poor and marginalized.[46]

Within this context, Jesus' journey to Jerusalem and his denunciation of the corruption of the Temple call into question the deification of religion, the collusion of the Jewish leaders with the Roman authorities in maintaining an unjust, but profitable, status quo, the idolatry of a "structural absolutism that sacralizes divisions." In the name of the one living God, he uncovers and denounces all idols, including systems and traditions that function as gods. "Jesus *had* to go to Jerusalem," insists Elizondo, because "it was the center of the powers that excluded and oppressed the masses." If he was to "attack oppression at its very roots," then the Jewish Galilean, the outsider, the *mestizo*, had to travel to the heart of the violence to expose its lie.[47]

Like other liberation theologians, Elizondo affirms that the cross was not necessary for salvation but was nevertheless inevitable: "Jesus knows that when he confronts the power structures he will be destroyed by them." And yet, "he also knows that it is the only way to triumph definitively over evil." Jesus' suffering and death are moments of truth—they reveal for all to see the brutality and moral bankruptcy of abusive power. By confronting violence with "dynamic nonviolence," insists Elizondo, Jesus embodies "the only power that can change not only external structures but human hearts as well." Even though Jesus died in apparent defeat, the fact that he never gave up on the possibility of love and forgiveness means that "he triumphed over violence without giving in to violent ways," thus opening up the possibility of a new humanity based on neither violence nor passivity but on active nonviolence. In his "refusal to resign himself to evil," to "sell out" to violence, Jesus wins a moral victory "through the power of truth" because with his death, "the final mask has been removed, and reality is seen for what it really is."[48]

Liberation from the power of evil and reconciliation with God take

place, says Elizondo, whenever violence is resisted with the power of truth
and love, whenever enslavement to idols is rejected in favor of commitment
to the one living God, whenever the absolutes of this world are relativized
through relationship with the only Absolute. For those "on the outskirts of
the established order," the mission is "to go to the centers of power and un-
veil the root causes of the evil that has become engrained in the structures
that shape socio-national life and hide the face of the true God" of love and
justice. In such resistance, in speaking truth to power, in struggling for humanization, "the true liberation of humanity has begun."[49]

Solidarity, Service, Salvation

There can be little doubt that the theology of colonial and neocolonial
Christianity has reinforced systems and practices of injustice. In particular, its
interpretation of atonement has reinforced fatalism and passivity among the
masses by making a virtue out of suffering, and it has sacralized violence
through carefully controlled metaphors of Christ the Conqueror and Victim.
In opposition to the Christ of Conquest with its two faces of power and powerlessness, however, has emerged a liberative theology, a theology undertaken
by and for the oppressed themselves, a theology that challenges all of
Christianity to reject idols of power, privilege, and profit in order to affirm the
one living God of justice and mercy. At the heart of liberation theologies is
the doctrine of atonement—the conviction that in the life and death of Jesus
the Christ, God has revealed God's definitive response to evil, thus liberating
humanity from enslavement to it and freeing us for right relationship with
God and world.

Liberation construals of atonement do not claim that evil has been abolished; naïveté is clearly not their way. They *do* claim that God has revealed
the one and only way to confront evil without buying into it. Boff, Sobrino,
and Elizondo are among the increasing number of liberation theologians who
claim that liberation and reconciliation occur through resistance to evil and
compassion for the suffering. In Jesus' life and death, this way of struggle and
solidarity is made a reality. In *this* life and *this* death, God is made known—
clearly, definitively. And because of this life and this death, the way of liberation and reconciliation has become a possibility for all.

Boff, Sobrino, and Elizondo agree that redemption is a praxis, a historical process, made viable and possible by Jesus but as yet incomplete. The
process is salvific because it is based on service and solidarity. This praxis of
"being-with" can save us from individual egoism and inordinate self-exaltation by turning us toward the other in mercy. In addition, it opens our eyes
to our complicity in their dehumanization and suffering. Finally, it summons
us toward repentance and conversion. This grace-filled power of life is also

the power of truth that can save us from idols of nationalism, racism, sexism, and consumerism by grounding us in the one true God of love and life who empowers us to speak truth to power. Only such a dynamic "proexistence" can save us from the power of fate by opening up possibilities for dignity and service in even the most hopeless situations.

This theology of liberation does not claim that evil has been defeated—only that the way of its defeat has been made clear. This way is the way of Jesus, in life and death. It is not an easy way; indeed, it is perhaps the most arduous way of all. But it is the only way, and it is possible. Jesus made it possible, and its pilgrims have been many, including Bartolomé de Las Casas, Archbishop Oscar Romero, Ignacio Ellacuria, Julia Elba, Dianna Ortiz, and the millions of other "crucified peoples" who have suffered in the struggle to abolish all crosses. In their resistance to evil and compassion for the suffering, they are reconciled with God and with the world. In them, Jesus is resurrected—"converted from one person into another."[50]

6

Mending and Discarding

The suffering and death of Jesus cannot be wished away or ignored but must be reckoned with theologically. However profound the problems with traditional interpretations of atonement may be, the refusal to attribute any redemptive significance to Jesus' passion represents a rejection of the clear convictions and experiences of the earliest Christians and of subsequent generations of Christian people for whom the cross reveals something indispensable about God and world. To deny such history while trumpeting the validity of a christology based solely on the life of Jesus reflects a convenient but untenable ahistoricism. We cannot, in one breath, insist on the sole theological centrality of Jesus' life and then, in another, ignore the lives of those who have found strength and solace in his death. We must find some kind of middle path.

Clearly, theologies of the cross—theologies whose central datum is the suffering and death of Jesus—have yielded ambiguous harvests, in some cases perpetuating injustice and domination, while in others empowering survival, resistance, and transformation. And yet, as convenient as it sounds, purging Christianity of the doctrine of atonement will not purge it of problems. It is increasingly clear to me that the insistence on such an easy "fix" to the problem of Christianity's complicity in attitudes and structures of injustice reflects a grave underestimation of both the problems and the possibilities of this religious tradition. The logic that uncritically reduces Christianity to patriarchy, or atonement to necrophilia, is a logic that eschews complexity, fragility, and conflict. It is a logic that is, in the final analysis, totalizing and otherworldly, desperately searching for certainty, innocence, and absolutes in a world far too nuanced to yield such easy unicity.

If we are to deal with Christianity as it really is, we must admit that it is an incredibly complicated, nuanced, and often contradictory phenomenon. Wishing that it were unequivocably liberating for all people and beings of all times simply does not make it so. Alternatively, rejecting it as evil incarnate is equally myopic. Perhaps the most difficult, but pragmatic, position to take is one that sees and attempts to respond to both the dysfunction and the delight that this religious tradition has spawned. From this perspective, uncritical acceptance *and* hypercritical rejection appear to suffer from a similar refusal to see the whole picture, to accept the complexity and ambiguity that characterize this two-thousand-year tradition.

I have become convinced that a primary source of misery and oppression in our world today is the inability or unwillingness of people, both privileged and marginalized, to accept complexity and ambiguity. We want so desperately to know how to live and whom to love that we are willing to force ourselves and those around us into false categories and moralities. We want so fervently to be right, to be certain, to be safe, that we assume that those who differ from us are wrong or dangerous or abnormal. Of course, those of us with relative social, political, economic, and theological power have been able to enforce our categories and moralities on others, and so we bear the weight of responsibility for the systems of scapegoating and sacrifice we have erected.

In such a world of desperate, narrow ideology and moralism, our theologies need at all costs to avoid a speculative Manichaeanism that oversimplifies reality, that divides and reduces reality and morality into neat binary opposites. What we *do* need are strategies for understanding the almost overwhelming complexity of our world and for negotiating ways to live in it that increase rather than decrease the possibility for ourselves and others to go on living in it. We need theologies that embrace and articulate the sacred and empowering power of love and life without denying the multiple and often strange ways in which such love and life are manifest and without sinking into a nebulous, feel-good religiosity that shrinks from the imperative to struggle against the attitudes, institutions, and policies that deny or diminish love and life. The courageous acceptance of complexity and ambiguity, then, does not mitigate the need to identify and resist human evil; it does, however, warn us against oversimplifying and reifying our conceptions of that evil.

Precisely this kind of sophisticated, pragmatic, prophetic "biophilia," or love of life, is at the heart of feminist theology as I understand it. Such a position challenges us to hold in play two seemingly antithetical stances. On the one hand, we need to affirm an openness to the nitty-gritty, complicated, conflictive character of reality and morality as we know them, which means a refusal to buy into "us versus them" mentalities and oversimplified reactions to groups and ideas that are different or bothersome. On the other hand, and

at the same time, we must be willing to struggle against life-diminishing realities at every turn. This latter imperative of prophetic justice-seeking is born
out of the experience, well known to those who are on the "underside" of history in some sense, that in this complex and conflictive world, despite our
best biophilic efforts, a necrophilic pedagogy seems to prevail. This pedagogy
masquerades as "free-market individualism," "family values," and "the American way." It deceives us with a facade of freedom and fairness that hides a
social Darwinism whose shortsighted cannibalism requires fresh victims at
every turn.

The problem is that contemporary Western culture has as one of its un-
seen foundations a socially constructed and maintained antireality that depends upon an "unworld" of subjugation and suffering: a steady supply of
cheap labor and raw materials (a permanent underclass, a ravaged earth, a
Third World), an unending fount of desire for consumable goods (among
which certain types of female bodies are the most highly coveted), a condon-
ing spirituality (for example, a Conquering Christ or Divine Victim). These
realities go unnoticed by the privileged and are unconsciously denied by the
underprivileged because taken seriously, they could eclipse all hope of transformation. Yet they are part of the framework within which both groups exist.

Is it any wonder that given such ignoble undercurrents, such systemic
dis-ease, such moral complexity, most of us opt for a simplified, if inaccurate,
picture of our world? Yet the danger of truly embracing the world's complexity is that we may lose any ground from which to denounce human rapacity
and callousness. For those caught in the vipers' den—for those who are the
victims of systems of inhumanity—complexity and ambiguity vanish in the
fight for survival. There is nothing ambiguous about poverty or rape when
you are on the receiving end. Talk of complexity and nuance can become one
more way to rationalize the violence, to stymie resistance to it. Feminists
know too well how dicta of politeness and social convention have been used
to silence protests of injustice; and we know how quickly charges of hysteria
or overreaction are brought against those who dare to speak in an "unfemi-
nine" voice. We know, too, the burden of debt we owe to prophets whose acts
of madness push the boundaries of society's (anti-)reason to their breaking
point and create a space for the rest of us to breathe.

In that space we search for fresh air—for new words and images with
which to express ancient insights, for old words and images with which to express novel experiences and newfound wisdoms. When it comes to the doctrine of atonement, we approach it with great caution, if at all, because its victims' cries ring in our ears or hoarsen our throats, and we refuse to shut them
up lest we forget their truth, which is ours as well. Amidst the din of betrayal,
hurt, and rage, we begin to work, piecing together shards of tradition—

mending and discarding, stitching and cutting, with no particular pattern in mind except that it must protect us from the elements and allow us plenty of room to stretch and move, to stomp and dance and climb trees, or just curl up in a ball and feel small. I am reminded here of Celie's pants in Alice Walker's *The Color Purple*—works of art born of a hurt so deep that it cuts the universe in half, emasculating it of all pretensions of innocence, simplicity, and easy optimism; slicing through its claims of equanimity to expose the ugly sores of human cruelty and unlove. But with the same needle, tacking on patches of love letters, shreds of song, glimpses of purple. Painstaking, tedious work it is to mend what has been ripped apart by such force. What emerges may not be pretty by most people's standards, but these pants are colorful and comfortable—one size fits all, but no two are alike—and for those who wear them, the world is a new creation.

Atonement and Eros

Many feminist theologians who have attempted to reconfigure the doctrine of atonement in recent years have embraced what might be called a theology of eros. If atonement is the process by which God and world are reconciled to each other, by which a broken relationship is mended or restored, then sin is defined as that which destroys relationship, while redemption is the experience of renewed connection or intimacy. Eros, or embodied love characterized by mutuality, is understood to be the criterion of relationship; that is, it is not merely *any* relationship that is reconciling, redemptive, healing, but only those based on a gentle reciprocity between partners, a mutual respect and uplift, a passion for the other in the midst of the recognition of the other's irreducible difference. Atonement, or reconciliation, takes place in and through "right relationship," through the establishment of relations of justice, empathy, and respect.

The criterion of right relationship has dramatic consequences for prevailing notions of atonement. It means a rejection of models and claims that require or result in the creation of victims. However, it also opens up fresh possibilities for rethinking the work of Christ. One of the most influential attempts to apply a relational hermeneutic to the redemptive activity of God in Jesus the Christ is found in the theology of Rita Nakashima Brock, whose critiques of traditional views we have already encountered.

As we have seen, Brock rejects traditional interpretations of atonement because they tend to make self-sacrifice the highest form of love; their definition of sin as pride or willfulness, she charges, undermines the agency of women and children and thus compounds their victimization. Brock also rejects notions of redemption that center on the powerlessness of humans and our absolute dependence on an external power to save us from sin and evil.

She argues that missing from this theology based on God's unilateral power and humanity's impotence are interdependence and mutuality. Mainstream Christian theology has rooted itself in a fundamentally destructive understanding of power, says Brock. According to traditional conceptions of atonement, power is understood as a commodity that can be possessed only at the expense of another; thus, humanity's quest for it is an affront to God, and only one who abdicates all power through voluntary submission to the authority of the omnipotent God can be reconciled. God's power requires our powerlessness. Brock argues that it is possible to move beyond this infantalizing logic by rejecting unilateral or positional power in favor of relational or erotic power: "We must move away from seeing power as a commodity possessed by a self toward seeing it as the bonds which create and sustain, and are created and sustained by relational selves."[1]

Erotic power, asserts Brock, is "the fundamental power of life." It is "born into us," giving each of us a desire for connection with others, for intimacy and caring.[2] Echoing Audre Lorde, Brock suggests that the erotic is the power of relationship; it is love in the concrete, a passion for connectedness, which is the foundation of life itself.[3] Erotic power, then, is not power at the expense of love, or love based on submission or obedience; rather, it is "both love and power"—defining and limiting each other. Far from requiring the diminution of self or other, erotic power "heals, makes whole, empowers, and liberates" by engendering both self-love and love of other. Human existence is essentially relational. This fact, says Brock, is both our strength and our fragility since our need for relationship means that we are vulnerable to those around us. Relational existence is "the heart of our being, our life source, our original grace," but it is also an entree for pain, hurt, and violence.[4]

Sin, according to Brock, is the denial of our "primal interrelatedness," and it is manifest in relationships of inequality and abuse. Suffering caused by such human evil, observes Brock, is a sign of the "brokenheartedness" of the world, the fracture of its original blessedness. What is needed to restore right relationship, to mend the world, is not the sacrifice of one but the empowerment of all. What we need, says Brock, is not "feeling by analogy," not "redemption through the suffering of another," but the reclamation of "our own fragile original grace"; the realization that we are all part of one another and are therefore responsible for the well-being of one another; the recollection that erotic power is the heart of the universe, that "the whole of life [is] sacred."[5]

Jesus plays an important role in our reconciliation with "the divine Eros"—not as spiritual conqueror or self-effacing innocent, but as the momentary locus of erotic power. Through healings and exorcisms, Brock suggests, Jesus made a decisive break with an oppressive social context—touching the unclean, loving damaged selves, learning from outcasts, summoning all to community based on self-worth, mutuality, and compassion. In Jesus' life we encounter "the revelation of a new understanding of power"—power-as-relation, erotic power. This power, not Jesus' possession of it, is redemptive. Brock insists that Jesus' death was not necessary or salvific. It was a tragedy. It bespeaks not triumph or even erotic power, but "the power of patriarchy to crush life." It reveals the carnage of unilateral power. The cross, then, is the site not of reconciliation but of violence; it reveals the face of human evil in all its ugliness and "power." If Jesus' suffering and death teach us anything, it is an awareness of our brokenness out of which we maim and murder.[6]

For Brock, the atoning import of Jesus' death lies not with Jesus but with the community's response to his death: "By not letting go of their relationships to each other, the members of Christa/Community do not let Jesus' death mean the end of their community." Despite the tragedy of the crucifixion, erotic power is not extinguished. We are reconciled to God, to the "Heart of the Universe," to "the divine Eros," not by Jesus' suffering and death but by our affirmation of erotic power, our courage to maintain connection with God and one another in the face of the death-dealing dynamics of unilateral power.[7]

Brock's christology shifts the focus from the individual of Jesus to the community of which he was a part. Because the redeeming, reconciling power that saves us from sin and evil is *relational* power, it cannot be located in only one person or being: "What is truly christological, that is, truly revealing of divine incarnation and salvific power in human life, must reside in connectedness and not in single individuals."[8] It is not, then, Jesus' suffering and death that reconcile us to God, nor even is it *his* life; rather, it is the incarnation of erotic power in the historical praxis of those who, in the face of the overwhelming violence of unilateral power—a violence that crucified Jesus and continues to accumulate victims on a daily basis—refuse to relinquish their relationships with one another and thus stand as testimonies of connection.

Brock's christology correlates well with Leonardo Boff's. Both theologians emphasize the importance of enhancing human agency and responsibility for evil and hence reject construals of atonement that assume the utter helplessness of human beings and our consequent dependence upon an external power for salvation. In addition, both Boff and Brock insist that Jesus' death was not necessary for redemption but was the cost of his commitment to "being-for-others" or "erotic power," which are the real salvific locii. Finally, both theologians argue that reconciliation with God and others was not a one-time event accomplished by one for all but is an ongoing process that must be taken up anew by each person and community.

Brock departs from Boff and other liberation theologians, however, when she decenters Jesus to such an extent that he becomes just one among many. As we have seen, Brock wants to remove Jesus from the center of Christianity because "the individualizing of Christ misplaces the locus of incarnation and redemption." She claims that while Jesus participates in the erotic, redemptive power of community in a central way, "he neither brings erotic power into being nor controls it."[9] For Brock, Jesus may be the most noticeable embodiment of erotic power, but that is mere coincidence. The difference between Brock and Boff here is that the latter wants to maintain Jesus' centrality by claiming that he brought into being something new, that his particular embodiment of "proexistence" was a novel incarnation of God's saving grace. Jesus does not "do for" the rest of us—he is not, in other words, the end point of redemption—but he *is* its starting point. With Schleiermacher, Teilhard, and process theologians, Boff suggests that Jesus creates a new possibility, a new option for the world; thus, his existence is not sufficient for our salvation, but it *is* necessary. Brock, on the other hand, proposes that erotic power is the incarnation of God, but she finds no necessary correlation between Jesus of Nazareth and that incarnation. In Brock's theology, Jesus functions as a convenient and well-known figure who happens to fit into her soteriological model, but he is, in the final analysis, dispensable. She detaches the *idea* of incarnation from the one who Christian tradition claims created the very *genre* of incarnation. This move raises the question of whether Brock's theology does not cut itself loose from a basic historical mooring. At the same time, it brings to the fore the fact that all theologies inevitably read back onto the historical Jesus their own christological assumptions and experiences. Thus, what may appear to be an anchor in history is actually just one more buoy constructed to keep a particular set of interests afloat.

Theologies of Risk and Accountability

For feminists like Brock, the claim of the ultimate importance of right relationship is rooted in the theological conviction that ultimate reality, God, is itself characterized by eros, by just love. The assumption is that God both exists and loves. From this perspective, the challenge is to live *with* reality, which requires struggle against idols of domination and violence that destroy mutuality and pervert right relationship. For others, however, reality is decidedly more opaque, and the affirmation of a God of love and justice is a calculated risk, based less on past and present validation than on future possibility, on the conviction that eros *ought* to be the heart of reality, that only such a world would be worth living in, and thus that living *as if it were so* is the only moral choice. These two approaches—one whose ethics is rooted in theology, and one whose theology is rooted in ethics—mark the broad boundaries of feminist theology, representing not opposing camps but differentiated allies who have more in common than not.

Perhaps the vitality of the second position, of an antitheology that calls into question not the meaning or necessity of theology but its pretensions of sure and pure foundations or referents, can help explain why feminists are more likely to reject atonement outright than are liberation theologians. For whatever reason, the latter tend to assume or to confirm *that* God exists and is on their side; they can find clear biblical support for a God who is particularly concerned for the poor, and they have warrants for charging that construals of atonement that compound the misery of the poor must be perversions of ultimate reality. To reject atonement outright, as some feminists do, could imply a rejection of morality itself, an abdication of a moral high ground from which important struggles for justice and freedom can be fought. Feminists, on the other hand, find far less support within biblical and theological tradition for their claims that sexism is "evil," that violence against women is "wrong." Indeed, it is difficult to deny that, as Renita Weems, Christine Gudorf, and others have made abundantly clear, "scripture itself accepts some forms of victimization, is blind to other forms, and is to some degree ambiguous about many forms."[10] Christian feminists have often had to look further than tradition to find warrants for our claims. In this process, we have come to realize that in a postmodern world in which the constructed, conflictive character of all truths and warrants has come to the fore, the very penchant for grounding claims in some self-evident or uncontestable "reality" may be a flight from the difficult task of negotiating contradictory discourses on the basis of our best estimations of good and evil, right and wrong.

From this perspective, interpretations of atonement based on relational power or the power of love, such as those endorsed by Brock and many other feminist theologians, can seem naive or overzealous in their assumptions insofar as they are based on convictions of a transhistorical, or metaphysical, or absolute being or power. Too often, feminist theologians take for granted that our theological language does indeed have a referent that is somehow "more than" a human construction. Consequently, we ignore the fact that such an assumption *is* contestable, that it is an assumption, and therefore ought to be recognized and thematized as a wager, a hypothesis, a "leap of faith." Insofar as theologies of eros uncritically posit a transcendent Eros, they inadvertently undermine the often messy work of negotiating values and truths in a non-ideal world, a world in which simple distinctions between good and evil are few and far between, and expectations of clear-cut "triumph" over evil create false hopes and fallen spirits. The result is that theological assumptions of clear and knowable absolutes actually subvert and hinder the proposed praxis of feminist theologies.

The challenge, as I see it, is to bring together the critique of power-as-control, which theologies of eros have articulated so persuasively, with a moral vision that, while recognizing its own constructed and hence limited character, dares to claim with as much authority as it can muster a vision of a world in which relationships and institutions are motivated by compassion and justice rather than pure self-interest. Such a vision would need to be materialized in concrete practices of struggle against violence and domination as they occur in our lives, communities, and institutions, as well as in others'. Categories of good and evil need not be understood to refer to transcendent absolutes to be persuasive. Without such a grounding, the way is cleared for self-critique, for asking questions about our complicity in evil, without jeopardizing our commitment to the good. In addition, the tendency to demonize other groups is mitigated when the presumption of a dualistic morality is rejected. Again, the contingency of our moral claims does not require a passive relativism. A middle ground *does* exist and needs to be claimed.

If the emergence of feminist and liberation theologies teaches us anything, it is that reality is not univalent. Feminist and liberation theologians need to recognize theology as "an aggregate of contesting, rival, often contradictory discourses,"[11] and rather than retreating to an imagined sure foundation, insisting that *we* are king or queen of the theological mountain because God is on our side, we need to focus our energies on creating a communal praxis based on the values we espouse as salvific. If that praxis does indeed function to save its practitioners from self- and other-destruction, then we have good reason to hope that others will find it persuasive enough to affirm. In regard to our discussion of atonement, claims that God has acted to reconcile the world to God's Self in Jesus' life and death—that we are saved from our own worst selves through a radical "proexistence" made possible by Jesus—are only as "true" as their effects. Just as the "lived-out consequences" of a theology are sufficient to discredit it, only they can validate it.

This radical historicism challenges us as theologians and people to situate ourselves and our ideas in *this* world, to risk judging our estimations of orthodoxy on the basis of the orthopraxy they spawn, to leap with our faith into the thick of the "real" world and put our hunches and convictions to the test. This does not mean, however, that only the strong survive. This is not a bottom-line, market-driven position that demands a display of quantitative success to justify its existence. I want to depart from a purely functional or pragmatist approach while maintaining its best insight—that "truth" is an ongoing communal project that can never be purely speculative but must become concrete, material. Our theologies do not have to "succeed," but they do need to have a clear praxic component, and they must be willing to put their claims on the line in a material way and to amend those claims if and when their embodiment contradicts their rhetoric.

Shifting Sands

Increasingly, contemporary theologians are affirming a "tragic" view of reality in an attempt to find an alternative to the dogmatism and moral positivism of absolute foundations, on the one hand, and the quicksand of nihilistic relativism, on the other. This turn to the tragic is particularly relevant to discussions of the Christian doctrine of atonement because its foundation is the recognition and thematization of evil. While many might argue that the Christian claim that salvation has been effected through the life and death of Jesus is an essentially nontragic, or comic, claim, I suggest that it is possible to affirm the liberative work of Christ within a framework that takes with ultimate seriousness the horror and intractability of human evil.

A tragic view begins with the sober recognition of tragedy—of undeserved, unresolvable human evil—and never lets that reality out of sight. It admits that the searing presence of evil calls all attempts to explain or redeem evil into question because evil remains and continues to claim victims despite our best theories and explanations. Wendy Farley suggests, "The cruelty of human suffering defies attempts to incorporate it into any order of justice. Instead of the just world we might envision, we seem to live in a tragic one." A tragic vision recognizes that the locus of suffering is existence itself; that the possibility of suffering is located within the fragility of human freedom; that finitude itself includes conflict and vulnerability, so that suffering is "both possible and inevitable." The problem of human evil, then, must be addressed within the broad situation of fragility.[12]

A tragic view recognizes the impossibility of "pure" knowledge and of absolute foundations for knowledge or for moral decision making and action. It allows the testimony of human evil to shatter the veneer of certainty and comfort offered by dominant construals of morality. We can no longer assume that our taken-for-granted worldview or morality is universal or transcendently grounded or validated. Indeed, the taken-for-granted character of our "truths" conceals their contingency and, too often, their oppressive consequences.

To think and live within a tragic context means that all our moral language and actions must be grounded in our best estimations of good and evil, justice and injustice, rather than in some unmediated, unquestionable, ahistorical truth. Inevitably, these estimations will change as new experiences and voices impact our moral community and negotiations. In our time, the voices of the marginalized and forgotten have revealed with particular clarity the falsity of dominant moralities. Their experiences and truths stand as a permanent caveat to the presumed universality and legitimacy of moral discourse, exposing the exclusionary, self-serving logic of the dominant regime of truth.

Theology in a tragic key grounds its truth claims not in exclusively or even primarily transcendent ideals but in concrete practices that embody a community's best estimations of what will enhance the survival and flourishing of the world. It recognizes that even acts of compassion and justice are subject to "the moral paradox that beings who want goodness cannot remain uncontaminated by evil," that there is no moral paradise in which to seek refuge as we go about the daily work of making the world go on.[13]

According to Kathleen Sands, Christian theology has tended to deny the tragic character of human reality by embracing simplistic attitudes toward evil. On the one hand, it has implied that evil is simply a lack of goodness or knowledge, thus encouraging neutrality toward it. On the other hand, Christian tradition has hyperbolized and reified evil such that struggle against it appears impossible or useless. Neither approach to evil can motivate real change because each eschews the moral ambiguity within which evil both exists and can be resisted. Both, says Sands, "describe complementary amnesic strategies. . . . Each, in its different circumstances, covers the absence and silences the grief that is tragedy." Sands rejects both moral traditions in favor of a tragic stance or view, which she defines as "the conflicted context where we must create what right and reason we can" rather than assuming transcendent norms as our foundation, or demonizing others in order to create moral clarity. Once the tragic character of reality is recognized, "once society is apprehended as a network of diverse and often conflicting powers," then it becomes possible to reject moral neutrality and to avoid the simplistic reduction of reality into pure good and pure evil; then it becomes possible to devise and mobilize strategies of resistance to the evil we communally identify, while remaining aware that truth and goodness are never in this world separable from "the most profound questions about violence, conflict, and loss."[14] The sooner we recognize this, the sooner we can navigate the moral ambiguity of the world in which live, making the best choices we can in less than ideal situations, recognizing that every choice includes some loss and conflict, that not one of our decisions or actions is innocent.

From within a tragic framework, then, the reality of evil cannot be explained or justified by neat theories or doctrines. The only way to respond to its searing presence is to resolve to live with it, treating its wound with compassion, and resolving to make the world go on; but "in a world of suffering and radical conflict," says Sands, "making the world go on is not an innocent faith but a *practice* of compassion" that can open up spaces of healing.[15] A tragic perspective embraces a world without the comfort of absolutes. Such a world is undeniably painful; its uncertainty can unnerve, and its brutality can

terrify; but it is also a world that is permanently open to critique and transformation; it is a world of both constant loss and infinite possibility.

Sandbars of Grace

Sands's embrace of the tragic leads her to reject theology and God altogether.
However, even while she dismisses all metaphysics as totalizing delusion, she
seems unaware of the ways in which her extreme reaction to the excesses of
theism does little more than mirror those excesses by positing yet another absolute—the absolute of secular humanism, the sure foundation of an ethical
atheism. Parting ways with Sands, other thinkers, myself included, find it intellectually and ethically possible to do theology without denying the tragic.
The conviction here is that living with our eyes wide open to the tragic dimension of existence does not have to blind us to the equally tangible presence of transformation and healing. Tragedy does not negate the possibility
of redemption but demarcates the field within which it can occur. My experience as one who struggles to weigh the transformative, liberative wisdoms
of the Christian religion against the undeniable brutality of much of its theology and history of effects motivates me to affirm that the "good news" of
Christianity does not magically dispel uncertainty and ambiguity; neither
must it blind us to the antimercy and suffering that mark existence. Instead,
it can, and occasionally does, come as a word of hope and of possibility for
those who have ears to hear. Its sacred texts and rich traditions give witness
to, among other things, an alter-world of compassion and justice that signals
the contingency and nonfinality of structures of domination. It hearkens to
the whispers of those who dare to base reality and morality on the incredible
experience of divine grace—of the experience of "the canary that sings on the
skull," of unexpected beauty and unforced intimacy in the very midst of the
world's apparent cruelty and absurdity.[16]

These testimonies bespeak the stubborn presence and efficacy of the
God of life and love. They uncover a bedrock of compassion and creativity
that runs deeper than despair and that grounds tragedy in the possibility of
redemption. To affirm this ground of being is a risky endeavor, for we never
encounter it apart from the shifting sands of history, and yet it is precisely in
and through history that this hope and this healing become incarnate.
Within the fragility and limits of finite existence, I believe, come revolutionary hope and unimagined possibility, transcending the bounds of the real with
the promise of transformation.

One theologian who has successfully combined the primary insights and
commitments of theologies of eros with a tragic perspective, while avoiding
both the hubris of foundationalism and the nihilism of radical relativism, is
Wendy Farley. She offers an interpretation of the human situation and of

God that is able to include the intransigent horror of radical suffering and the possibility for divine and human transformation. However, her theology leaves no room for the doctrine of atonement, for an understanding of redemption as occurring through the life *and death* of Jesus. On this point, I argue that Farley's assumptions about atonement are so narrow that they force her theology into an unnecessarily anti-christological posture that ultimately diminishes the theological scope and impact of her project.

According to Farley, traditional "solutions" to the problem of evil are impotent in the face of the massive evil and suffering that have marked the twentieth century. Theologies that presume to include human evil within an ultimately comic context offer "too neat a solution," for they "[quell] outrage over suffering by explaining it and, worse, by justifying it." To adopt a tragic posture or view, says Farley, is to recognize that "certain kinds of suffering are irredeemably unjust," that not all suffering can be made meaningful. Because guilt is not the primary problem, "atonement and forgiveness cannot help transcend tragedy."[17]

Yet even if tragic suffering cannot be atoned for, Farley insists that it can and must be defied, resisted. She suggests that defiance of suffering takes place when we refuse to give up our passion for justice in the very midst of injustice; when we identify the conditions of suffering and thus transcend its immediacy; when we treat victims of dehumanization with dignity, not allowing suffering to destroy their very humanity. Such resistance does not abolish tragedy or deny its continued reality, but neither does it let evil stand uncontested. In specific acts of resistance to dehumanization, asserts Farley, "another layer of the world order is peeled back" and "one is permitted to glimpse something beyond the apparent finality of evil." Tragedy "is redeemed but not abolished." For Farley, radical suffering creates "a fundamental cleavage and brokenness at the heart of human life," a rupture so profound that "even the death of a Messiah cannot atone for the anguish of the world."[18]

If atonement means the justification of evil, or the claim that it has been abolished—if atonement implies that the death of Jesus has wiped evil away, that it has expunged tragedy—then Farley rejects it as otherworldly, unreal, because the world we inhabit is a tragically structured one in which suffering is inevitable. Rather than rationalizing evil away, or theologizing it into acceptability, we must find ways of resisting human evil that interrupt its dehumanizing logic with a logic of compassion.

Compassion, says Farley, is a fundamentally different kind of power from the power of domination or coercion. It is an "empowering power" that "gives people their own power" to resist injustice and to fight despair and guilt themselves. Compassion "is a mode of relationship and a power that is wounded by the suffering of others and that is propelled into action on their behalf." It mediates dignity and respect as well as a sense of the contingency of suffering, and "in this way becomes an agency to resist the dehumanizing effects of suffering." The key to combating evil, insists Farley, is the recognition that "it cannot be resisted on its own terms," that "one must repudiate the desire for domination" and choose a fundamentally different way, the way of compassion. The paradox of the power of compassion is that "it is a power but it cannot coerce. . . . Compassion repudiates the methods of force and coercion and wears the disguise of weakness." Compassion, then, is the power to struggle against evil with the noncoercive but defiant power of love. In the final analysis, contends Farley, the practice of compassion does not redeem us *from* the fragility of historical existence but "*for* responsibility and joy within this existence." To be able to "taste the presence of divine love even through the torment" of existence is to transcend evil, to expose its nonfinality. In Farley's theology, then, we have a recognition of the scarring and irrevocable presence of human evil *and* an affirmation that such evil does not have to have the final word, that hope and struggle and transformation continue to be possible, even if they cannot erase the tragedy to which they respond.[19]

Yet even while she affirms the possibility of grace-filled moments and acts, of a God of compassion whose empowering love and thirst for justice mark the limits of evil's destruction, Farley rejects all notions of atonement. She insists that "evil must remain a surd, with no resolution, no atonement."[20] At the same time, however, her theology bears striking resemblances to those of Boff, Sobrino, Elizondo, and Brock. For them, as we have seen, the work of Christ does not accomplish the abolition or justification of evil but opens up a way to resist evil, to resist power-as-domination or power-as-control with the power of mercy or eros. In the historical praxis of resistance to evil we avoid being consumed by it. In choosing an entirely different logic, we circumvent evil—not by avoiding its effects but by escaping enslavement to it. Perhaps Farley would be less willing to dismiss the relevance of atonement were she to consider it not in terms of the absolution of individual sin but in broader terms as God's response to evil—as the Christian church's interpretation of the ultimate meaning of Jesus' life and death, a meaning that, when materialized in concrete ways, has the potential to free us from bondage to evil in its multiple and ever-changing forms, and to reconcile us to God, to one another, and to our own best selves. I argue in the next and final chapter that a contemporary reconstruction of the "patristic" model of atonement offers just such a scenario for interpreting the character and meaning of human evil and of God's salvific response to it.

By way of conclusion, let me suggest that in terms of the doctrine of atonement, the implications of this chapter's ruminations on the shifting sands of the discursive and moral universe and on a tragic framework for viewing the world are at least twofold. First, atonement should not be maintained as part of the theological repertoire if it does more harm than good. Interpretations of the salvific efficacy of the suffering and death of Jesus that yield a praxis of domination instead of freedom are illegitimate—the rotten fruit they produce discredits their theory. At the same time, however, we must recognize that the effects of any given idea are multiple, they vary over time, and they are often impossible to predict or control; thus, the issue of what constitutes an effective praxis, and therefore an acceptable theory, is rarely self-evident and is necessarily open to discussion, debate, and revision. Feminists and others who criticize atonement orthodoxy because of its violent history of effects should not back down from our claims, but we ought to take care that in the heat of the argument we do not invalidate our position by embracing the very tactics of stereotype, reductionism, and scapegoating for which we denounce that orthodoxy, lest we, too, produce rotten fruit.

A second implication follows from the first. In a context of irreducible plurality; in a world whose most sophisticated knowledges confirm that diversity is indispensable for the survival and health of planet Earth and its multiform inhabitants; in a world in which the other-effacing consequences of regimes of absolute truth and authority have become undeniably clear, theology should not have as its goal the articulation of singular interpretations and univocal truths but should aim to multiply possibilities, to open up various vistas of meaning, to diversify methodologies and canons, and to devise multiple strategies for transformation, recognizing at all times the contingent, contestable character of all our constructs. In regard to atonement, this means that rather than trying to come up with the one interpretation that can account for all contingencies, respond to all concerns, and please all people and beings, we ought to encourage a multiplicity of models that can be put into dialogue with one another in a process of ongoing, mutual critique and revision. On this point we can learn from biblical tradition, and particularly the Gospel narratives, whose different and often conflicting versions of Jesus' life and significance, as William Placher points out, "accept diversity, let multiple voices speak, leave ambiguities in place, and thus do not attempt to impose a neat master narrative on Christian existence."[21]

One goal of this book has been to explore several contemporary attempts to respond to the weaknesses of traditional construals of atonement with alternative interpretations. Boff, Sobrino, Elizondo, and Brock offer important variations on the work of Christ that, though they have significant commonalities with one another and with certain strands of theological tradition, cannot be narrowed to one absolute type or interpretation. It is precisely as their different threads of meaning and layers of experience are woven together into a momentary synthesis of color and texture that the larger fabric of the doctrine of atonement is enriched and remade, only to unravel with the force of change and the weight of critique. In the spirit of this never-ending process of whole-making and scrapping, I offer in the final chapter yet another rendering of the meaning of the life and death of Jesus, setting it alongside these others in the hope that the overlaps and contrasts might contribute to a more interesting, useful, and humane account. My interpretation of the work of Christ is greatly indebted to both Christian tradition and contemporary critiques of that tradition. I seek to recast, reinvigorate, and reconstruct an ancient set of ideas and images from the perspective of a feminist hermeneutic of suspicion that rejects victimizing theologies, that takes place within and accepts the boundaries of a tragic framework, and that yet attempts to give voice to a contemporary word of resistance and redemption emerging from within the Christian past.

7

Undermining Evil

As I was reading Augustine's *On the Trinity* several years ago, I happened upon a most intriguing passage: "It pleased God that for the sake of rescuing men from the power of the devil, the devil should be overcome not by power but by justice . . . power ought to follow not precede justice."[1] At my bedside table were Brock's *Journeys by Heart* and several other feminist theologies of eros or relationship; they were my "fun" reading, the ideas I resonated with deep in my soul, the texts I turned to when my mind was frayed or my spirit worn. By them I had become convinced that theology was at heart a discourse about power, about human power and divine power and how they ought to be understood in relation to each other. I was also convinced that power defined as control is at the root of injustices such as sexism, racism, and homophobia; that our inability to live in a world that we cannot completely understand, much less control—a world of limitations, mystery, and intransigent ambiguity—can unnerve us to such an extent that we try to secure our identity and group by bifurcating reality into "us" and "them," "good" and "evil," "pure" and "defiled," "normal" and "deviant." Such conceptual neatness gives us sure ground on which to stand, a stable self- and group-identity, and it works fairly well to stave off the chaos of complexity, ambiguity, and blurred boundaries, but it also requires that there be losers, victims. Injustice, I believed, is inevitable when power-as-control becomes a way of life, the hallmark of a marriage, an economic system, a social policy, a church polity. I realized that the only way really to combat injustice is to cultivate a different understanding of power, one that allows us to identify ourselves as agents—to act on and in the world—in a relatively noncoercive fashion.

What I found, and still find, in relational theologies is not only a convincing analysis of human evil as a problem of power-as-control, but also a clear and persuasive vision of a different kind of power guided primarily by a commitment to justice, to the common good, to the beloved community, to the dominion of God, rather than by self-interest. I was surprised and delighted to find in Augustine's thought this recognition—that only power guided and limited by justice has the potential to save us from our own worst selves. His ruminations on the defeat of the devil through justice rather than power are part of an identifiable tradition often referred to as the "classic" model of atonement, a model first given systematic expression by Gustav Aulén in his 1931 book *Christus Victor*. Since the "classic" designation is Aulén's, and since I intend to part ways with his interpretation of this tradition, I refer to it simply as the "patristic" model because it was widely espoused by the early "fathers" of Christian theology.

This patristic tradition regarding the interface of God and evil is what I intend to explore in this chapter. In my interpretation of this so-called theory, I bring an ancient set of ideas and images about God and Christ into conversation with contemporary concerns about the scope and intransigency of human evil, about victim-making theologies, and about the possibility of finding saving grace and redemptive resistance in the life and death of Jesus. I begin by setting forth the traditional contours and claims of the model; then I explore several problems that seem to make this model an unlikely candidate for contemporary resuscitation, especially by those who share the concerns about power, justice, and tragic suffering outlined throughout this book; finally, I argue that despite these shortcomings, this model offers contemporary Christian people a way of characterizing human evil and God's response to it that is too provocative, and potentially enlightening, to ignore.

The Patristic Model

Because the patristic model is actually a set of images, or a broad mythic motif, the following summary is less a step-by-step explanation of a systematic or linear theory than a series of expository reflections on a root narrative. This narrative depicts atonement in terms of conflict and victory and was especially popular between the second and sixth centuries of the common era. According to this view, the event of atonement is characterized by struggle—between God, the one who sets free, and the devil, the one who binds and enslaves. God and humanity are thought to be reconciled with each other because the powers of evil that kept them apart are decisively defeated by God, who confronts and triumphs over evil and thus loosens its stronghold over human beings. Within this drama of struggle for liberation, Jesus plays a crucial role, for it is in and through the life and death of Jesus the Christ, who is God incarnate, that the powers of evil are stripped of their authority.

The central image of this model is liberation from bondage, the result of a dramatic and surprising confrontation between the forces of good and evil. Human beings are understood to be held captive by the devil, to be bound by sin and evil, and atonement is the process by which our release is won. The battle is often viewed as a cosmic struggle—between God and Satan, good and evil, justice and injustice—whose locus is the life, death, and resurrection of Jesus the Christ.

Two central concepts often used to explain the nature of and relationship between human beings, evil, God, and redemption are the ideas of "ransom" and the "deception of the devil." Patristic theologians were convinced that human beings are held captive by sin and evil; consequently, they reasoned, humans must be redeemed by paying a "ransom," a release fee as it were. They found in the Christian Scriptures ample motivation and support for the view that Christ's ransom freed humankind from bondage to evil. In the Gospels, they drew on passages such as Matthew 20:28, in which Jesus claims that "the Son of Man came . . . to give his life a ransom for many"; on John, where the cross is presented as a victory over the powers of darkness and death; and on the countless "tyrants" who oppose Jesus, from Herod, to the Pharisees, to the devil himself. Pauline imagery, rich with references to redemption as victory over the demons, offered additional fodder for the patristic view. However, there was much disagreement about what should comprise the ransom and to whom it should be paid. Despite considerable debate, a consensus gradually emerged that Christ was the ransom who was paid to the devil—or, collectively, the powers of evil—as the price that would purchase the freedom of humanity. As Origen of Alexandria argued in the third century, "We were doubtless bought from the one whose servants we were. . . . He held us until the ransom for us, even the soul of Jesus, was paid to him."[2] Salvation, according to this model, is liberation from captivity that was effected by Christ's life, understood as a ransom paid to the devil in order to free humans from bondage to evil.

According to this view, the devil was understood to have certain rights over human beings. The fact of original sin meant that the devil had some sort of hold over human beings that the justice of God could not ignore. Moreover, human decisions to turn against God in various ways constituted a rejection of the good and a kind of allegiance to the powers of evil. As a result of human sin, therefore, the devil was thought to have a significant degree of legitimate authority in the world. It was consequently thought that the ransom presented to the devil was done in accordance with the rules of "fair play," for humanity was understood to be justly held by the devil and hence subject to death instead of life eternal.

However, unlike other human beings, Jesus was completely without sin and hence not under the devil's authority or subject to death. As we will see, early Christian thinkers such as Irenaeus and Gregory of Nyssa reasoned that by killing this sinless One, over whom he had no rights, the devil made a terrible blunder; he overstepped his boundaries, overreached his power. This "tragic overstepping or *hamartia*"[3] caused the devil's defeat by revealing the illegitimacy of his claim to Jesus' life and, consequently, by undermining any further claims to power he might make. Because of his fateful error, the devil had to forfeit his rights to the souls of those who follow Christ. According to the patristic model, it was in this event hinging on the devil's hubris and avarice that humanity was liberated from bondage to evil; and in this process, we will see, the life and death of Jesus were crucial components.

The ideas of ransom and the overreaching of authority helped early Christians understand the nature and consequences of evil, personified as the devil. But what about *God's* role in the drama of redemption? Early Christian thinkers frequently employed the "deception of the devil" motif to explain God's activity in the defeat of evil. The central piece in this rationale was God's incarnation in the person Jesus. By becoming incarnate, it was argued, God fooled Satan into thinking that Jesus was just another human being— sinful and subject to death. Popular images that conveyed this pattern of deceit were often quite vivid, if theologically grotesque; the most popular one portrayed Jesus as the bait that lured the devil onto a hook, which ensnared Satan in his attempt to catch another sinner.[4] Other images used to express the incarnation-as-deception idea included a mousetrap and a snare. All were metaphorical attempts to express the conviction that the powers of evil were defeated at the very point of their apparent victory, and that, paradoxically, Christ was triumphant at the moment of his defeat on the cross.[5]

The patristic view of atonement is often rejected as anachronistic, bizarre, grotesque, and theologically incorrect; and no doubt a case can be made that it is each of these. However, it was enormously convincing to many sharp-minded people for hundreds of years during early Christianity, and it has cropped up from time to time in other ages as well. Like other models of atonement, this view sought to express basic biblical insights and theological convictions in contextually relevant ways.

The worldview of early Christianity was characterized by widespread belief in and daily encounters with hostile powers and tyrants, both mythological and empirical; hence the appeal of the idea of ransom, of a way of release from bondage. Within the Christian Scriptures, the list of tyrants that threaten human life and health and that separate human beings from God can be divided into three groups: (1) sin, law, and death; (2) the principalities and powers, which include systems and institutions that become demonic when treated as idols; and (3) Satan, who represents the sum total of all evil.[6] As we have seen, the patristic model refers most often to "the devil" or "Satan," titles used to name the gamut of evil, cosmological and historical, individual and collective. As we have also seen in the discussion of the ransom and deception themes, "the devil" has a dual role. Satan, on the one hand, is the evil one who opposes God and enslaves human beings but, on the other hand, is understood to have certain rights, a certain jurisdiction, which even God appears to respect.[7]

When demythologized, then, the patristic model suggests a sophisticated construal of evil as that which, when succumbed to, seems to have enormous power and to take on a life of its own—to rival, it would seem, even the power of God—but which is, ultimately, *not* greater than God. Such a view claims biblical backing, for whereas the Christian Scriptures usually present Satan as the enemy of God and humankind, the Hebrew Scriptures offer also another view in which Satan has a legitimate place in Yahweh's service: "The 'Satan' or 'Adversary' appears in God's heavenly court as the public prosecutor, accusing sinners before the bar of divine justice."[8] Thus while the patristic view has been rejected from the start by those who object to the idea that the devil has rights and that therefore a ransom is paid to him—for such a perspective, it is argued, flies in the face of God's majesty and omnipotence—it is precisely this model's portrayal of evil as powerful and complex, though not invulnerable, that has striking parallels with contemporary attempts to understand evil within a tragic context.[9]

Limits of Tyranny

Irenaeus, the premier Christian thinker of the second century, was the first to anticipate the ransom theme, although he argued against the notion that the devil had rights to sinful humanity, claiming that the devil was always a usurper.[10] Like other Christian theologians of his time, Irenaeus emphasized the justice of God, particularly as he tried to express the precise way in which God successfully confronted and defeated the powers of evil. Claiming that "God is neither devoid of power nor of justice," Irenaeus suggested that through the incarnation, God expressed such a perfect balance of power and justice that "he who had led man captive (Satan), was justly captured in his turn by God; but man, who had been led captive, was loosed from the bonds of condemnation."[11]

According to Irenaeus, Jesus the Christ "gave Himself as a ransom for those who had been led into captivity":

And since the apostasy [Satan, or the kingdom of Satan] tyrannized over us unjustly, and, though we were by nature the property of the omnipotent God, alienated us contrary to nature, rendering us its own disciples, the Word of God, powerful in all things, and not defective with regard to His own justice, did righteously turn against that apostasy, and redeem from it His own property, not by violent means, as the [apostasy] had obtained dominion over us at the beginning, when it insatiably snatched away what was not its own, but by means of persuasion, as became a God of counsel, who does not use violent means to obtain what He desires; so that neither should justice be infringed upon, nor the ancient handiwork of God go to destruction.[12]

In this remarkable passage, Irenaeus sounds two noteworthy themes. First, he depicts evil not only as apostasy, or the falling away from or rejection of God, but also, and primarily, as tyranny, as the unjust use of power, as insatiable appetite or acquisitiveness.[13] Second, he suggests that God responds to such evil not by using force or violence but by deliberately eschewing such tactics, choosing instead the nonviolent means of persuasion, of wise counsel. In another passage, Irenaeus argues that by becoming human, by fully embracing what is seemingly ignoble and weak, God "baffled His adversary" the devil and "exhausted the force" of his attack.[14] Thus, in the thought of Irenaeus we see the main contours of what I am calling the patristic model—the recognition of the reality and profound influence of evil; the definition of evil as the unjust or avaricious use of power; and the conviction that in the person of Jesus, God has acted not only to reveal the true nature of evil but also to decenter and delegitimate its authority by luring it into exposing its own moral bankruptcy and thus defeating itself, hence opening up the possibility for human beings to escape enslavement to evil.[15]

For Gregory of Nyssa, writing in the fourth century, the question of why God became incarnate—of why "that incomprehensible, inconceivable, and ineffable reality, transcending all glory of greatness, [wrapped] Himself up in the base covering of humanity"—finds its answer in the clear need of human beings for healing and liberation from bondage to evil:

Here is the cause of the presence of God among men. Our diseased nature needed a healer. Man in his fall needed one to set him upright. He who had lost the gift of life stood in need of a life-giver, and he who had dropped away from his fellowship with good wanted one who would lead him back to good. . . . The captive sought for a ransomer, the fettered prisoner for some one to take his part, and for a deliverer he who was held in the bondage of slavery.[16]

In the incarnation, says Gregory, God accomplished this liberation according to the criteria of true justice, "not exercising any arbitrary sway over him who has us in his power, nor, by tearing us away by a violent exercise of force from his hold, thus leaving some colour for a just complaint," but through a method "consonant with justice . . . devised by Him Who in His goodness had undertaken our rescue."[17] This method, continues Gregory, was "to make over to the master of the slave whatever ransom he may agree to accept for the person in his possession."[18] Yet the life of Jesus was not simply *any* ransom; its value was so great that it appealed to the devil's pride, enticing him to believe that he could actually possess its greatness, control its power:

> He then, who . . . shut his eyes to the good in his envy of man in his happy condition, he who generated in himself the murky cloud of wickedness, *he who suffered from the disease of the love of rule, that primary and fundamental cause of propension to the bad and the mother, so to speak, of all wickedness* that follows,—what would he accept in exchange for the thing which he held, but something, to be sure, higher and better, in the way of ransom, that thus, by receiving a gain in the exchange, he might foster the more his own special passion of pride? (Emphasis added)[19]

Thus, concludes Gregory, the devil's grasp of Jesus—that is, the putting to death of the One who, because sinless, did not deserve death—became the devil's undoing. In his arrogance and greed, the devil ignored his own limits, lost sight of Jesus' divinity, and erroneously thought he had the power to quash even God.

Gregory's account indicates that the devil was brought to his demise by two things—first, and most important, his lust for power; and second, and derivatively, the inventiveness of God who, recognizing the devil's insatiable appetite for power, disguised the Divine Self "under the veil of our nature, that so, as with ravenous fish, the hook of the Deity might be gulped down along with the bait of flesh."[20] In trying to swallow God—to consume or control the Other absolutely—the absurdity and delusion of the devil's pretension are laid bare, and he is left to choke on his arrogance. In the life and death of Jesus, the devil's lust for infinite power finds its limit, for his attempt to control God, to squash even divinity, ultimately fails as the meaning and vitality of Jesus' existence do not die with him on the cross but are resurrected and renewed by the Christian community, which embraces the Spirit of the risen Christ. Gregory's account suggests, it seems to me, that God's response to evil is to expose and dramatize the violence and greed at its root, allowing the force of its own avarice to discredit it in the eyes of the moral community and empowering that community to embrace power guided and limited by compassion and justice.

Later in the fourth century, Augustine sounded the ransom theme again, making the issue of God's justice central to his understanding of atonement: "What is this justice, therefore, by which the devil was conquered? What, unless the justice of Jesus Christ? And how was he conquered? Because, although he [the devil] found in Him [Christ] nothing worthy of death, yet he slew Him. And it is certainly just that the debtors, whom he held, should be set free, since they believed in Him whom he slew without any debt."[21] Augustine is convinced that in the life and death of Jesus, God responded to the powers of evil with justice rather than power, and in that choice, God exhibited salvific goodness and wisdom. "The essential flaw" of the devil, says Augustine, is the "perversion" that "made him a lover of power and a deserter and assailant of justice." The seductive effect of such evil on sinful humanity is that humans "neglect or even detest justice and studiously devote themselves to power, rejoicing at the possession of it or inflamed with the desire for it."[22]

For Augustine, as with Irenaeus and Gregory of Nyssa, the death of Jesus on the cross signaled the defeat of evil by exposing the injustice and immorality at its root. In the murder of Jesus, the absolute unfairness of the devil's motives and tactics become devastatingly clear; the true face of evil is unmasked for all to see, its claim to authority discredited, and its seductive potential squelched. According to this scenario, God cunningly uses the devil's lust for power against him, baiting him with the lure of power until he eventually grasps for more than he can hold and causes his own demise. At the crucifixion, says Augustine, we "see the devil overcome when he thought he himself was overcoming."[23] Applauding the ingenious wisdom of God that facilitated such a demise, Augustine concludes, "The devil does not know how the most excellent wisdom of God makes use of both his snares and his fury to bring about the salvation of His own faithful ones."[24]

Although the patristic themes of ransom, deception, and justice remained popular throughout the medieval period, particularly in the literary and visual arts of that age, other ideas and emphases gradually eclipsed them.[25] They resurfaced briefly in Luther's thought, most noticeably in his numerous references to the divine-demonic conflict and to the way in which the Hidden God caused the devil to defeat himself; but this "classic" dimension was soon forgotten by Lutheran theology and, indeed, by Christian theology in general.[26]

Liabilities

Like all theological constructions, the patristic model of atonement has its drawbacks. In advocating for a contemporary rereading of the model, my intention is not to overlook or ignore its liabilities but to address them forthrightly. Obviously, I am convinced that the model's potential for illuminating contemporary theological discourse and for engendering a humanizing praxis makes it worth serious consideration. In what follows, I discuss both its problems and its possibilities, arguing that the former pale when compared with the latter.

Perhaps the most problematic element of the patristic view of the work of Christ is its dualistic framework for understanding evil. Typical interpretations of this material depict the drama as a cosmic battle with a clear-cut, metaphysical distinction between good and evil, God and the devil. The universe and everything in it are understood according to a rigid moral framework believed to reflect a transcendent order. However, this kind of moral absolutism bypasses the complexity and subtlety of evil as we know it, feeding illusions of purity and innocence, on the one hand, and permitting the demonization of those people and groups viewed as unclean or damaged, on the other. As we have seen in the case of sexual violence, this innocent/ damaged duality creates a moral universe that, for victims, breeds self-hatred and guilt and that, for perpetrators, disallows the possibility of transformation by reducing persons to crime. The simplicity of a dualistic morality may be intellectually and politically convenient, and it may even be used to inspire important struggles for justice, but it is an illusion; human experience is simply not divisible in this way, and it is time our conceptions of good and evil responded to, rather than ignored, the uncompromising ambiguity of life in a finite world.

The centrality of the figure of the devil in the patristic model compounds these concerns. As Elaine Pagels argues, Christian theology has throughout its history made recourse to Satan in order to ground and justify its existence and identity. This process of self-preservation and self-promotion has been based on the theological vilification of various groups, including Jews, pagans, and dissident Christians. Once these groups were identified with the devil, with evil itself, their repudiation appeared to have divine sanction. Pagels explains that understandings of Satan underwent a dramatic shift during the emerging years of Christianity, when the turmoil of navigating a turbulent, unpredictable, and often hostile social and religious landscape prompted early Christians to interpret the conflicts in which they were embroiled in terms of a spiritual struggle against evil itself. Satan, who in Jewish tradition originally represented one of God's angels, a penultimate adversary or member of the loyal opposition, was reinterpreted to signify outright opposition to God, rebellion against God, an ultimate force that threatened God's dominion. By using this framework of transcendent, conflicting moralities to make sense of their own conflicts, early Christians were able to identify themselves as God's people and their enemies as God's enemies, justifying their own righteousness at the expense of those with whom they disagreed. The Gospel writers used this discursive framework to understand the life and death of Jesus, depicting Jesus and his disciples as embroiled in a cosmic struggle against demons and the devil, and allowing the early Christians to identify with the disciples and to demonize their opponents as incarnations of evil.[27]

Tragically, as Pagels points out, this dynamic was not unique to the first centuries of Christianity but became a defining logic of Western Christendom, contributing most notably to a powerful tradition of anti-Semitism.[28] This theology has been used for two millennia to secure divine sanction for processes of self- and group-identification and cohesion that depend upon the projection onto an "other" of whatever is deemed negative, impure, or threatening. According to this logic, Christian identity requires scapegoats, victims, demonized others. "Such moral interpretation of conflict," admits Pagels, "has proven extraordinarily effective throughout Western history in consolidating the identity of Christian groups"; however, "the same history also shows that it can justify hatred, even mass slaughter."[29]

Clearly, an understanding of God's salvific activity in and through the life and death of Jesus that legitimates the demonization of otherness is merely one more tool of theological violence, of power-as-control, which results in the ideological and/or physical domination of some by others. Insofar as the patristic model of atonement expresses and condones the establishment of a transcendent, bifurcated moral universe in which the identity of "the good" depends upon the creation and then destruction of "the evil," it reflects a logic of domination that those concerned about expanding the possibility of fullness of life for all will want to resist. The invocation of Satan as a tool for understanding human evil and conflict is dangerous, indeed.

However, this cosmic dualism emerged during a time of tribulation for the early Christians, a time in which they were a minority whose ideas and claims challenged prevailing norms and traditions and who were made to suffer for their heterodoxy. Survival was most likely the primary force behind their theological and moral conceptualizations. In the face of persecution, injustice, and impending extermination, the moral landscape *can* appear bifurcated; the stark reality of a life-or-death situation permits few moral equivocations and may even require dramatic action and fierce language. Nevertheless, passion and conviction do not have to be grounded in an other-effacing absolutism. Pagels concludes her social history of Satan by reminding her readers that despite the tragic fact that Christians have tended to establish their identities and communities by vilifying "others," there have also been those who "have believed they stood on God's side without demonizing their opponents."[30]

In addition to its dualist framework, a weakness of the patristic model of atonement is its tendency to depict redemption as a purely cosmic affair, an otherworldly fight from which God emerges triumphant, securing humanity's liberation from Satan without the participation, or even knowledge, of human beings. Such a depiction undermines human responsibility for evil and implies that the real work of struggling against evil takes place outside the historical realm. In terms of its portrayal of Jesus, the patristic model attributes salvific import to his death *and* life, but it tends to emphasize obedience as the theologically significant component of his life—an emphasis that, as we have seen, is highly problematic.

Even though God, according to this model, does not act arbitrarily or even unilaterally to confront evil and hence effect atonement, the history of interpretation of this model has, I would argue, misunderstood or distorted its implied conception of the Divine. The result is that God has been reduced to a kind of cosmic superhero who goes undercover to meet Satan in an all-out battle of the superpowers and who, after agreeing to a shady deal with the devil, emerges triumphant, if morally bruised. This comic-book caricature appears to be at the root of the overwhelming tendency in both mainline and feminist theologies to dismiss the patristic model as simplistic, absurd, and/or grotesque. While I am convinced that there is much more to the model than the superhero reading depicts, I am wary of its amenability to such an interpretation.

A final concern I want to raise has to do with the tendency of the patristic model to portray atonement as a "done deal" and the work of Christ as resulting in absolute and universal triumph over evil. According to Aulén's now paradigmatic interpretation, Christ is victor, totally triumphant over the forces of evil. For Aulén, writing as he did at the end of World War I, perhaps the forces of evil appeared to have been vanquished by the forces of good, making this a tenable reading of atonement; but for those of us who live at the end of that same century and are heirs to a legacy of human evil whose effects and continued presence are impossible to ignore—from the Holocaust to Nagasaki, from Cambodia to Watts to Rwanda and Bosnia—the suggestion that good has defeated evil, even from an eschatological perspective, seems impossible to confirm. Sharon Welch's critique of an imperialist concept of God is relevant here; insofar as traditional understandings of atonement imply that sin and evil have been defeated once and for all, they function "to remove some of the risk of history," to remove "people from the bloody arena of historical struggle and responsibility," for if evil has been vanquished, then we no longer need to struggle against it. Such an emphasis on "victory" and "triumph" makes it problematic insofar as it belies what Welch calls "a pathological obsession with security . . . that leads to a blinding Christian triumphalism."[31]

Welch argues that the context of triumph often leads to an "ethic of control" in which we delude ourselves into thinking that our actions can determine the shape of the future, that "the aim of moral action [is] the attainment of final, complete victory." Such a view encourages us to act only in situations in which success is certain, which means that our activities are necessarily supportive of the status quo. If genuine transformation or change is to occur, then we have to relinquish our "utopian imagination" and embrace "an ethic of risk" in which we dare "to care and to act although there are no guarantees of success." To avoid despair in the face of repeated failure, Welch encourages us to get rid of our delusions of victory and triumph, and affirm instead the ambiguity and limitations of existence, for it is only within the latter context that hope and resistance in the face of suffering and evil become possible.[32]

Another theologian who is critical of the assumption of the defeat of sin and evil is Nel Noddings, who argues that the false assumption that evil can be defeated, and the concomitant desire to do just that, "often results in perpetuating and renewing it." To counter false views of evil, such as that implied in Aulén's interpretation of the patristic model of atonement, Noddings suggests that we need to develop "a morality of evil" with which we can learn to avoid and manage evil, to reduce its effects, rather than deluding ourselves into thinking we can conquer it.[33] Reflecting on his experience with sexual abuse survivors, James Poling concurs that a clear-cut, win-lose context for understanding evil is not helpful. As he points out, a "core issue in healing from sexual abuse is the ability to live in the midst of ambiguity. Ambiguity is a necessary component in forming a self that can flourish during the healing process."[34] Thus in a world in which we must learn how to live *with* evil, the challenge is not to vanquish it or to imagine it already defeated but to learn to recognize its many faces and then to struggle to avoid it when possible, to confront it when it cannot be avoided, and to resist its dehumanizing effects when we find ourselves its victims. Noddings expresses this thought: "It takes great conscious effort to subdue evil by living with it rather than stirring it up in misguided attempts to overcome it once and for all."[35] To live with ambiguity requires patience; it is a never-ending task that must be taken up daily.

An appropriate construal of atonement must take seriously the ambiguities and fissures of history, the very real possibility that good may not triumph, that the possibility of failure is real. After all, daily living attests to the countless occasions in which the good does not prevail but instead is frustrated, humiliated, exploited, betrayed, and murdered. Our understandings of human evil must not imply easy solutions, whether of victory or violence; rather, what is required is a sober recognition of the intractability of evil and of the necessity of finding "the courage to act and to think within an uncertain framework," for such a framework is life.[36]

Openings and Connections

Having discussed the liabilities of the patristic model of atonement, I turn now to an exploration of its strengths, arguing that its metaphorical character gives it a pliability conducive to multiple readings, one of which is a feminist liberation interpretation of the work of Christ that brings together contemporary concerns about power, justice, and relationality in ways that could shed new light on Christian understandings of and responses to human evil. Toward that end, I begin by noting again that this model is not a theory at all. It functioned during the first several centuries of Christianity as a loosely cohering cluster of themes and images that centered on bondage, liberation, ransom, and deception, and it was frequently employed in conjunction with other schema, such as satisfaction and sacrifice, signifying its nonexclusive formal character. I find this atheoretical character appealing, for while its images can whet our theological appetites and energize our imaginations, it does not give us a clear-cut or simple formula into which we can plug the life and death of Jesus and come up with a neat solution to the problem of evil. Even its form, I would argue, is subversive of totalizing discourses as it eludes systematization, linearity, and rigid conceptualization. This does not mean that it cannot yield concepts or theories, but these are second-order affairs and none of them can claim interpretive hegemony. Its narrative character opens rather than closes discussion, invites rather than discourages participation, question, and innovation. I agree with Boff, who asserts in a different context: "Perhaps the most theological way to discourse upon radical human problems such as suffering, death, love, life, and so on, is in the language of symbol and myth. These do not explain a great deal. But they 'make us think.' The solution they indicate is not a formula, not the conclusion of an argument, but a journey we make together, in solidarity."[37]

The patristic model of atonement finds expression in the language of myth, and here I find an opening for myself to enter into dialogue with this ancient story of the redemptive activity of God in Christ, bringing my horizon of meaning to encounter, learn from, and question its horizon, attempting to open up a discursive universe not limited by dogma. In what follows, I explore the relevance and significance of several key components of the patristic model for contemporary discussions of the character of human evil and of the meaning of Jesus' life and death, suggesting ways in which many of the problems of today's atonement orthodoxy can be avoided without rejecting the idea of atonement altogether, and bringing together some of the major concerns and commitments of feminist and liberation theologies. I attempt a demythologization of this ancient model, based not on a rejection of myth or symbol but on the conviction that a contemporary framework poses quite different questions to the model and so, not surprisingly, yields different meanings from the original.

As we saw in chapters 1 through 3, Christian theology has been harshly criticized for narrowing atonement to the heroic, once-and-for-all absolution of individual human sin—understood in terms of willfulness, disobedience, and pride—through the life and death of the perfectly innocent, obedient, and humble Jesus, whose voluntary sacrifice of himself either pays humanity's debt to God or perfectly exemplifies God's saving love for humanity. Such an interpretation, I have argued, constitutes theological violence insofar as it contributes to the deification of unilateral power and undermines the agency and well-being of the socially disadvantaged, thus perpetuating unjust relationships and policies. A contemporary reading of the patristic model, by contrast, offers a markedly more expansive and pragmatic understanding of human evil and of salvation, suggesting that liberation from evil occurs through a historical praxis of resistance and compassion that was embodied by Jesus in his life and death and that continues to have the potential to disrupt and discredit the powers of evil, breaking the chains of its hegemony and opening up spaces of freedom and possibilities for healing and transformation.

In my retrieval of the patristic model of atonement, what is confronted and overcome by Jesus the Christ is not merely individual or personal sin, as is the case with most construals of atonement; rather, Satan or the devil represents the sum total of evil, and so it includes not only individual sin but the countless ways in which human evil manifests itself interpersonally, communally, institutionally, and globally. In contrast to those who define human evil in terms of individual rebellion, willfulness, or pride, this model implies a definition of evil as the abuse of power,[38] a definition broad enough to include a wide range of attitudes, actions, and policies; a definition that can be adapted to the particular character of different times and contexts; a definition of evil that has both individual and systemic relevance. In Jesus' life and death, abusive power is confronted with the apparent impotence of truth and compassion, yielding a praxis that can liberate not only from individual sins of egocentrism, idolatry, and indifference, but also from corporate sins such as racism, ethnocentrism, and anthropocentrism. Thus, the patristic view of atonement shares with feminist and liberation theologies an understanding of sin as both individual and social. To talk about evil as "cosmic," I argue, is not necessarily to render it ahistorical or transcendent but to identify the scope and impact of human rapacity and ignorance, the depth of social dis-ease. In sum, a contemporary reconstruction of the patristic model suggests an understanding of human evil expansive enough to speak to the countless ways in which human beings are mired in, even bound by, the powers of evil.

Redemption is understood in similarly expansive terms, with the primary trope being liberation from bondage. According to this model, to be saved is to be freed from enslavement to evil.[39] When evil is defined as the abuse of power, salvation is not reducible to either the personal or the institutional but includes both. Redemption understood in this way does not imply the abolition of evil itself but a transformation in one's relationship *to* evil. To be liberated from bondage to evil means that evil no longer determines one's being and actions, that one is free to resist evil and to try to reduce it. We are saved not *from* the vicissitudes, vulnerabilities, and inevitable suffering of finite existence, but *for* a particular way of responding to those inevitabilities, a way that, as we will see, Jesus exemplified in his life and death. Redemption, then, is a profoundly this-worldly affair, though it implies a radical transformation of our conception of and place in the world.

In addition to a broad understanding of both sin and salvation, a strength of this model is the seriousness with which it takes human evil. In this respect, it has more in common with the Anselmian view, according to which sin creates an objective and infinite barrier between human beings and God, than some versions of the Abelardian model that depict sin as a sign of temporary confusion or immaturity. According to the patristic model, evil not only exists—it rivals God! The powers of evil are pervasive and potent enough to warrant *serious* action. They bind; they captivate; they enslave. When this seriousness is combined with a social understanding of sin as outlined above, we have a theological framework within which human evil is depicted as expansive *and* insidious, a framework that can account for systemic evils such as sexism and colonialism.[40]

According to the original patristic interpreters of the model, the good versus evil dualism is not absolute but relative—"relative" because only God was understood as absolute, while all else, including evil, was contingent; but still a "dualism" inasmuch as the framework of thought was characterized by a profound recognition of the presence of evil in the world and of God's struggle against it. For these thinkers, evil obstructs but does not ultimately negate or defeat good. For them, the certainty of God's omnipotence meant that evil was always penultimate, ultimately subject to God. By contrast, contemporary Christians who do theology in a postmodern, tragic context may find claims about the "defeat" of evil to be naive and counterproductive. Rather than assuming good and evil as metaphysical givens and then uncritically asserting the ultimacy of good and the contingency of evil, we recognize that all definitions of good and evil are social constructs, and we join the public debate about how they are defined, arguing in favor of the conceptions that we judge will be most helpful in our efforts to cocreate a world that enhances the survival and well-being of all.

As people of faith, we cling to the promise of God's mercy and justice; we remember and celebrate the stories of God's liberating love that pervades history, enabling individuals and communities to resist the temptations of power-as-control by embracing and embodying the healing power of compassion; and we try to fashion a *basileia* praxis, an ethic of courage and care infused with a biophilic spirit. In this process, we *hope* that good will prevail. Acting on that hope, we theologize and act in certain ways rather than others, knowing that neutrality is never an option. And on those occasions when the good does prevail, we treasure the moment; we try to learn what went right and how to do it again. Like Frederick the field mouse in the children's tale by Leo Lionni, we store up the memory of that act, so that in the winter of our discontent its beauty and efficacy can feed our souls, warm our hearts, and color our world, giving us courage to keep on keeping on, to make love where violence abounds, to stand together where divisiveness thrives, to defy injustice through concrete acts of mercy and civil disobedience.[41] In such acts, we are freed from the bonds of evil, if only for a moment, to taste the sweetness of freedom; we are lifted beyond the limits of violence and greed, exposing their contingency, their inability to define our lives completely, their nonfinality.

But while we may hope for and work toward a world without evil, and even see it wane now and then, we know too well its vitality and tenacity to assume its defeat or disappearance. Taking evil seriously, as the patristic model of atonement does, means that we recognize its reality and power, admitting that within this finite, fragile world, good and evil are locked in battle, that moral existence has the character of struggle, and that it is up to us to keep hope alive by loving and living the good and resisting evil in concrete acts of compassion and celebration.

Even as this model highlights the unfinished nature of the struggle against evil and the necessity of locating this struggle within the finite world—that is, within the realm of human activity and responsibility—it also recognizes that human effort alone is insufficient. It reminds us of our fragility, our captivity to impoverished views of self and world, our inability to extricate ourselves from destructive patterns of relating. The patristic model thematizes the sad fact that we *are* enslaved to evil, for our power alone is impotent in the face of it; and even our power together, in groups and communities, when it manages to avoid mimicking the dynamics of domination it purports to oppose, eventually fizzles into exhaustion or despair. This recognition is less a theological assumption than a hard-won conclusion based, on the one hand, on the failures and frustrations of countless well-intentioned attempts throughout history to construct a world-transforming and -sustaining ethic, politics, or philosophy on purely secular foundations; and, on the other hand, on experiences, also without number, of revolutionary grace, of a life-affirming power that is *not* generated or manipulable by human desire or convention but that nonetheless reveals its reality and vitality in and through the finite world.

It is this mysterious presence, this transformative power, that Christians call God; and it is this life-affirming Spirit that Jesus of Nazareth is said to have embodied in a definitive way and that pervaded and empowered the community at whose center he stood. In the life and teaching of Jesus, this power was manifest as compassion—a caring so profound that it threatened to undo the world. Indeed, for those who share Jesus' vision, the world itself appears to unravel under the weight of its own pretension, its own inability to redeem itself from the banality of evil. But in the very midst of this cosmic undoing is the promise of a new world—the *basileia* of God—proclaimed by Jesus and made concrete in his praxis of healing and compassion.

In a feminist retrieval of the patristic model, Jesus' unspectacular ethic of care manifests God's presence in the world. Furthermore, the *immanental* character of this divine power confounds the bearers of demonic power, for they assume that Jesus' commitment will bend under fire, that his spirit will break under duress or disappear when dominated. Ironically, if his commitment had been his alone, crucifixion would surely have crushed it. However, what the powers of evil did not anticipate, what they did not see, was the infinite font of life that spawned Jesus' struggle and that continues to spring forth long after his death. This sacred power transcends the bounds of any one person, activity, community, or institution, and yet it can become concrete only in such ones. Irreducibly different yet intimately present, erotic power grounds Christian identity and community; it is the pulse of life that pervades all being, the one breath enlivening the embodied billions, luring each toward individual fulfillment within an organic whole and thus coming to expression in a *basileia* praxis of justice and compassion.

Resistance as Redemptive

Such a praxis, however, in Jesus' day as in our own, is at odds with the world as we know it and thus takes on the character of struggle against injustice and unlove. The emphasis on struggle is one of the most central and important features of the patristic model of atonement. Keeping in mind the legitimate concerns about a dualistic morality discussed above, I argue that the model's image of cosmic battle need not yield an absolute dualism, a suprahistorical drama, or an assumption of the final defeat of evil, but can be interpreted to point to the morally ambiguous character of finite existence and to the constant challenge of recognizing and resisting human evil. Seen in this way, the patristic model's image of conflict between God and Satan, between the forces of good and evil, has much in common with recent emphases on struggle as a crucial theological category.

For Jon Sobrino, as we have seen, what Jesus' life and death brought into clear view is the struggle between two conceptions of God—a God of life and liberation, and a God of oppressive power.[42] The struggle between these two deities did not happen "once upon a time" but is occurring in every moment as human individuals and groups choose which values will be of ultimate concern to them. According to Leonardo Boff, Jesus' being-for-others was in constant conflict with power-as-domination, and this same agon characterizes contemporary existence. Boff and other Third World theologians have little choice but to recognize "the stubborn presence of an antihistory" of human evil to which resistance and struggle are the sole alternatives. "The problem of evil," insists Boff, "is a problem not of theodicy but of ethics. Evil—its burden and its defeat—is understood not by speculating about it, but by taking up a *practice of combat for good,* by embracing those causes that produce love and deliverance from the crosses of this world" (emphasis added).[43] For Virgilio Elizondo, we recall, Jesus' "refusal to resign himself to evil" reveals the salvific power of truth; and for those who seek liberation from the bonds of evil, Elizondo admonishes that "it is not sufficient to do good and avoid evil: the disciple must do good and *struggle against* evil."[44]

African theologian Jean-Marc Éla argues that it is because of Jesus' life of "unending struggle against oppressive socioreligious forces and structures" that he "transforms the cross from an instrument of humiliation into an instrument of struggle against slavery and death."[45] His life of protest stands as a challenge to us, asking "us to decide whether we are in fact in solidarity with those who struggle against the forces of death at work in history."[46] Our redemption from evil, then, is effected not through his struggle but through our own, as we dare to bear concrete witness to the amazing grace that creates and sustains life in the face of death-dealing powers. According to Eleazar Fernandez, the history of colonization undergone by Filipino men and women has given birth to a "theology of struggle," which understands anger and protest as important theological resources and tools and which, additionally, recognizes that "only in struggle and by struggle are suffering and hope saved from being a futuristic escape." In the long and protracted struggle against human evil, says Fernandez, Filipinos identify with "the suffering but struggling Jesus," and yet this identification "does not mean 'empathizing' with a once-upon-a-time figure and his struggle, but waging their own struggle as Jesus did."[47] The theme of struggle plays a central role in Korean *minjung* theology as well. According to Andreas A. Yewangoe, Jesus is understood "as the One who sets free," the One whose own struggle for survival and transformation in a brutal world inspires the *minjung,* the people, to do likewise. "The *minjung,*" he says, "are those who resist in a situation where they are oppressed, those who do not lie down under their fate."[48]

And yet struggle is not always understood in such proactive terms. Sometimes survival itself is a struggle, endurance a victory of sorts. Walter Altmann reminds us, "Passive resistance . . . could be indispensable in order to get through periods of captivity that seem endless."[49] To understand the work of Christ as a struggle against evil, then, is not to posit a theology of heroism but a theology based on a praxis of survival and resistance whose specific form will vary depending on the possibilities at hand.

Among feminists, Third World theologians have consistently stressed the importance of the categories of struggle and resistance in responding to human evil. According to Ada María Isasi-Díaz, struggle is a dominant way of life for poor people. Utopian ideas fade quickly when confronted with the never-ending brutality of daily existence, and struggle becomes a necessity if survival is to be a possibility. In the midst of the dehumanizing effects of human evil, the only alternative to fatalism is protest. For Hispanic people, says Isasi-Díaz, "what is central to our self-understanding is not our suffering oppression but rather our struggle to overcome that oppression and to survive."[50] Thus for Isasi-Díaz, struggle is a major theological category—not a luxury but a necessity—and in the life and death of Jesus she finds a paradigm of the liberative strategy of struggle against evil. In a similar vein, Delores Williams suggests that rather than Jesus' *death* effecting salvation, his life of resistance has redemptive significance; by resisting the temptations of worldly power and material wealth, and by utilizing a variety of survival strategies in the midst of death-dealing forces, Jesus gives "humankind new vision to see the resources for positive, abundant relational life."[51] Jesus' praxis of resistance to evil forges a new path for all who follow, a possibility for responding to evil that can save us from its enslaving grasp, even if it cannot liberate us from the existence of evil itself.

First World feminists are increasingly recommending that struggle and liberation be kept at the center of theological constructions, lest our theologies function as tacit support for an unjust status quo. Building on the work of Dorothee Sölle, Rebecca Chopp, and Sharon Welch, Christian feminists declare common cause with liberation theologies, insisting that the practice of protest and resistance to oppression is the focus of Christian faith and theology, that Christians ought to rebel against evil, actively opposing dehumanization and violence.[52] For Ellen Wondra, the theme of resistance offers a middle path between the passivity implied in themes such as suffering and endurance and the heroic activism of the theme of triumph. To make resistance a central theological category, she asserts, allows for the recognition of the dehumanizing effects of human evil, but it also "gives more weight to agency than passivity," illuminating not only the reality and brutality of human suffering but also the possibility of re-creating meaning by struggling against the delimitations of suffering and by keeping the memory of victims alive to contest the victors' version of history and truth. Resistance, then, is "part of a dialectical movement from domination to transformation."[53] It exposes the savagery of human violence and keeps alive the possibility of a different way of being, generating hope for transformation in the very midst of injustice.

To understand resistance to evil as a theological imperative is to wager that God is a God of life; that God is the ground of being, the power of being itself; that God is on the side of life and its fulfillment. But it is also to locate these claims within a materialist context that calls for constant historical instantiation of all truth claims. Thus, it is on the basis of concrete experiences of God's transformative biophilia in our lives, or in the lives of those whose memories we keep, that the struggle to enhance the possibility and quality of life is waged. Precisely in such struggles we are saved from both nihilism and idolatry.

The theme of struggle against evil, of a battle for life and truth, is at the heart of the patristic model of atonement as I interpret it. A contemporary reading of this model highlights the relevance of this emphasis on struggle for understanding the significance of the life and death of Jesus and the being and presence of God. It reminds us that evil is no illusion—its victims are flesh and blood, as are its perpetrators; we know them, we are them. It presents evil as subtle, complex, pervasive, and intractable. As we will see, this model depicts God not as a triumphant superhero who squashes evil in one fell swoop but as One who circumvents convention in surprising ways. Jesus' life and death become revelations of how to respond to evil without becoming it. Such is the challenge of finite existence, then and now. To respond to evil by struggling against it is both to recognize its reality and to defy its ultimacy by keeping the possibility of difference alive.

We can understand Jesus' life and death as manifestations not only of his individual struggle but of God's as well, and of the ongoing challenge with which we all are faced. In this challenge that is life, the story of Jesus' refusal to be inscribed by the forces of evil surrounding him becomes for us a sacred memory that keeps possibility and hope alive, reminding us that because a praxis of resistance was actualized "once upon a time," it can be yet again. Moreover, to claim that Jesus' struggle is also God's is to wager that resistance to evil is better and truer than acquiescence or resignation, that such a praxis is our best hope for making the world go on. The patristic model challenges us to recognize that in the life and death of Jesus, the moral ambiguity of human existence is revealed in full clarity—the conflict between good and evil is thrown into sharp relief; and a way of navigating that ambiguity is manifest—a way based on the identification of evil as dominating power and on the resistance of evil in concrete acts of power-as-compassion.

Confounding Evil

According to the patristic model, God is the one who, through Jesus the Christ, liberates humankind from bondage to evil. In this liberating event,

God is understood to act in accordance with the rules of "fair play," recognizing the reality and even legitimacy of the devil's hold over human beings, and working to overcome the power of evil not through using brute force, not by simply destroying Satan or wiping evil from the face of the earth, but by exposing the injustice at the root of evil and allowing this injustice to discredit the devil and hence to loosen its hold over humankind.[54]

The true character of evil is manifest in the life and death of Jesus. His message and praxis of proexistence—of identification with the poor and outcast, of prophetic denunciation of religious and social practices that put custom or profit above physical and spiritual well-being, of power as empowerment of others—were met with suspicion, fear, hostility, and violence by those whose status or worldview depended on an unjust status quo. Here the face of evil was revealed as the abuse of power—the use of one's talents and situation to control the people and things around one so that the uncertainty and instability of finite existence can be avoided or denied; the securing of one's status or authority at the expense of the well-being or existence of others; the uncritical or fatalistic acceptance of the status quo so as to avoid the vulnerability of engagement; the creation of institutions whose *raison d'être* is their own perpetuation and aggrandizement instead of the enhancement of the common good. In the violent response to Jesus' prophetic message and presence of compassion and justice, human evil was exposed with ultimate clarity.

Jesus' untimely death was inevitable because of the kind of *life* he lived. Rather than treating the life of Jesus as a practically dispensable prelude to the real action of his atoning death, my reading of the patristic model suggests that his concrete praxis of mercy and resistance confronted evil in a definitive way. In and through Jesus, God is understood to struggle against evil, but not with the tools of evil itself—not with coercive power, not with unjust force—but unconventionally, indirectly, immanently, incarnationally, using "weakness" to confront and confound "dominance." Human evil is a this-worldly affair; it cannot be defeated from on high but must be addressed *within* the world, within history, within the particular acts of real people and communities. Human evil always takes the form of violence, against self or other; and according to this model of atonement, the one hope for resisting it is to eschew its means, to choose not coercion but nonviolence, not power-as-control but power-as-compassion. This was God's choice; this was Jesus' choice; this is the only choice that can circumvent the cycle of violence.

The theme of the deception of the devil illuminates the nature and method of redemptive power. While the idea of divine deceit may appear immoral to some, it points to the reality that any struggle against oppression and injustice that seeks to avoid violent means or that emerges from a context of relative powerlessness must rely on cunning and ingenuity rather than ascribed authority or power. The centrality of the trickster theme in African and African American narrative traditions reflects this realization. Figures like Brer Rabbit and Signifying Monkey demonstrate that confronting power from the underside requires a gritty resourcefulness, a willingness to take what is at hand and turn it into a tool of subversion. Those who are forced to exist at the margins of social power, and those among the privileged who choose to abdicate unilateral power, have no recourse but to make creative use of what is available to them. Black women, says Bernice Johnson Reagon, "have to do whatever we have to do in order for there to be a new day":

> *It's called*
> *making a way out of no way*
> *I'm not talking about magicians.*
> *I'm talking about people who have to handle the things that they*
> *   find in the society . . . so*
> *that they can deliver the goods*
> *when there is no way laid out to deliver the goods.*[55]

When resources are scarce, survival itself requires ingenuity. Beyond that, genuine transformation of an unjust status quo may require a deliberate side-stepping of the power establishment. Parody, satire, and other mischief-making ploys can unsettle the comfortable and change popular conceptions of the Real, creating a space of alterity in which the grip of unilateral power is loosened and the limits of its strength exposed.

In a similar vein, French feminist Luce Irigaray's work suggests—contrary to Audre Lorde's well-known claim—that the master's tools *can* be used to dismantle the master's house.[56] Indeed, in a world in which patriarchy is so entrenched in our patterns of socialization, education, politics, and religion, its tools are the only ones available. According to Irigaray, the best strategy for resistance, for opening up a space that is authentically different, for speaking in a voice that is not the same as the dominant discourse, is what she calls mimesis—a kind of playful imitation of the normative that exposes the absurdity, arbitrariness, and ruthlessness of its reduction of multiplicity and difference to One voice, authority, and truth. This kind of mimetic strategy has been used for centuries by women who have sought to express their agency and creativity within the suffocating confines of patriarchal authority and politics. In the twelfth century, for instance, Hildegard of Bingen brought together popular misogynist conceptions about women's "nature" with medical theories about humoral theory in such a way that women's perceived weaknesses became strengths. Using the sexist assumption of women's natural "airiness" to support her claims to "receptivity to the wind of the Holy Spirit," Hildegard laid claim to spiritual and ecclesial authority normally reserved for men.[57]

In dire circumstances, surprise, humor, play, and subterfuge may offer the best hope for transformation. Once obsessions with divine omnipotence are overcome, and once the illusion of moral Manichaeanism is shattered, the patristic model's suggestion that God uses guile to unseat evil may find a kind of commonsense resonance. Faced with the contradiction, futility, and moral bankruptcy of fighting violence with violence, God takes the devil by surprise by opting *not* to employ unilateral power, by choosing the road less taken. Using cunning and creativity rather than force, God outsmarts evil. God not only becomes human—abdicating omnipotence and eternality for the fragility of finite existence—but embodies an unspectacular praxis of voluntary poverty, table fellowship with undesirables, and concern for the outcast. Not expecting divinity to look like this, the devil assumes Jesus is just another human, ripe for temptations of worldly power and social success. When Jesus resists such evil and, through a public praxis of healing, compassion, and denunciation of the status quo, calls into question the legitimacy of reigning conceptions of power, of ruling classes and dominant moralities, he creates a crisis; he threatens the moral authority of those in power and hence provokes their wrath, forcing them to exert the only power they know—power-as-domination, violence.

According to the symbolics of the patristic model, we recall, the devil actually causes his own defeat by overstepping his boundaries, making an idol of his power, ignoring his limits, assuming he can have what is not his. His concupiscence—his desire "to have it all," his "limitless greed"—is his undoing.[58] This kind of assumption of entitlement is at the root of contemporary ills as diverse as spousal abuse, poverty, and ecological destruction, and this, according to the patristic model, is the essence of human evil. When demythologized, then, this model points not only to the dynamics of human evil as the distorted use of power, but also to the predatory tendencies of evil; to its subtle proliferation in the lives of individuals and institutions to such an extent that it becomes habitual, normative. To depict abusive power as demonic is to recognize its power to seduce, to captivate, and to destroy. It is to take with absolute seriousness the death-dealing reality of human evil.

In this context, sin is directed primarily or directly not against God but against creation, against concrete others.[59] Reconciliation takes the form of the reconstitution of power in terms of nonviolence, the redefinition of self as self-in-relation, the relocation of agency within the limits of reciprocity and sustainability, rather than the sacrifice of the innocent. According to the patristic model, this redemptive relocation and redefinition take place in moments of crisis when the glutton chokes on his food—when the greed or violence of the powerful becomes so indisputable, so clear, that it ignites moral outrage and is discredited in the public eye.

History reflects numerous examples of people and groups who responded to their marginality with surprising, and sometimes revolutionary, creativity and cunning, forcing the excesses of the powerful into the open and providing the opportunity for an alternative morality to find public support. Without the resources of the powerful or affluent, the underprivileged learn to take advantage of the preconceptions, expectations, and pride of the powerful, using their narrow assumptions against them in unexpected ways. Perhaps the clearest example of this dynamic of subversion and transformation is to be found in movements of nonviolent resistance. In these circumstances, as in the patristic scenario, we have the deliberate creation of a situation of "unavoidable moral confrontation" whose purpose is to lure the wielders of unjust power into exposing and discrediting themselves. Eugene TeSelle explains, "Non-violent direct action takes control of the situation away from the ruling powers, poses a dilemma to them, puts them in a double bind: they must either consent to an act of disobedience (and thus appear weak, or give legitimacy to the dissenters) or exert their authority against it (and thus seem bullying and be morally discredited). It is a kind of moral 'jujitsu' that uses an opponent's strength to defeat him."[60]

The patristic model illuminates the fatal flaw of power-as-control—its Achilles' heel. Its symbolics demonstrate that the collapse occurs at the point of overextension; in this moment, this space, the truth about human evil is revealed. But it is also here that an alternative, a salvific possibility, is manifest.

In Jesus' suffering and death the conflict between two powers, two value systems, two gods, comes to an absolute impasse. Paradoxically, his suffering and death do not signal his defeat but reveal the righteousness of his cause, the moral persuasiveness of his praxis, for they bring into clear public view the violence and injustice of the reigning powers. The execution of Jesus brings to a head the moral battle to which his life had been dedicated; it reveals for all to see the misuse of power, the tyranny of human evil, the avarice of authority, the ugliness of violence. And it presents the public with a choice—power-as-control or power-as-compassion. To choose the latter is to choose the hard path, the unorthodox way; it is to give up the certainty of social norms, the comfort of conformity, the dream of being number one; but it offers the only possibility for mutual love and respect, for the creation of relationships, communities, and institutions that enhance the survival and flourishing of all life, for the continuation of life itself.

In Jesus' day and in our own, the basic choice is the same: violence or nonviolence, domination or mutuality, idolatry or community. However, the tenacious complexity and ambiguity of existence mean that moral decisions are rarely easy to negotiate, that the boundaries between control and compassion are not always clear, which is why even our most passionate choices must be open to critique and revision. It is also why we need communities within which to reflect on the meaning and consequences of our moral decisions—relationships and communities that can hold us accountable for our theories and practices and that can support us in the daily effort to live responsibly, compassionately, and joyfully.

A Novel Possibility

The doctrine of atonement thematizes Christianity's response to the problem of evil, suggesting that it was in the life and death of Jesus of Nazareth that human evil was decisively confronted and redemption from it made possible. In this book I have argued that despite the considerable problems of many traditional construals of atonement—particularly their tendency to buttress human evil rather than to mitigate it—the theological attempt to understand evil and Jesus' relation to it is an important and necessary task for Christian theology.

Toward that end, I have tried to suggest that a contemporary demythologization of the patristic model of atonement preserves the most significant insights of the Anselmian and Abelardian traditions while avoiding their most debilitating weaknesses. With the Anselmian model it affirms that human evil is a deadly serious affair—that it upsets the cosmos; that sin severs our relationship to God, to the power of life and love, by making us forget our radical dependence upon this power, our essential connectedness to all of life, and hence our responsibility to nurture, protect, and honor life in its myriad forms. In our distortion of power we alienate ourselves from God, from others, and from our own best selves. This alienation is so profound that it disfigures self-understanding, interpersonal relationships, social institutions, public policies, economic practices; indeed, it remakes the world so that extrication from the bad habit of power-as-control is no simple task. It requires the in-breaking of something new—a liberating impulse that pervades the dynamics of control from the outside, presenting a wholly fresh perspective, posing a completely novel possibility, and so breaking the hegemonic hold of the Same.

The testimony of hundreds of generations of Christian women and men is that this in-breaking of saving power and re-creative possibility has been present from the beginning of time but was made fully vital in the life and death of Jesus.[61] Like the Abelardian tradition, the patristic model affirms the continuity of Jesus' life and death, seeing his death as the tragic consequence of a lifelong commitment to the principle of mercy. In this life, the transformative power of compassion broke into the historical world with unprecedented immediacy, creating a brand-new option, a radical alternative to the enslaving idolatry of power-as-control. For those who had ears to hear, this message of hope and possibility became an unprecedented turning point, a moment of pure grace that empowered conversion—a turning around—from control to compassion, from isolation to connection, from concupiscence to right relation. Despite its revolutionary effect, however, this saving power was made known not through force but in freedom; it did not abolish the free will of those who encountered it but *enabled* true freedom—freedom from bondage to evil—by making available in an undeniably potent way the transformative power of compassion.

Atonement, then, was not a one-time event in the past achieved by one for all. But there *was* an event in the past—the life and death of Jesus—which brought into the world with unsurpassed vitality the power of life and love that is God. This power breaks the chains of abuse, oppression, and violence not with force but with persuasion, not directly but indirectly, in the lives, communities, and institutions of those who dare to actualize its possibility.

It is my contention that this feminist reprisal of the patristic model of atonement is a genuine alternative to both the Anselmian and the Abelardian traditions. Like the Anselmian school, it safeguards divine power and salvific efficacy, suggesting that spiritual healing is a requirement for the flourishing of human life and reminding us that the possibility for such healing is not something we ourselves can create or control but is a mystery to be embraced and celebrated with awe and thanksgiving. At the same time, however, it insists on the necessity of a continued human praxis of liberative transformation, for without the daily incarnation and actualization of saving power, salvation is merely an idea, a lifeless point of dogma with no liberative power. In my interpretation, Jesus' life and death are affirmed as the revelation of amazing grace and liberative power, but their redemptive possibility depends absolutely on their continued instantiation in the concrete acts of historical people, communities, and institutions. This reconstructed patristic model, then, represents a third possibility, a novel middle way, which eludes the narrowness of the traditional models while affirming their most important insights. It offers contemporary Christians a genuine alternative to both the Anselmian and the Abelardian traditions.

It also, I suggest, creates a kind of bridge between feminist and liberation concerns, a shared narrative that includes the central critiques and honors the commitments and experiences of each. As we have seen, feminist theologies have argued persuasively that Jesus was the victim of human evil, of fear and violence, but they have had considerably less to say about how we might understand Jesus to have revealed a redemptive response to evil. In particular, they have been loath to attribute salvific significance to his suffering and death, fearing the sacralization of suffering and a theology that functions to support death-dealing political, economic, and social policies and practices. Liberation theologies, by contrast, have found in the passion of Jesus a story not unlike the story of the world's poor—a tale of poverty, suffering, and injustice. For them, Jesus' suffering and death are revelations of God's passion, of God's concern for the victims of injustice, of God's special identification with the poor and the disenfranchised. In Jesus' death, God's compassion for those who suffer, God's solidarity with victims, is made undeniably clear. But whereas feminist theologians tend to reject any meaning making with regard to Jesus' suffering and death—ignoring the witness of centuries of the faithful and assuming that hardship and injustice can never yield growth or transformation—liberation theologians often focus so intensely on the divine pathos manifest in Jesus' suffering and death that they overlook the active resistance to evil that Jesus' praxis exhibits and evokes.

As I have sought to demonstrate, a contemporary appraisal of the patristic model of atonement offers the possibility of understanding the salvific work of Christ in a way that takes into account both feminist criticisms and liberationist appropriations. According to this model, the life and death of Jesus are understood to manifest with novel clarity the complexity and intractability of evil as well as the reality of moral existence as a constant struggle to resist evil and to affirm the good. At its root, evil is revealed as the abuse of power—the use of power to dominate and violate, or the relinquishment of power so as to avoid the hard work of moral struggle. Jesus' encounter with human evil is seen as a groundbreaking response. His use of courage, creativity, and the power of truth to uncover and disrupt the hegemony of power-as-control becomes a prototype for further strategies and action. He actively opposes violence with the nonviolent power of truth, exposing evil for what it is and challenging those around him, and all those who hear his story, to recognize the victim-producing effects of unilateral power and to risk embodying a different kind of power—relational power, erotic power, power-as-compassion.

Jesus' cross is understood as the actual and symbolic meeting point of good and evil, of justice and injustice. It is the site of violence and of fierce but loving resistance to violence. In his death we see a subversion of traditional notions of power as unilateral, of justice as retributive, and of violence as necessarily mimetic. His existence and praxis suggest that the power of love is the *only* alternative to the power of violence; it is the only strategy that can discredit injustice and violence while not becoming them. Fighting violence with violence may result in momentary victory, but it will never bring true peace and justice. To be liberated from evil in a world that remains so clearly in its grasp means refusing to let evil define our options and existence. It means struggling against evil with passion, creativity, cunning, and tenacity, but without violence, without cruelty or hatred, without callous indifference. As impossible as that way may seem, it *is* possible—Jesus opened that way, and it remains a possibility for all who follow him. To call him Christ is to affirm that this way, this possibility, did not die on the cross of violence but is universally available. To call him Christ is to wager that the path of resistance and compassion is a liberative one, reconciling us with the power of life itself.

The claim of the patristic model of atonement, then, is that this way of resistance and compassion illuminated by Jesus has the potential, when followed, to liberate from evil, to reveal a way of confronting our evil and the evil of others, which exposes the moral perversity of injustice and offers a clear alternative. This redemption is not a thing of the past effected for us by another, but a constant challenge, a real possibility. Its prize is not the abolition of evil or even of ambiguity, but the satisfaction of being transformed toward fuller life, freedom, and responsibility; of experiencing the expansion of our being through relationships of love and respect; of tasting the sweetness of freedom from evil. Such satisfaction is always piecemeal, transitory; the liberations are forever partial; but they are the best of the possible, and they may just be enough to sustain and enrich us in the daily work of cultivating meaning and making love.

Notes

Introduction

1. Robert J. Daly, *The Origins of the Christian Doctrine of Sacrifice* (Philadelphia: Fortress Press, 1978), v–37.

2. Anthony J. Tambasco, *A Theology of Atonement and Paul's Vision of Christianity* (Collegeville, Minn.: Liturgical Press, 1991), 99.

3. For my purposes, "sexual violence" refers to intra- and extra-familial sexual abuse, including but not limited to stranger rape, acquaintance rape, marital rape, sexual harassment, pedophilia, and incest. "Domestic violence" refers to all types of familial violence, including emotional and physical spousal abuse, child abuse, and sibling abuse.

4. Sharon Welch uses the term "erotics of domination" in *A Feminist Ethic of Risk* (Minneapolis: Fortress Press, 1990), 114.

5. This phrase was coined by theologian Ignacio Ellacuria, *Freedom Made Flesh* (Maryknoll, N.Y.: Orbis Books, 1976).

6. *Cur Deus Homo* in *St. Anselm: Basic Writings,* trans. S. N. Deane (La Salle, Ill.: Open Court Publishing, 1962), 216.

7. Christ chose to die, says Anselm, because "he had agreed with the Father and the Holy Spirit, that there was no other way to reveal to the world the height of his omnipotence, than by his death." Ibid., 208.

8. Ibid., 217, 219. When Anselm's dialogue partner and foil, Boso, states, "It is a strange thing if God so delights in, or requires, the blood of the innocent, that he neither chooses, nor is able, to spare the guilty without the sacrifice of the innocent," Anselm retorts firmly, "I wish to have it understood between us that we do not admit anything in the least unbecoming to be ascribed to the Deity." Ibid., 214.

9. Ibid., 220. Anselm is quick to add that God's honor is not at stake in any ultimate sense: "It is impossible for God to lose his honor; for either the sinner pays his debt of his own accord, or, if he refuse, God takes it from him." Ibid., 221.

10. Ibid., 223. This point is usually overlooked by those who, in an attempt to defend the Anselmian model, emphasize that the central issue is not the offended honor of the Deity but the disruption of the order and beauty of the world. Recent formulations of this opinion include Colin Gunton, *The Actuality of Atonement* (Grand Rapids, Mich.: Eerdmans, 1989), 90; and Mary Grey, *Redeeming the Dream* (London: SPCK, 1989), 114. Anselm found both interpretations convincing while also recognizing that, in the final analysis, they yield the same result.

11. Anselm, *Cur Deus Homo*, 249–50.

12. Ibid., 260.

13. Linwood Urban raises one objection to this logic: "In the end, it seems to be an act of God's mercy to accept Christ's suffering and death in lieu of something owed by human being—but if it is a matter of mercy, why can't God simply forgive us without any reparations?" *A Short History of Christian Thought* (New York: Oxford University Press, 1986), 119.

14. Anselm, *Cur Deus Homo*, 272.

15. John Calvin, *Institutes of the Christian Religion*, trans. Henry Beveridge, vol. 2 (Edinburgh: Edinburgh Printing Co., 1845), 43, 60.

16. Ibid., 65, 63.

17. Karl Barth, *Church Dogmatics*, vol. 3, bk. 2 (Edinburgh: T. & T. Clark, 1960), 211, 212. Barth also employs the category of representation to denote Jesus' divinity; see ibid., 3.2:144.

18. For a recent discussion of Barth's variation on the Anselmian theme, see David L. Wheeler, *A Relational View of the Atonement* (New York: Peter Lang, 1989), 132–52.

19. Peter Abelard, "Exposition to the Epistle to the Romans," in *A Scholastic Miscellany: Anselm to Ockham*, trans. and ed. Eugene R. Fairweather (New York: Macmillan, 1970), 282–83. As Abelard points out, if human beings owed a debt to God as a result of the dishonor of sin, the death of Christ—far from ameliorating the severed divine-human relationship—would only have exacerbated the situation since human beings murdered him: "If that sin of Adam was so great that it could be expiated only by the death of Christ, what expiation will avail for that act of murder committed against Christ?" (p. 282).

20. Ibid., 282. Unlike Anselm, Abelard relativizes the importance of Jesus' death by stressing the salvific significance of his life. However, Abelard is insistent that the horrible *death* perfectly exemplifies the dramatic depth of divine love and has the greatest potential to move and influence the human heart. Thus despite his emphasis on the life of Jesus, Abelard seems to be saying that the death *is* the critical moment of atonement because it can tap most directly into the wells of human emotion and evoke the greatest response. Although he does not go so far as to make the death of Christ *necessary* for atonement, as Anselm does, Abelard nevertheless presents it as the crucial impetus toward reconciliation.

21. Ibid., 283.

22. Paul Fiddes, *Past Event and Present Salvation: The Christian Idea of Atonement* (Louisville, Ky.: Westminster/John Knox Press, 1989), 143.

23. Peter Abelard, *The Letters of Abelard and Héloïse*, trans. Betty Radice (New York: Penguin, 1974), 153.

24. As R. S. Franks points out, this view of the work of Christ was anticipated by Athanasius, who interpreted the death of Christ as an example, and the resurrection as a faith-awakening impetus. *The Work of Christ: A Historical Study of Christian Doctrine* (London: Thomas Nelson, 1962), 204.

25. Abelard, *The Letters of Abelard and Héloïse*, 150–51.

26. Frederick William Dillistone, *The Christian Understanding of Atonement* (Philadelphia: Westminster Press, 1968), 327.

27. For example, Schleiermacher asserts that "we are not entitled to say that sin . . . would conflict with the original perfection of man and thus annul it. On the contrary, we must rather insist upon the fact that sin in general exists only in so far as there is a consciousness of it; and this again is always conditioned by a good which must have preceded it and must have been just a result of that original perfection." Friedrich Schleiermacher, *The Christian Faith*, ed. H. R. Mackintosh and J. S. Stewart (Edinburgh: T. & T. Clark, 1986), 277.

28. Ibid., 436.

29. Ibid.

30. Ibid., 456–58. Schleiermacher says, "He cannot have done so *in our place* in the sense that we are thereby relieved from the necessity of fulfilling it. . . . Neither can He have fulfilled the divine will in any way *for our advantage*, as if by the obedience of Christ, considered in and for itself, anything were achieved for us or changed in relation to us." Ibid., 456.

31. See Walter Rauschenbusch, *A Theology for the Social Gospel* (Nashville: Abingdon Press, 1917). For process theology, see works by John Cobb and David Griffin, Charles Hartshorne, and Marjorie Suchocki.

1. Surviving Traditional Notions of Sin

1. See Max Horkheimer, *Critical Theory*, trans. M. J. O'Connell (New York: Herder and Herder, 1972), and Jürgen Habermas, *Knowledge and Human Interests*, trans. J. J. Shapiro (Boston: Beacon Press, 1971); for a full discussion of this point, see *Feminism and Methodology*, ed. Sandra Harding (Bloomington: Indiana University Press, 1987).

2. Elisabeth Schüssler Fiorenza uses this phrase in her book *Jesus: Miriam's Child, Sophia's Prophet* (New York: Continuum, 1994), 14. She encourages her readers "to understand oppression not in terms of dualistic oppositions but as diverse social, interactive, and multiplicative structures of power," so that the focus is on socioculturally constructed relations of domination, of which sexism and racism are examples. Ibid., 36–37.

3. In the following discussion, "sin" and "evil" will usually be used in conjunction with each other to connote their interconnectedness. For the purposes of this discussion, I have in mind something along the lines of the distinction and definition offered by Mary Potter Engel, who says that "evil and sin together may be called 'wickedness'"—"the complex condition of the lack of right relations in the world in which we live naturally, socially, and individually." Engel distinguishes evil as systemic or structural arrangements "that distort our perceptions or restrain our abilities to such an extent that we find it difficult to choose or do good." By sin she means "those free, discrete acts of responsible individuals that create or reinforce these structures of oppression." See her "Evil, Sin, and Violation of the Vulnerable," in *Lift Every Voice: Constructing Christian Theologies from the Underside*, ed. Susan Brooks Thistlethwaite and Mary Potter Engel (San Francisco: Harper & Row, 1990), 154–55.

4. This is not to say that every element of traditional understandings of sin and evil has been or should be identified as problematic. Nor is it to deny the significant points of continuity between some traditional (male) views and feminist appropriations of them; for example, the consonance on this issue between Sallie McFague and Augustine, or Mary Daly and Paul Tillich. However, as we will see, it is possible to point to several traditional emphases, assumptions, and assertions that are profoundly disturbing from a feminist perspective.

5. This commitment includes the realization that the full humanity of women cannot be attained at the expense of men or the nonhuman world. Indeed, it is based on a recognition of the need to dismantle *all* relations of domination, while attempting at the same time to preserve difference and diversity. Emphases on interconnectedness, justice, and diversity are typical of feminist theologies; see, for example, the works of Rosemary Radford Ruether and Sallie McFague.

6. Vanguards of this trend include Marie Fortune, Alice Miller, Susan Brooks Thistlethwaite, Joanne Carlson Brown, and Rita Nakashima Brock.

7. Another way of putting this conviction is that orthodoxy and orthopraxy are mutually dependent, as liberation theologians have emphasized. When applied to atonement theories, this conviction supports the insight that "right belief" results in "right action," so the evidence that links religious beliefs about atonement with the victimization of women and children points to the necessity of rejecting such beliefs in their present form. Thus, feminist critiques of atonement theories tend to function with a pragmatic definition of truth—that is, one that makes the historical effects of truth claims a constitutive part of these claims. For the classic articulation see William James, *Pragmatism* (1907; reprint, Indianapolis: Hackett Publishing Co., 1981); for a feminist articulation and application, see Sharon Welch, *Communities of Resistance and Solidarity: A Feminist Theology of Liberation* (Maryknoll, N.Y.: Orbis Books, 1985).

8. Shelley Wiley, "Diving Down Many Layers," *Daughters of Sarah* 18, no. 3 (summer 1992): 33. Commenting on the results of their study of incest survivors in Norway, Annie Imbens and Ineke Jonker suggest that the religious upbringing of the survivors—the specific

values, norms, and images they were taught were Christian and therefore ordained by God and society—in part contributed to their victimization, and hence Imbens admonishes her readers that we have to recognize "the actual way in which these teachings and passages affect people, and especially children" because most people "do not consider that a certain teaching might have been written in another context and was meant for use in a different situation from the one in which they find themselves." Imbens and Jonker, *Christianity and Incest,* trans. Patricia McVay (1985; reprint, Minneapolis: Fortress Press, 1991), 5.

9. Valerie Saiving, "The Human Situation: A Feminine View," in *Womanspirit Rising: A Feminist Reader in Religion,* ed. Carol Christ and Judith Plaskow (San Francisco: Harper & Row, 1979), 25–42. Saiving's article was originally published in 1960 in the *Journal of Religion.* Although this initial attempt at a feminist critical analysis of sin and evil is inevitably dated by what might be seen as today's feminist standards, the questions Saiving raises, and her insistence that theology recognize and seek to correct its androcentrism, represent valuable contributions upon which others have built.

10. Mary Daly, *Beyond God the Father: Toward a Philosophy of Women's Liberation* (Boston: Beacon Press, 1973), 45.

11. Ibid., 77, 100, xvi, 47–48.

12. Ibid., 81–82. Daly offers an alternative interpretation of Mary, which has the potential to emphasize the values of independence and original blessedness for women; yet she realizes that this reinterpretation stands in opposition to the one that has dominated mainstream Christian theology; see 83–87.

13. *Christianity and Incest,* 4–5, 273, 30, 55, 44.

14. Imbens and Jonker comment: "When survivors resisted, they are also bad because they are disobedient, rebelling against men and the natural order created by God, in which women are intended to be subservient to men, and children obedient to fathers." Ibid., 217.

15. Cited by Marjorie Procter-Smith, "The Whole Loaf: Holy Communion and Survival," in *Violence against Women and Children,* ed. Carol J. Adams and Marie M. Fortune (New York: Continuum, 1995), 469–71.

16. Ibid., 470.

17. Rita Nakashima Brock, *Journeys by Heart: A Christology of Erotic Power* (New York: Crossroad, 1988), xii, 6.

18. Brock, "Ending Innocence and Nurturing Willfulness," in *Violence against Women and Children,* 71–84.

19. Jennifer L. Manlowe, "Seduced by Faith: Sexual Traumas and Their Embodied Effects," in *Violence against Women and Children,* 336.

20. Ibid., 333.

21. Rosemary Radford Ruether, *Sexism and God-Talk: Toward a Feminist Theology* (Boston: Beacon Press, 1983), 37.

22. Ibid., 163.

23. For a provocative analysis of this view of evil, see Edward Farley, *Good and Evil: Interpreting the Human Condition* (Minneapolis: Fortress Press, 1990).

24. Engel, "Evil, Sin, and Violation of the Vulnerable," 154, 164, 156.

25. Ibid., 154–56. Engel points out that some family systems approaches assume equal participation and guilt in sexual abuse, which is highly problematic.

26. Ibid., 159.

27. Mary Pellauer suggests this view in *Sexual Assault and Abuse: A Handbook for Clergy and Religious Professionals,* ed. Mary D. Pellauer, Barbara Chester, and Jane Boyajian (San Francisco: Harper & Row, 1987).

28. Engel, "Evil, Sin, and Violation of the Vulnerable," 157.

29. Ibid., 158.

30. Ibid.

31. Engel does not appear to recognize this possibility, yet it seems to me to warrant consideration, especially as concerns children victims of family violence, whose understandings of

what it means to be in right relationship, or to express affection in appropriate ways, are easily influenced by the definitions of elders.

32. Engel, "Evil, Sin, and Violation of the Vulnerable," 160.

33. See her discussion in *The Body of God: An Ecological Theology* (Minneapolis: Fortress Press, 1993), especially chapter 4, 99–129.

34. Engel, "Evil, Sin, and Violation of the Vulnerable," 162.

35. Ibid., 160.

36. Noddings, *Women and Evil* (Berkeley: University of California Press, 1989), 200–201.

37. Two recent expositions of this position are offered by Sallie McFague, *The Body of God*, and Marjorie Suchocki, *The Fall to Violence*.

38. Sallie McFague has developed this idea of the world as the body of God in *Models of God* and *The Body of God*.

2. Wrestling with God

1. For discussions of religious language and symbols, see Paul Tillich, *Dynamics of Faith*; Elizabeth Johnson, *She Who Is*; and Sallie McFague, *Metaphorical Theology*.

2. McFague, *Metaphorical Theology* (Philadelphia: Fortress Press, 1982), 9.

3. See Gordon Kaufman, *Theology for a Nuclear Age*; and McFague, *Models of God*.

4. Sharon Welch, *Communities of Resistance and Solidarity: A Feminist Theology of Liberation* (Maryknoll, N.Y.: Orbis Books, 1985), 70.

5. Sharon Welch, *A Feminist Ethic of Risk* (Minneapolis: Fortress Press, 1990), 111–12.

6. Rita Nakashima Brock, *Journeys by Heart: A Christology of Erotic Power* (New York: Crossroad, 1988), 25.

7. Annie Imbens and Ineke Jonker, *Christianity and Incest*, trans. Patricia McVay (1985; reprint, Minneapolis: Fortress Press, 1991), 116.

8. Ibid., 101.

9. McFague, *Metaphorical Theology*, 9.

10. Here I part ways with those who insist that parental models are necessarily harmful. Brock, for instance, argues that regardless of the good intentions of parents, their very position *as parents* carries ascribed authority that is usually unquestioned by children and creates a situation ripe for abuse. James Poling articulates a similar position. However, I understand both these critiques to be directed toward the *patriarchal* family model in which authority is exclusive and power is unilateral; it is within *this* context that parental metaphors are inherently problematic.

11. Susan Brooks Thistlethwaite, *Sex, Race, and God* (New York: Crossroad, 1989), 113. Imbens and Jonker, *Christianity and Incest*, 20.

12. Imbens and Jonker, *Christianity and Incest*, 194. Alice Miller, *Thou Shalt Not Be Aware* (New York: Farrar, Straus and Giroux, 1984), 221.

13. Hunter's argument is set forth in an unpublished paper, "Fear, Respect, and Love: Divine and Human Bonds of Connection and Control," written for the annual meeting of the American Academy of Religion in 1992. She graciously provided me with a copy of the paper. Hunter, 8–10.

14. Hunter quotes Alice Miller; ibid., 18.

15. Ibid. Based on their work with incest survivors, Imbens and Jonker concur: "The destructive impact of incest in combination with [an] oppressive image of God is expressed in fear and confusion aroused by this image. God is good, almighty, all-seeing, and just—and allows this [the incest] to happen. Consequently, these women doubted themselves, and experienced God as terrifying;" *Christianity and Incest*, 206.

16. Hunter, "Fear, Respect, and Love," 21.

17. Ibid., 22, 24–25.

18. Ibid., 24–26.

19. James Poling asserts that "the sexual abuse of children has been disregarded for much of history because it is often perpetrated by the very men who are socially responsible for the

protection of children. . . . The lie that respectable men cannot be child rapists . . . actually serves to increase the danger to children by hiding from them the real danger within the family. Patriarchy protects men as a group from suspicion of sexual violence." *The Abuse of Power: A Theological Problem* (Nashville: Abingdon, 1991), 141–42.

20. Michel Foucault, *Discipline and Punish: The Birth of the Prison,* trans. Alan Sheridan (New York: Pantheon Books, 1977), 200 ff. Foucault's analysis is based on Jeremy Bentham's *Panopticon.* Anne Marie Hunter made this connection in an unpublished paper presented at the annual meeting of the American Academy of Religion in 1991. This information is taken from my notes of the paper, which was untitled and not available for distribution.

21. Imbens and Jonker, *Christianity and Incest,* 33, 58, 206, 207.

22. Cited by Elizabeth Clark, "Sex, Shame, and Rhetoric: En-gendering Early Christian Ethics," *Journal of the American Academy of Religion* 59, no. 2 (summer 1991): 235–36. While Augustine directed this particular admonition to his male congregants, other similar ones were geared toward female hearers.

23. Capps, *A Child's Song* (Louisville, Ky.: Westminster/John Knox Press, 1995), 52.

24. The initial study of traditional values in Mediterranean societies was conducted by Julian Pitt-Rivers, *The People of the Sierra* (London: Weidenfeld & Nicolson, 1954); see also his article, "Honor," in *Encyclopedia of the Social Sciences,* 2d ed. (New York: Macmillan, 1968), 503–11.

25. See Julian Pitt-Rivers, "Honour and Social Status," in *Honour and Shame: The Values of Mediterranean Society,* ed. J. G. Peristiany (Chicago: University of Chicago Press, 1966). See also Bruce Malina, *The New Testament World* (Louisville, Ky.: John Knox Press, 1981), 28 ff.

26. Pierre Bourdieu, "The Sentiment of Honour in Kabyle Society," in *Honour and Shame,* 199, 212.

27. Ibid., 219.

28. Sheila Delaney, "Seeds of Honor, Fields of Shame," in *Honor and Shame and the Unity of the Mediterranean,* ed. David Gilmore (Washington, D.C.: American Anthropological Association, 1987), 40.

29. Karen Jo Torjesen, *When Women Were Priests* (San Francisco: HarperCollins, 1993), 137.

30. Ibid., 136.

31. Jane F. Collier, "From Mary to Modern Woman: The Material Basis of Marianismo and Its Transformation in a Spanish Village," *American Ethnologist* 13 (1986): 101; cited by Kathleen Zuanich Young, "The Imperishable Virginity of Saint Maria Goretti," in *Violence against Women and Children,* ed. Carol J. Adams and Marie M. Fortune (New York: Continuum, 1995), 283.

32. Commenting on Saint Maria Goretti, Young concludes: "Maria Goretti died in order to preserve her hymen; her physical intactness was the only metaphor for her value to her family, her church, her community, and her culture. Any other contribution she might have made didn't count." "The Imperishable Virginity," 285.

33. Delaney, "Seeds of Honor, Fields of Shame," 40.

34. Each author cited above concurs that honor and shame continue to be relevant, useful, and important notions. See also Stanley Brandes, "Reflections on Honor and Shame in the Mediterranean," in *Honor and Shame and the Unity of the Mediterranean,* 121.

35. However, many scholars support the historical and cultural plasticity of the honor/shame dialectic.

36. The relationship between God and human beings can be understood as a patron-client relationship, which is a relationship between unequals based on the common quest for honor. For a discussion of patron-client relationships and their interplay with honor, see S. N. Eisenstadt and L. Roniger, *Patrons, Clients, and Friends* (Cambridge: Cambridge University Press, 1984).

37. Although Calvin's reformulation of Anselm's theory of atonement deemphasizes honor and focuses instead on God's wrath, Calvin's emphasis on sin as the breaking of God's *law* makes it possible to substitute his wrath/law interpretation for Anselm's offended honor/chal-

lenge scheme. In challenging or resisting the divine law, humankind disrupts the "law and order" of the universe and hence brings on itself God's infinite, though justifiable, wrath. In Calvin's version, God's hands are also tied because to ignore the requirements of divine law would be to violate God's very being as Divine Judge; hence mercy is not an option for God. The main difference between Anselm and Calvin at this point is that while Anselm assumes that God offers humankind two options—either punishment or shame—Calvin reduces the "choice" to punishment. Thus, Anselm claims that Jesus' death compensates God for the dishonor and disorder caused by human sin, while Calvin insists that in dying, Jesus bears the punishment that should have been humanity's. Barth's version of the Anselmian model prefers Calvin's focus on the wrath of God and the substitutionary rather than compensatory nature of the death of Jesus.

38. Since males have the ascribed honor that allows them to enter into the challenge-response "game," God is clearly figured as male.

39. *St. Anselm: Basic Writings*, trans. S. N. Deane (La Salle, Ill.: Open Court Publishing, 1962), 221.

40. Ibid., 217, 219, 220. In "Honor, Shame, and the Outside World in Paul's Letter to the Romans," Halvor Moxnes explains that language of payment and indebtedness "was widely used to describe the relations between rulers and subjects, patrons and clients"—an insight that illumines Anselm's use of such language when he claims that human sin constitutes a "debt of honor which we owe to God." *St. Anselm: Basic Writings*, 214.

41. Imbens and Jonker, *Christianity and Incest*, 40, 54–55.

3. Saved by the Divine Victim?

1. Elizabeth Johnson, *She Who Is: The Mystery of God in Feminist Theological Discourse* (New York: Crossroad, 1993), 151. This basic perspective is shared by most feminist theologians, with the important exception of post-Christian feminists like Mary Daly and Emily Culpepper, who argue that Christianity is *essentially* patriarchal. From this perspective, Joanne Carlson Brown suggests that feminists who remain within the Christian church/tradition are themselves battered women unable or unwilling to leave their abuser [Joanne Carlson Brown and Carole R. Bohn, eds., *Christianity, Patriarchy, and Abuse: A Feminist Critique* (Cleveland: The Pilgrim Press, 1989), 3]. For my part, I try to take this possibility seriously because Christianity as it exists is ridden with sexism, racism, and elitism; however, I am unconvinced that it is any more saturated with such evils than society at large, and I do not think "leaving" patriarchy is an option for any except those privileged enough to set up utopian communities on uninhabited islands(!). I agree with Elisabeth Schüssler Fiorenza that "those of us who have experienced and are committed to the liberating power of traditional Christian vision must claim and exercise our own spiritual-theological authority and power of naming for the sake of life in the global village." *Jesus: Miriam's Child, Sophia's Prophet* (New York: Continuum, 1994), 11. In addition, I concur with Rita Nakashima Brock that since Christianity "has functioned as an iconoclastic tool of liberation and life-giving power" among some marginalized groups, it "cannot be dismissed as hopelessly oppressive of women, unless all women are regarded as middle class and white." *Journeys by Heart: A Christology of Erotic Power* (New York: Crossroad, 1988), xv.

2. Schüssler Fiorenza, *Jesus*, 120.

3. As Adolf Harnack suggested at the turn of this century regarding certain models of atonement, the "God-man need not have preached, and founded a kingdom, and gathered disciples; he only required to die." *History of Dogma*, trans. N. Buchanan, vol. 6 (1900; reprint, New York: Dover, 1961), 76.

4. Mary Daly, *Gyn/Ecology: The Metaethics of Radical Feminism* (Boston: Beacon Press, 1978), 59.

5. Francis Fiorenza, "Critical Social Theory and Christology: Toward an Understanding of Atonement and Redemption as Emancipatory Solidarity," *Catholic Theological Society of America Proceedings*, vol. 30 (1975): 72.

6. From the United Methodist liturgy; cited by Marjorie Procter-Smith, "The Whole Loaf: Holy Communion and Survival," in *Violence against Women and Children*, ed. Carol J. Adams and Marie M. Fortune (New York: Continuum, 1995), 473.

7. Sarah Bentley, "Bringing Justice Home: The Challenge of the Battered Women's Movement for Christian Social Ethics," in *Violence against Women and Children*, 155.

8. Schüssler Fiorenza, *Jesus*, 106.

9. Carol J. Adams, "Toward a Feminist Theology of Religion and the State," in *Violence against Women and Children*, 30.

10. Procter-Smith, "The Whole Loaf," 472.

11. Christine E. Gudorf, *Victimization: Examining Christian Complicity* (Philadelphia: Trinity Press International, 1992), 91.

12. Nel Noddings, *Women and Evil* (Berkeley: University of California Press, 1989), 24.

13. Gudorf, *Victimization*, 72.

14. Jennifer L. Manlowe, "Seduced by Faith: Sexual Traumas and Their Embodied Effects," in *Violence against Women and Children*, 329.

15. Sally B. Purvis, *The Power of the Cross: Foundations for a Christian Feminist Ethic of Community* (Nashville: Abingdon Press, 1993), 14.

16. Gudorf, *Victimization*, 61–62.

17. Ibid.

18. Wendy Farley, *Tragic Vision and Divine Compassion: A Contemporary Theodicy* (Louisville, Ky.: Westminster/John Knox Press, 1990), 42, 53.

19. Joanne Carlson Brown and Rebecca Parker, "For God So Loved the World?" in *Christianity, Patriarchy, and Abuse*. There are problems with the "divine child abuse" scenario proposed by Brown and Parker and others, although the majority of feminist theologians seem to agree that it raises a legitimate point of critique of theological tradition. For recent debates, see *Daughters of Sarah* 18, no. 3 (summer 1992).

20. Imbens and Jonker, *Christianity and Incest*, 212.

21. Ibid., 30.

22. Daly, *Beyond God the Father*, 76.

23. Delores S. Williams, "Christian Scapegoating," *The Other Side*, May-June 1993, 43–44.

24. Gudorf, *Victimization*, 60.

25. Rita Nakashima Brock, "Ending Innocence and Nurturing Willfulness," in *Violence against Women and Children*, 79.

26. Ibid., 80.

27. Ibid., 80–81.

28. According to Imbens and Jonker, Mary was "the prime example of virginity and obedience"; Maria Goretti was "the martyr of chastity," who "allowed herself to be murdered rather than lose her virtue"; and Saint Lidwina "patiently bore her suffering." Thus, the survivor of sexual violence "fails to live up to the examples of Mary and Maria" because of her loss of virginity, while the example of Lidwina "only encourages her to accept her fate." *Christianity and Incest*, 142.

29. "The Imperishable Virginity of Saint Maria Goretti," in *Violence against Women and Children*, 279, 281. Imbens and Jonker, *Christianity and Incest*, 49.

30. "Born Again, Free from Sin?" in *Violence against Women and Children*, 345.

31. Imbens and Jonker, *Christianity and Incest*, 34, 66.

32. Young, "The Imperishable Virginity," 284.

33. Smith, "Born Again," 345.

4. Cross and Sword

1. The question of where and when liberation theology began is not the main point here; rather, the commonalities among various liberationist perspectives are the issue. In addition, while some scholars use "liberation theology" to refer exclusively to certain Latin American theologies, I use it in a more expansive way to include all theologies sharing a basic set of

methods, commitments, and convictions to be identified shortly. Such a broad designation is not intended to reduce the multiplicity or distinctiveness of the various theologies that fit the broad description but to allow for the identification of broad trends and claims.

2. Cited by David Batstone, *From Conquest to Struggle* (Albany: State University of New York, 1991), 14.

3. Walter Altmann, "A Latin American Perspective on the Cross and Suffering," in *The Scandal of the Crucified World,* ed. Yacob Tesfai (Maryknoll, N.Y.: Orbis Books, 1994), 81.

4. The phrase about reading the Bible "with Third World eyes" is used by Robert McAfee Brown in *Unexpected News: Reading the Bible with Third World Eyes* (Philadelphia: Westminster Press, 1984). More recently, liberation theologians are being challenged to deal with the profound moral ambivalence and ethnic/national exclusivity implied by biblical portrayals of God. To claim that Yahweh is a liberating God, for instance, works well if one takes the perspective of the Israelites; but when one considers Yahweh's actions toward Israel's opponents, such a claim becomes impossible.

5. Robert McAfee Brown, *Liberation Theology* (Louisville, Ky.: Westminster/John Knox Press, 1993), 32.

6. Pablo Richard, "1492: The Violence of God and the Future of Christianity," in *1492–1992: The Voice of the Victims,* ed. Leonardo Boff and Virgilio Elizondo (Philadelphia: Trinity Press International, 1990), 66.

7. Batstone, *From Conquest to Struggle,* 15.

8. Cited by Saúl Trinidad, "Christology, *Conquista,* Colonization," in *Faces of Jesus: Latin American Christologies,* ed. José Miguez Bonino (Maryknoll, N.Y.: Orbis Books, 1984), 55.

9. Yacob Tesfai, "Introduction," in *The Scandal of a Crucified World,* 4.

10. The prophecy Columbus refers to is Isaiah 60:9; Trinidad, "Christology, *Conquista,* Colonization," 56.

11. Cited by Trinidad; ibid., 57.

12. Ibid.

13. Leonardo Boff and Virgilio Elizondo, "The Voices of the Victims: Who Will Listen to Them?" in *1492–1992,* vii.

14. Richard, "1492: The Violence of God and the Future of Christianity," in *1492–1992,* 59, 61.

15. Maximiliano Salinas, "The Voices of Those Who Spoke Up for the Victims," in *1492–1992,* 107.

16. Johann Baptist Metz, "With the Eyes of a European Theologian," in *1492–1992,* 116.

17. Georges Casalis, "Jesus—Neither Abject Lord nor Heavenly Monarch," in *Faces of Jesus,* 74.

18. Cited by Trinidad, "Christology, *Conquista,* Colonization," 56–57.

19. Casalis, "Jesus," 74.

20. Although I have chosen to focus on liberation theology in its Latin American form, clear parallels to the Christ of Conquest exist among other Third World theologies. In Asia, for instance, liberation theologians often speak of "the Gold-crowned Jesus" as the symbol of the interpretations and practices of Christianity that contribute to the oppression of Asian peoples. See the articles by C. S. Song, Byung Mu Ahn, Virginia Fabella, and Chung Hyung Kyung in *Asian Faces of Jesus,* ed. R. S. Sugirtharajah (Maryknoll, N.Y.: Orbis Books, 1987). See also A. A. Yewangoe, *Theologia Crucis: Asian Christian Views of Suffering in the Face of Overwhelming Poverty and Multifaceted Religiosity in Asia* (Amsterdam: Rodopi, 1987). Among African American theologians, a distinction is often made between "slaveholding religion" with its white Christ and "slave religion" with its black Jesus or Christ; see Jacquelyn Grant, *White Women's Christ, Black Women's Jesus,* and Kelly Douglas Brown, *The Black Christ.* Similarly, African theologian Jean-Marc Éla speaks of the "slavetrading Christ" of imperial Christianity; see "The Memory of the African People and the Cross of Christ," in *The Scandal of the Crucified World,* 33.

21. Casalis, "Jesus," 72.

22. João Dias de Araújo, "Images of Jesus in the Culture of the Brazilian People," in *Faces of Jesus*, 32.

23. "Christ in Latin American Preaching," in *Faces of Jesus*, 43.

24. Casalis, "Jesus," 72-73.

25. Virginia Fabella, "Christology from an Asian Woman's Perspective," in *Asian Faces of Jesus*, 215, 218.

26. Hugo Assmann, "The Actuation of the Power of Christ in History: Notes on the Discernment of Christological Contradictions," in *Faces of Jesus*, 135.

27. Trinidad, "Christology, *Conquista*, Colonization," 51.

28. A variation on this model is the "pacifist Christ." As Trinidad explains, this is "a non-violent, nonpredatory" Christ, "a Christ of the works of beneficence" who is often commended as an alternative to the Christ(s) of Conquest. However, this image does not in practice avoid the problem because while this Christ is no longer "a heavenly monarch and inquisitor," he is still "a monarch—of the philanthropical stripe now." In the last analysis, argues Trinidad, "the path of pacifism is the best way to dominate, for it encourages the submission of the will itself." Trinidad, "Christology, *Conquista*, Colonization," 54.

29. Ibid.

30. Assmann, "Actuation of the Power of Christ," 136.

31. Trinidad, "Christology, *Conquista*, Colonization," 50.

32. See his discussion in *Passion of Christ, Passion of the World* (Maryknoll, N.Y.: Orbis Books, 1987), 79-83.

33. Ibid., 83.

34. Batstone, *From Conquest to Struggle*, 147.

35. Ibid.

36. Takatso A. Mofokeng, *The Crucified Among the Crossbearers* (Kampen: Uitgeversmaatschappij J. H. Kok, 1983), 93.

37. Simon S. Maimela, "The Suffering of Human Divisions and the Cross," in *The Scandal of a Crucified World*, 37-38. Maimela continues, "The racial divisions that South Africans have suffered over the years are the product of European cultural and religious triumphalism, which has given rise to and feeds on the theology of glory. This reflects the 'success motif' of Western Christendom. It has forgotten its origin in the crucified Christ and has allowed Christianity to be transformed into a religion of the successful and the mighty." Ibid., 45.

5. Atonement from the Underside

1. Gustavo Gutiérrez, *A Theology of Liberation* (Maryknoll, N.Y.: Orbis Books, 1973), 102-3.

2. Jon Sobrino, *The Principle of Mercy* (Maryknoll, N.Y.: Orbis Books, 1994), 4, 9.

3. Jon Sobrino, *Christology at the Crossroads* (Maryknoll, N.Y.: Orbis Books, 1978), 51.

4. Ibid., 53.

5. Sobrino, *The Principle of Mercy*, 100.

6. Sobrino, *Christology at the Crossroads*, 51.

7. Ignacio Ellacuria, *Freedom Made Flesh* (Maryknoll, N.Y.: Orbis Books, 1976), 115.

8. Ibid., 103.

9. Ibid., 106.

10. This way of interpreting the meaning of Jesus' death originated with German theologian Jürgen Moltmann, especially as articulated in his book *The Crucified God* (San Francisco: HarperCollins, 1991). Moltmann's reading owes much to Japanese theologian Kazoh Kitamori's work, *Theology of the Pain of God* (Richmond, Va.: John Knox Press, 1965), as well as to the theology of Karl Barth. Moltmann's work has been a major influence on liberation construals of atonement.

11. See *Theology of the Pain of God*.

12. Leonardo Boff, *When Theology Listens to the Poor* (San Francisco: Harper & Row, 1988), 104.

13. Boff, *Passion of Christ, Passion of the World* (Maryknoll, N.Y.: Orbis Books, 1987), 72, 134.

14. Boff, *Jesus Christ Liberator* (Maryknoll, N.Y.: Orbis Books, 1978), 290.

15. Boff, *Passion of Christ,* 87–88.

16. Ibid., 87–89.

17. Ibid., 7.

18. Boff, *Passion of Christ,* 9.

19. Boff, *Jesus Christ Liberator,* 25–26, 53, 111.

20. Boff, *When Theology Listens to the Poor,* 113–16.

21. Ibid., 119.

22. Boff, *Jesus Christ Liberator,* 219. Boff and other liberation theologians who speak of Jesus' "proexistence" or "being-for-others" are indebted to Dietrich Bonhoeffer's christology.

23. Ibid., 83.

24. Boff, *Passion of Christ,* 18.

25. Ibid., 111–16.

26. Ibid., 121–22, 107.

27. Boff, *When Theology Listens to the Poor,* 119–21.

28. Boff, *Jesus Christ Liberator,* 219.

29. Boff, *Passion of Christ,* 134.

30. Boff, *When Theology Listens to the Poor,* 117, 119.

31. No assumptions are made here regarding whose work may have influenced whom.

32. Sobrino, *Christology at the Crossroads,* 179–80.

33. Ibid., 204.

34. Sobrino, *Christology at the Crossroads,* 55.

35. Sobrino, *The Principle of Mercy,* 9.

36. Sobrino, *Christology at the Crossroads,* 203–4, 208–9.

37. Ibid, 208–9, 55.

38. Sobrino, *The Principle of Mercy,* 17.

39. Ibid., 15, 61, 65, 15.

40. Virgilio Elizondo, *Galilean Journey* (Maryknoll, N.Y.: Orbis Books, 1983), 5.

41. For a recent discussion of the power of religious narratives such as the *payson* "to help ordinary people to make sense of their experiences, to articulate collective and personal identities, and to mobilize action" for change, see Anna L. Peterson, "Religious Narratives and Political Protest," *Journal of the American Academy of Religion* 64, no. 1 (spring 1996): 27–44.

42. Elizondo, *Galilean Journey,* 41.

43. Ibid., 50, 55, 53.

44. Ibid., 62.

45. Ibid., 58–63.

46. Ibid., 63, 65.

47. Ibid., 70, 68.

48. Ibid., 72, 77–78.

49. Ibid., 105, 118.

50. Spoken by Rosa, a Salvadoran woman; cited by Peterson, "Religious Narratives and Political Protest," 27.

6. Mending and Discarding

1. Rita Nakashima Brock, *Journeys by Heart: A Christology of Erotic Power* (New York: Crossroad, 1988), 34.

2. Ibid., 25.

3. See Lorde's essay, "Uses of the Erotic: The Erotic as Power," in *Sister Outsider* (Freedom, Calif.: Crossing Press, 1994), 53–59.

4. Brock, *Journeys by Heart,* 25.

5. Ibid., 7, 24–26.

6. Ibid., 87, 94.

7. Ibid., 100, 49.

8. Ibid., 52.

9. Ibid., 68, 52.

10. Christine Gudorf, *Victimization*, 26. See also Renita Weems, *Battered Love: Marriage, Sex, and Violence in the Hebrew Prophets* (Minneapolis: Augsburg Fortress Press, 1995), and Elisabeth Schüssler Fiorenza, *Jesus: Miriam's Child, Sophia's Prophet* (New York: Continuum, 1994).

11. Schüssler Fiorenza, *Jesus*, 26.

12. Wendy Farley, *Tragic Vision and Divine Compassion: A Contemporary Theodicy* (Louisville, Ky: Westminster/John Knox Press, 1990), 19, 31.

13. Kathleen Sands, *Escape from Paradise: Evil and Tragedy in Feminist Theology* (Minneapolis: Fortress Press, 1994), 64.

14. Ibid., xi, 2, 5, 6.

15. Ibid., 16.

16. Annie Dillard, *Pilgrim at Tinker Creek* (New York: HarperPerennial, 1985), 7.

17. Farley, *Tragic Vision*, 12, 22, 29.

18. Ibid., 22, 29, 63.

19. Ibid., 86, 87, 69, 80, 92–94, 115, 117.

20. Ibid., 125.

21. William Placher, *Narratives of a Vulnerable God* (Louisville, Ky.: Westminster/John Knox Press, 1994), 87–88.

7. Undermining Evil

1. Augustine *On the Trinity* 13.13.17, in *Nicene and Post-Nicene Fathers*, ed. Philip Schaff, vol. 3 (Buffalo: Christian Literature Co., 1887), 176.

2. Cited by L. W. Grensted, *A Short History of the Doctrine of the Atonement* (Manchester, England: Manchester University Press, 1920), 37–38. Other thinkers who affirmed the notion include Gregory of Nyssa, Ambrose, and Augustine.

3. Eugene TeSelle, "The Cross as Ransom," *Journal of Early Christian Studies* 4, no. 2 (1996): 151.

4. H. E. W. Turner identifies this type of logic as the *Logos Victor* theory, in which Christ's humanity is reduced to bait to lure Satan, as opposed to the *Christus Victor* theory, in which Christ's humanity is seen "as the very element in and through which his vicarious victory was achieved." *The Patristic Doctrine of Redemption* (New York: Morehouse-Gorham Co., 1952), 20. My reading of the patristic materials suggests that Turner's distinction is too strict; in several cases the two "theories" stand side by side and are simply not as easily extricable as Turner's categories imply. As I will argue, the deception motif's greatest strength is its portrayal of the crucial importance of the incarnation, of an embodied God, who does not destroy evil in a unilateral show of force, but who persuades and lures evil into undoing itself.

5. Sometimes the disguise motif was used by the patristic theologians as a lens for understanding other well-known events in the life of Jesus. From this viewpoint, keeping the secret of Christ's divinity was the rationale for his being born to a *betrothed* virgin; and it explained his numerous efforts to conceal his identity as well as his silence during his trial and his feigned fear of death on the cross. See Martin Werner, *The Formation of Christian Dogma* (London: Adam & Charles Black, 1957), 97.

6. Paul Fiddes, *Past Event and Present Salvation: The Christian Idea of Atonement* (Louisville, Ky.: Westminster/John Knox Press, 1989), 115–24.

7. As R. W. Southern explains, there is presumed to be "a certain order and justice in the Devil's empire, not to be broken by an arbitrary exercise of God's omnipotence." See *Saint Anselm and His Biographer: A Study of Monastic Life and Thought 1059–c. 1130* (Cambridge: Cambridge University Press, 1963), 94.

8. Fiddes, *Past Event and Present Salvation*, 118.

9. Other support comes from those, like Emil Brunner, who stress Satan's subordination to and use by God; see Brunner, *The Christian Doctrine of Creation and Redemption*, trans. Olive Wyon (Philadelphia: Westminster Press, 1952), 145–46.

10. See, for instance, *Against Heresies* 3.23.3, in *Ante-Nicene Christian Library*, ed. Alexander Roberts and James Donaldson, vol. 5 (Edinburgh: T. & T. Clark, 1869), 364–65.

11. *Against Heresies* 3.23.2, 3.23.1; ibid., 364, 363.

12. *Against Heresies* 5.1.1, in *Ante-Nicene Christian Library*, ed. Alexander Roberts and James Donaldson, vol. 9 (Edinburgh: T. & T. Clark, 1869), 56.

13. Elsewhere, Irenaeus suggests that evil is power that transgresses all boundaries. *Against Heresies* 5.21.3; ibid., 113.

14. *Against Heresies* 5.21.2; ibid., 112. Elsewhere, Irenaeus argues that in the temptations in the desert, Jesus used scripture to "put our adversary to utter confusion." *Against Heresies* 5.12.1; ibid., 114.

15. Although these themes are indeed present in Irenaeus's writings, they exist alongside other, quite different, construals of the work of Christ. Thus, the claim here is not that Irenaeus—or any of the church fathers—affirmed what I am outlining as the patristic model of atonement as their sole soteriological framework. Rather, it tended to exist alongside, and sometimes in conflict with, other traditions.

16. Gregory of Nyssa, *The Great Catechism* 15, in *Nicene and Post-Nicene Fathers*, ed. Philip Schaff and Henry Wace, vol. 5 (New York: Christian Literature Co., 1893), 487.

17. *The Great Catechism* 22; ibid., 492–93.

18. Ibid., 493.

19. *The Great Catechism* 23; ibid., 493.

20. *The Great Catechism* 24; ibid., 494.

21. Augustine *On the Trinity* 13.14.18, in *Nicene and Post-Nicene Fathers*, 3:177.

22. *The Trinity* 4.14.14, in *The Works of St. Augustine*, trans. Edmund Hill, ed. John E. Rotelle, vol. 5 (Brooklyn: New City Press, 1991), 356.

23. *The Trinity* 5.13.19; ibid., 358.

24. *On the Trinity* 4.13.18, in *Nicene and Post-Nicene Fathers*, 3:79.

25. For a discussion of the popularity of these themes in medieval art, see Ruth Mellinkoff, *The Devil at Isenheim: Reflections of Popular Belief in Grünewald's Altarpiece* (Berkeley: University of California Press, 1988), 28–31.

26. The next and best-known appearance of these themes came in 1931, when Swedish theologian Gustav Aulén brought them together under the rubric of the "classic" or "dramatic" view of atonement. Thanks to Aulén's provocative retrieval, this model has been increasingly recognized as a legitimate construal of the event of atonement. See Gustav Aulén, *Christus Victor: An Historical Study of the Three Main Types of the Idea of Atonement*, trans. A. G. Hebert (1931; reprint, London: SPCK, 1960). For the purposes of my reconstruction of the model, Aulén's reading offers an originating thesis whose importance cannot be overstated; however, my desire is to explore quite different aspects of the material from what he did.

27. Elaine Pagels, *The Origin of Satan* (New York: Random House, 1995). Pagels suggests that this shift was begun in sectarian Jewish circles—for instance, as the Essenes began to make distinctions not simply between Israel and its external enemies, but between "real" Jews and those who had adopted foreign practices: "More radical than their predecessors, these dissidents began increasingly to invoke the *satan* to characterize their Jewish opponents; in the process they turned this rather unpleasant angel into a far grander—and far more malevolent—figure. No longer one of God's faithful servants, he begins to become what he is for Mark and for later Christianity—God's antagonist, his enemy, even his rival." Ibid., 47.

28. It also became part of racist discourse. See Robert Hood, *Begrimed and Black* (Minneapolis: Fortress Press, 1994), 78, 94.

29. Pagels, *The Origin of Satan*, xix.

30. Ibid., 184.

31. Sharon Welch, *Communities of Resistance and Solidarity: A Feminist Theology of Liberation* (Maryknoll, N.Y.: Orbis Books, 1985), 70, 72. Although her analysis is applicable here, Welch does not discuss the patristic model of atonement.

32. Sharon Welch, *A Feminist Ethic of Risk* (Minneapolis: Fortress Press, 1990), 33, 47, 68.

33. Noddings, *Women and Evil* (Berkeley: University of California Press, 1989), 35. For the sake of clarity, it should be noted that Noddings does not address the issue of atonement, although her analysis is applicable.

34. Poling, *The Abuse of Power*, 110-11.

35. Noddings, *Women and Evil*, 50.

36. Welch, *Communities of Resistance and Solidarity*, 78.

37. Leonardo Boff, *Passion of Christ, Passion of the World* (Maryknoll, N.Y. Orbis Books, 1987), 111.

38. See Jean Rivière, *The Doctrine of the Atonement*, trans. Luigi Cappadelta (London: Kegan Paul, Trench, Trübner & Co., 1909). For a recent discussion of this point, see TeSelle, "The Cross as Ransom," 147-70.

39. Perhaps it is because of its strong emphasis on liberation that the patristic model is widely rejected by mainstream theologians, who tend to discount it as primitive or crass, but is increasingly attractive to those who are held captive by poverty and oppression (those whom history tends to designate as primitive and crass). I wonder, further, if it is mere coincidence that this model, which was so popular during the early centuries of Christian history, fell out of favor just as Christianity gained acceptability and power. My suspicions are seconded by Justo González, who argues that it is because of its sociopolitical dimension and implications that this model appeals to Hispanics; see *Mañana: Christian Theology from a Hispanic Perspective* (Nashville: Abingdon Press, 1990), 154.

40. It is also used by some psychiatrists to depict the bondage of mental illness; see, for example, Don S. Browning, *The Atonement and Psychotherapy* (Philadelphia: Fortress Press, 1966).

41. Leo Lionni, *Frederick* (New York: Knopf, 1967).

42. Jon Sobrino, *Christology at the Crossroads* (Maryknoll, N.Y.: Orbis Books, 1978), 203-4.

43. Boff, *Passion of Christ*, 102, 114.

44. Virgilio Elizondo, *Galilean Journey* (Maryknoll, N.Y: Orbis Books, 1983), 77, 72.

45. Jean-Marc Éla, *My Faith as an African* (Maryknoll, N.Y.: Orbis Books, 1988), 109.

46. Ibid.

47. Eleazar Fernandez, *Toward a Theology of Struggle* (Maryknoll, N.Y.: Orbis Books, 1994), 55, 103, 99.

48. Andreas A. Yewangoe, "An Asian Perspective on the Cross and Suffering," in *The Scandal of a Crucified World*, ed. Yacob Tesfai (Maryknoll, N.Y.: Orbis Books, 1994), 70.

49. Walter Altmann, "A Latin American Perspective on the Cross and Suffering," in *The Scandal of a Crucified World*, 82.

50. Ada María Isasi-Díaz, *En la Lucha: A Hispanic Women's Liberation Theology* (Minneapolis: Fortress Press, 1993), 22.

51. Delores S. Williams, *Sisters in the Wilderness: The Challenge of Womanist God-Talk* (Maryknoll, N.Y.: Orbis Books, 1993), 165.

52. See Sölle, *Suffering* (Philadelphia: Fortress Press, 1984), Chopp, *The Praxis of Suffering* (Maryknoll, N.Y.: Orbis Books, 1986), and Welch, *Communities of Resistance and Solidarity*.

53. Ellen K. Wondra, *Humanity Has Been a Holy Thing: Toward a Contemporary Feminist Christology* (New York: University Press of America, 1994), 91, 328.

54. As Eugene TeSelle explains, this model "suggests that God effects the liberation of human kind not by violence, not by power, but in a manner that expresses goodness, justice, and wisdom." TeSelle, "The Cross as Ransom," 148-49.

55. "My Black Mothers and Sisters, Or On Beginning a Cultural Autobiography," *Feminist Studies* 8, no. 1 (spring 1982): 85, 86.

56. See, for example, *This Sex Which Is Not One* (Ithaca, N.Y.: Cornell University Press, 1985).

57. Henrietta Leyser, *Medieval Women: A Social History of Women in England 450–1500* (New York: St. Martin's Press, 1995), 98.

58. Sallie McFague, *The Body of God: An Ecological Theology* (Minneapolis: Fortress Press, 1993), 115.

59. For excellent discussions of this point, refer to McFague, *The Body of God,* and Marjorie Suchocki, *The Fall to Violence: Original Sin in Relational Theology* (New York: Continuum, 1995).

60. Taking his cue from Linwood Urban's brief discussion in *A Short History of Christian Thought* (New York: Oxford University Press, 1986), Eugene TeSelle explores the connections between the ransom theme and the strategies of nonviolent direct action. See TeSelle, "The Cross as Ransom," 162–70.

61. I do not intend here to exclude the possibility that this redemptive opening or actualization may also occur apart from its concretization in Jesus—for instance, in other religious traditions. My intention is to offer an interpretation of salvation within Christianity (and, hence, focused on the figure of Jesus), not to claim that I know the full extent or shape of God's liberative possibilities or presence.

Index